MW01101123

ROUTLEDGE LIBRARY EDITIONS:
LITERARY THEORY

Volume 2

WOUNDED FICTION

WOUNDED FICTION
Modern Poetry and Deconstruction

JOSEPH ADAMSON

Routledge
Taylor & Francis Group

LONDON AND NEW YORK

First published in 1988 by Garland Publishing, Inc.

This edition first published in 2017
by Routledge
2 Park Square, Milton Park, Abingdon, Oxon OX14 4RN

and by Routledge
711 Third Avenue, New York, NY 10017

Routledge is an imprint of the Taylor & Francis Group, an informa business

British Library Cataloguing in Publication Data
A catalogue record for this book is available from the British Library

ISBN: 978-1-138-69377-7 (Set)
ISBN: 978-1-315-52921-9 (Set) (ebk)
ISBN: 978-1-138-68882-7 (Volume 2) (hbk)
ISBN: 978-1-315-53804-4 (Volume 2) (ebk)

Publisher's Note
The publisher has gone to great lengths to ensure the quality of this reprint but
points out that some imperfections in the original copies may be apparent.

Disclaimer
The publisher has made every effort to trace copyright holders and would welcome
correspondence from those they have been unable to trace.

JOSEPH ADAMSOM

WOUNDED FICTION

Modern Poetry and Deconstruction

GARLAND PUBLISHING, INC.
NEW YORK & LONDON
1988

Library of Congress Cataloging–in–Publication Data

Adamson, Joseph, 1950–
Wounded fiction : modern poetry and deconstruction / Joseph
Adamson/
p. cm. — (Garland publications in comparative literature)
Bibliography: p.
ISBN 0–8240–7480–7
1. Poetry, Modern—20th century—History and criticism. 2.
Deconstruction. 3. Stevens, Wallace, 1879–1955—Criticism
and interpretation. 4. Vallejo, César, 1892–1938—Criticism
and interpretation. 5. Char, René, 1907– —Criticism and
interpretation. I. Title. II. Series.
PN1271.A34 1988
809.1'04—dc19
88–21185

The volumes in this series are printed on
acid–free, 250–year–life paper.

Printed in the United States of America

To Jean and Lois

Acknowledgments

I would like to express my deeply felt thanks to the following people for their generous encouragement and guidance: Peter Nesselroth, Patricia Parker, Jean Wilson, Rigmore Adamson, Linda Hutcheon, and Eleanor Cook.

TABLE OF CONTENTS

ABBREVIATIONS

René Char:

FM   *Fureur et mystère*. Paris: Gallimard, 1967.

LM   *Les Matinaux*, followed by *La Parole en archipel*. Paris: Gallimard, 1962.

NP   *Le Nu perdu et autres poèmes*. Paris: Gallimard, 1978.

Wallace Stevens:

CP   *The Collected Poems*. 1954; rpt. New York: Alfred A. Knopf, 1978.

NA   *The Necessary Angel: Essays on Reality and the Imagination*. New York: Random House, 1951.

OP   *Opus Posthumous*. Ed. Samuel French Morse. New York: Alfred A. Knopf, 1957.

César Vallejo.

PC   *Poesía completa*. Ed. Jan Larrea. Spain: Barral Editores, 1978.

INTRODUCTION: A POETRY THAT THINKS

> Poetic writing is the most advanced and refined
> mode of deconstruction; it may differ from critical
> or discursive writing in the economy of its articula-
> tion, but not in kind.
> Paul de Man, "Semiology and Rhetoric"[1]

> There are thus two interpretations of inter-
> pretation, of structure, of sign, of play. The one
> seeks to decipher, dreams of deciphering a truth or
> an origin which escapes play and the order of the
> sign, and which lives the necessity of interpretation
> as an exile. The other, which is no longer turned
> toward the origin, affirms play and tries to pass
> beyond man and humanism, the name of man being
> the name of that being who, throughout the history
> of metaphysics or of ontotheology — in other words,
> throughout his entire history — has dreamed of full
> presence, the reassuring foundation, the origin and
> the end of play.
> Jacques Derrida, "Structure, Sign, and Play"[2]

This book does not concern the theory of poetry so much as the poetry of theory: a poetry that theorizes, that has — to play on the etymology of that word — a "view" on things, that thinks. The idea of a thinking poetry calls to mind Heidegger's insistent exploration of the relationship between poetry and thought, which has shown how the two, whatever differences divide them, however different their modes, share a significant common power of disclosure and meditation. But to use Heidegger as an authority in this matter only reminds us that to say that poetry "thinks about" things raises other questions. What or what things does poetry think about? For that matter — and to continue in the spirit of a Heideggerian questioning — what do we mean by thinking? One thing that the three poets here — Wallace Stevens, César Vallejo, and René Char — all reflect upon is, of course, poetry itself. Another may be, indeed, that other thing both opposed and closely related to it: thinking.

1

We naturally enough make a primordial separation between poetry and thought or philosophy, and Heidegger has perhaps come closest of anyone to recognizing what they share, while never relinquishing the abysmal difference that divides and distances them even in their greatest proximity. Proximity, nearness, for Heidegger, is in fact only possible in the first place because of primordial difference, this being the case for the neighboring of poetry and thinking as well:

> Yet we have placed thinking close to poesy, and at a distance from science. Closeness, however, is something essentially different from the vacuous leveling of differences. The essential closeness of poesy and thinking is so far from excluding their difference that, on the contrary, it establishes that difference in an abysmal manner. This is something we moderns have trouble understanding.[3]

Their closeness establishes their difference, or, rather, establishes the fact that their difference articulates their proximity, "the essential closeness of poetry and thinking." If "This is something we moderns have trouble understanding," it is not something any of these three "modern" poets have particular problems with. Both the convergence and the divergence of poetry and thought are at play in their writings. It is not just that they do not let their poetry fall under a purely esthetic judgement. More importantly, the value they implicitly lend to the poetic text presupposes a certain articulation of poetry and thinking, an intricate crossing of concerns that are never finally separable anyway. Stevens, for one, makes their interrelatedness explicit and theorizes about their profound commonality and their radical difference, and their *différance*. He speaks of that limit where philosophy, for all its might, can no longer progress, but where poetry, as though borne on wings over an abyss, goes on without it, like the flighty and flying Canon Aspirin in "Notes," that master of both fugue and flight, who reflects, "humming an outline of a fugue / Of praise," and, having finally reached that "point / Beyond which thought could not progress as thought," dramatically chooses a more successful interdependency:

> He had to choose. But it was not a choice
> Between excluding things. It was not a choice
>
> Between, but of. He chose to include the things
> That in each other are included, the whole,
> The complicate, the amassing harmony. (*CP* 403)

This interdependency or "complicate" and "amassing" interconnectedness of things is the meshing and fitting together of different modes of thought as well, a complex fusion which does not dispel their difference but, on the contrary, is only articulable and binding because of it. In "A Collect of Philosophy," in a typically elegant and provocative reversal, Stevens makes the point that this means that philosophy is always, when at its best, part poetry, always more and less than philosophy:

> The most significant deduction possible relates to the question of supremacy as between philosophy and poetry. If we say that philosophy is supreme, this means that the reason is supreme over the imagination. But is it? Does not philosophy carry us to a point at which there is nothing left except the imagination? If we rely on the imagination ... to carry us beyond that point, and if the imagination succeeds in carrying us beyond that point ..., then the imagination is supreme, because its powers have shown themselves to be greater than the powers of the reason. Philosophers, however, are not limited to the reason and, as the concepts, to which I have referred, show, their ideas are often triumphs of the imagination. To call attention to ideas in which the reason and the imagination have been acting in concert is a way of saying that when they act in concert they are supreme and is not the same thing as to say that one is supreme over the other. (*OP* 200-01)

The very style of this deceptively simple passage (a beautiful mixture of questioning aporia, hypothesis and speculation, and just plain assertion) reflects perfectly Stevens' characteristic strategy of carefully prepared reversal, which is such a source of rhetorical power throughout his poetry. Its goal is the achievement of some momentary balance among shifting differences and extremely opposed positions: not the abolishment of differences but their measuring, and the finding of a measure between them, what Heidegger calls "the carrying out and settling of differences."4 Stevens' extraordinary sense of equilibrium does not result, however, in a simple equalization or uniformization. It is, on the contrary, rooted in the capacity for testing extremes and entertaining the differences among diverse things. Faithful to the great American tradition of *skepsis*, of carefully considered judgement in face of polarities, he refuses to pronounce on the supremacy of one limited position over another, of poetry over thought in this case. He recognizes instead their concerted supremacy, their profound interdependency and participation. They are both part and apart. Part of, and participating in, apparently separate concerns, their difference both sets them apart and makes them belong to the same, bringing them together in a chiasmatic and supplementary fashion.

But if neither poetry nor thought is counted supreme, both Heidegger and Stevens suggest, as do Vallejo and Char in their own ways, that poetry is possessed of a certain archetypal priority, that it has a certain primordial advantage over philosophy and therefore comes first. Poetry's limits, which are always primitive elements, are really its strengths: that it cannot explain itself rationally is also a necessary condition of its intuitive power. This does not mean that poetry's "intuition" lacks structure. Rather, the way it structures its thinking lacks stricture. It does not, that is, recognize the need to resolve difference, contradiction, paradox, and contraries into identity, logical consistency, truth, and unity. Philosophy restricts its own investigation of things by invalidating from the start certain *other* ways of posing problems. Derrida has shown us, for example, the problems of metaphor in the philosophical text, which the philosopher, to protect the coherence and consistency of his discourse, must desperately seek to tame and neutralize.

But for a philosopher like Heidegger, philosophy, like Antaeus returning to the vital earth, draws strength and insight from metaphor. Heidegger, indeed, goes to poetry as a source of philosophical insights presumably absent in the discipline of philosophy itself. In his interpretation of the poets — Hölderlin most obviously, but Rilke, Trakl, George, and Char, as well as others — he treats poetry as an oracle of thought not yet thought. Because of its power of disclosure, a power inaccessible to mere thought by itself, poetry is like an origin and has a certain priority. On the other hand, poetry implicitly depends on philosophy, since what it "thinks" must be thought again, must be wrested from it and re-thought in another mode, even though the poetic text is a more "sacred" text than the philosophical idiom that is its vehicle and is therefore impossible ultimately to translate (hence Heidegger's own "style" which, in its poetic use of metaphor, is a crossing of poetry and thought). This is why we do not progress with poetry. There is a critical point — the very point of signif- icant disclosure — when poetry, most itself, closest to itself in its essence, does not contribute to the project of thought; that is, it cannot by appropriated or "used" by philosophy, without significant loss. Poetic thinking is fundamentally different from philosophical thinking. Nevertheless, this point of untrans- latability, when poetry's "thought" is no longer accessible or apprehensible except as an enigmatic knot, may also be the most provocative and, paradox- ically, the most fruitful for thought.

Stevens, Vallejo, and Char have, indeed, all exerted their most insistent pressure at that critical point where poetry both escapes thought and yet extends it profoundly. On the basis of any superficial reading, however, there is initially little to connect these very different poets, even if the three are contemporaries. Beyond this obvious historical conjunction, the disparity is manifold: linguistic, national, religious, ideological, biographical, generic, stylistic, thematic, philosophical, political, and — to use a perhaps outmoded and impressionistic, but nevertheless quite useful word here — *temperamental*. The temper — the consistency and tone — of their writings is so different as to make any particular resemblance all the more remarkable. This resemblance is ultimately theoretical. Each of these poets throws into question certain philosophic values essentially connected with truth-oriented discourse, the whole tradition of *logos* as speech, reason, science, light, etc. But if they subvert these values, they also revalue them, in the Nietzschean sense, and go beyond any simple self-congratulatory and self-justifying gesture of demystification. They are by no means nihilistic. They do not do away with the truth without putting something else in its place. They advocate a more general, unrestricted economy of values, an alternate organization for thought, another means of thinking about the world and human experience, of productively harnessing the energy born from contradiction and difference.

This poetics is not simply destructive, as Paul Bové claims of much modern poetry. These poets do not proclaim an irrational ideology of illegibility, of the death of meaning, or some semic chaos beyond any determinable organization or logic. They are in fact all eminently *readable*, interpretable, and make sense, even if they do not make *one* sense. They make senses, when they make most sense, senses that remain enigmatic and unresolved into one. Contradiction and inconsistency, for them, are not an admittance of semantic defeat, of the failure to make meaning cohere and to impose a unique view of reality. They are the mark of irreconcilable differences which have a ponderable significance. The complexities of these works are not amenable to simple solution, but betray a semantic depth calling for interpretation, even if this interpretation is a potentially infinite task.

Each poet's work has, then, a describable organization and logic, and consequently a pattern of significance, an economy of meaning. But this economy is not, for instance, what Derrida would designate as a "proper" economy or "law of the house." These works only make sense as anti-economies: improper, unrestricted, general economies of discourse, subversive of the strictures that govern the *official* discourse of Western thought, which may be summed up as the determination to reduce all signification to the unity of a proper order, meaning, name, identity, or state of being. To eternalize a plenitude of meaning, to idealize and fix a hierarchy of presence and truth, are tendencies all three poets actively question and disrupt by diverse strategies of contradiction and reversal, by paradoxical logics and impossible conjunctions, and finally — most powerfully — by affirmations irreducible to the proffering of a truth.

* * *

At one point or another, each poet summons the same singular metaphor to convey that which in their poetry, intruding from some *other* place, both escapes and comes from somewhere beyond voice, presence, truth, light. The metaphor is that of the wound, which is an image of apartness, dispersal, severance, loss, but at the same time enigmatically one of participation, articulation, attachment, of a separation that gathers, as in Heidegger's painful "threshold" where difference brings near and relates insurmountably different things.[5]

Vallejo, for example, uses the wound as figure for the gravity of the blow that has struck and impaired the discourse of Western thought. "¡Vámonos! ¡Vámonos! Estoy herido" (*PC* 641), the poet cries out in "Intensidad y altura": "I am hit, wounded." What Vallejo calls in "Panteón" the "lesion of the unknown," seen in the "lesion of the response" ("Y Si ví en la lesión de la respuesta, / claramente, / la lesión mentalmente de la incognita" [*PC* 647]), has radically shaken the faith of the philosopher, profoundly violated the unity of the logos, of voice and reason, which are scattered without hope of remission. Poem after poem returns us again and again to that limit point at which the illimitable dimension of human experience definitively disrupts metaphysical discourse. The wound, the deadly blow to the logos — that one more blow reserved for philosophical knowledge of which Derrida writes in "Tympan"[6] — has become insufferable, bleeding away the meaning of life for the human individual. The exceptional power of Vallejo's poetry stems, indeed, from the disparity involved in the great eloquence with which he uses discourse to convey the catastrophe that has befallen it. Vallejo is an important test case, precisely because what is positively at work in the other two poets is undecided in his own: namely, the idea of poetic invention as a powerful curative element, which nevertheless is still antagonistic to any strictly proper order of meaning or state of being.

For this reason, Vallejo naturally comes first in the discussion. His poems relentlessly satirize the metaphysical dream of plenitude and presence. In Bakhtin's sense, they uncrown and *degrade* their object, "bringing it down to earth," down to "the material bodily lower stratum."[7] In "Panteón," for example, the earth is said to "let itself be understood and named" and the philosopher's nostrils are described as "funeral, temporal" (*PC* 647). In this process of subversion, Vallejo's language loses its power to affirm and becomes extremely parodic, as he destroys through irony any conception of informing transcendent presence, of historical orientation and human destiny. All that is left is the unaccountable, incomprehensible event of life. His poetry thus finds itself in the curious dilemma of expressing the desire for that which it can only ridicule and mock, for to a large extent Vallejo still conceives of human discourse as finding its sole possible justification in the validity of the logos. Being incapable of either affirmation or denial, and yet compelled towards both, his poetry reaches a point of extreme tension. Confronted with the contradictory and ambivalent nature of existence, he adopts a radically *neutral* perspective, which never resolves itself as an "either/or" but remains an extreme state of "neither/nor."

For both Stevens and Char there is, by contrast, a cure of the wound. This cure lies, paradoxically, in the wound itself, a cure of the wound by the wound that comes about, although in distinctive ways, through the affirmation of poetic invention. For all their obvious differences, both Stevens and Char believe in the healing power of poetry.

"The fiction of the leaves," in Stevens' "The Rock," when fully "digested" ("And if we ate the incipient colorings") and made identical with "the poem, the icon and the man," becomes "a cure of the ground and of ourselves, / In the predicate that there is nothing else" (*CP* 526). Paradoxically, the fact that "there is nothing else" may well provide us with everything else, all of our life in the world, "A particular of being, that gross universe." Paul Bové's reading of the same poem by Stevens illustrates the unfortunate negative zeal of some deconstructive approaches. Bové unduly focuses on the poem's negations, seeing the poem as an exposing of the unromantic "truth" of poetry's groundlessness and falsity. The poem, however, might better be regarded as an affirmation, however groundless, of the fictional, as the celebration of "A vital assumption," which is "An illusion so desired" that it becomes uncannily effective and not merely deceptive and mendacious. "The self so wants a comforting illusion," claims Bové, "that it creates a soothing, yet impermanent illusion to populate the cold emptiness which truly endures. The flowers cover the barren rock and satisfy the self by putting sight of something in the place of a vision of nothing."[8] The problem with this reading is that it simply repeats and confirms, albeit in a contrasting negative key, the traditional opposition between fiction and truth, when Stevens is testing and throwing into question this very opposition. For Bové, Stevens presents fiction as having a purely negative, compensatory value. Not that such an interpretation is inexact; in fact, the exactitude is part of the problem. It reduces the very paradox that a poem like "The Rock," through the presence of contradictory elements, brings into play. The exactitude of such an interpretation is too exacting; it excludes too much. It emphasizes an irremediable loss of meaning, the senselessness and emptiness of fiction, when the poem itself insists upon the curative influence of fiction and poetry, and not only in spite of, but *in view of* this recognition of nothingness: "As if nothingness contained a métier." The lack of ground for such an affirmation is not a negative, invalidating factor; it is indeed a necessary aspect of the affirmation. To overlook this creative paradox represents an unnecessarily literalist deprivation of the poem's significance, which only gains richness as the very reverse of Bové's paraphrase.

The cure afforded by the encounter with poetry, by which the poisoned ground of poetry — the recognition that its foundation is abysmal — becomes in its turn the source of a healing, suggests the work of a *pharmakon*, a "pharmaceutical" element, like the one described by Derrida in "Plato's Pharmacy."[9] Precisely this effect is missing in Vallejo's loss of faith in the logos as the foundation of effective discourse. Vallejo does not exploit *différance* and supplementarity as positive factors. Although both Char and Stevens see the supplementary logic of language as ambivalent, they understand this ambivalence as a beneficial condition of poetry. The wound, for both poets, becomes a medium of disclosure.

Stevens recognizes a potentially poisonous aspect of language in what he calls "the metaphor that murders metaphor" (*NA* 84). But this fatal element is also, potentially, a tonic and restorative as well. If extravagant metaphor can murder itself, it can also cure us of an equally dangerous tendency to seek a "beyond" of metaphor, a state of proper meaning and being where we would be — perhaps finally, terminally — transfixed by the truth or by an excessively strict definition of reality. Stevens' metaphor follows precisely the logic of Derrida's *pharmakon*, and works as a dangerous but at the same time saving supplement. The viciousness of metaphor is, at a different moment, the affirmative "finding fang" (*CP* 420) of an invented fictive world. This world not only supplements the loss of an idealized fuller, truer world, but also serves as a powerful antidote protecting us against the potentially fatal wound of a restrictive truth. In "Someone Puts a Pineapple Together" truth is described as being, originally, green's "implacable sting" (*NA* 84), in the context a positive expression, which nevertheless indicates the need for *différance* that is part of the network of truth and metaphor in Stevens' poetry. The "sting," if it is capable of curing us of murderous metaphor, may — by the very fact of its being a sting (and an implacable one at that) — be just as naturally thought of as a poisonous wounding, which would become effective in a different context. Truth and metaphor are definable and measurable only in their difference — and in their *différance*. In the case of truth, this means that the truth as a positive term does not exist, and therefore there is no truth as such, since it could only exist as the foundation, the ground of linguistic figuration, not as always already part of language's system of differences. Stevens, in short, treats the truth as signifier: "Where was it one first heard of the truth? The" (*CP* 203). Thus its determining force is only of a relative nature, like all signifiers in the chain. This changes, of course, our understanding of metaphor as well, and of figurative language in general, since any deviation of language is only measurable where there exists a strict relation to truth, to proper meaning or identity. But this change of perspective, catastrophic as it may be for the metaphysical tradition, does not simply ruin metaphor and truth. It lifts the stricture in the structure of their relation and of our relationship to them, and prepares the way for a curiously liberated affirmation, a joyful wisdom, a *gaya scienza*, a knowledge — to invoke Bakhtin's idea of carnival — of the "gay relativity of all things," and of all signs and words as well. There is a powerful healing influence in language joyously affirmed as it rolls "on the expressive tongue, the finding fang" (*CP* 420).

René Char equally affirms this paradox of a *vital wound*. When he asks, for example, in *Lettera Amorosa*, "Pourquoi le champ de la blessure est-il de tous le plus prospère?" (*LM* 95), he is nt only being faithful to the oxymoronic conventions of romantic love poetry. He is also drawing on the ambivalence of the *pharmakon* that is an essential effect in his poetry. For Char, the identity of a proper name or meaning is finally only discoverable as a profound contradiction, riddle, or enigma. The process whereby this contradictory identity is attained is often dramatized as an agonistic contest with another self or sovereign equal, one of Char's "loyaux adversaires" (*FM* 87). This opponent against which one tests oneself is finally an image of our — the reader's — encounter with the text, the "identity of the text"[10] being the result of a violent but creative contradiction, which remains unresolved and the extreme image of which is a potentially fatal wounding. In this way the highly defensive and oppositional nature of the poetic text is, paradoxically, at the same time the opportunity of its disclosure, in Heidegger's sense of *Entschlossenheit*,[11] which refers to a point of extreme decision or resolution that is also a dis-closure: a removal of closure, an aperture, an open-endedness. This aperture is a space for the play of signification, which remains active. Another way in which Car poses this definition of the poetic text is as a marriage, a "hymen" or union of violently opposed extremes or contraries. What Derrida characterizes as the undecidability of writing in "The Double Session" (*D* 173-286) is, for Char, the *conditio sine qua non* of the poem. One of his figures for this necessary condition is the serpent, the emblem of an energy that is essentially "pharmaceutical." It involves, as already mentioned, the idea of a poison that is also antidote, of a wounding that is both curative and creative. In Char's poetry, as in Stevens', the idea of a *pharmakon* thus joins with the figure of the *pharmakos*. The serpent as a scapegoat, as the figure of a destructive power, is reversed and positively revalued as the symbol of an indispensable creative energy.

* * *

Two final remarks, then, concerning my strategy.

The first has to do with the way I have organized the discussion. Since the first challenge in such a comparison of poets is to preserve as much as possible the individual character of their writings, I have staged things "paratactically" and respected the peculiarities and particulars of each. The analysis of each poet's work is separate, self-contained, and independent of the others. I have made no attempt at transition from one chapter to another, a syntactical omission which has, nevertheless, the great advantage of presenting each poet on his own terms. The last thing I wanted to do was to dissolve their differences, to shorten, as it were, the significant distances between them.

But this *parataxis*, this absence of bridges over the abysses between the three, may have another justification. One of my themes is the difference that gathers, that separates and brings together at the same time. This "articulation" takes place best in the silences, and with the simple placing of the three poetries side by side, what is *proper* to them all should emerge "silently," on its own — through their differences and not in spite of them.

Secondly, and in conclusion, I have sought to be theoretical only *along with* the poetry; that is, only to the extent that it is itself theoretical and theorizes, thinks, even if that thinking is, strictly speaking, "improper": metaphoric, paradoxical, enigmatic, contradictory. I have tried to "think" these poetries — and not just to paraphrase them — with the recognition that, to use Heidegger's words regarding "his thinking the same thing that Hölderlin is saying poetically":

> Poetry and thinking meet each other in one and the same only when, and only as long as, they remain distinctly in the distinctness of their nature. . . . We can only say "the same" if we think difference. It is in the carrying out and settling of differences that the gathering nature of sameness comes to light. The same banishes all zeal always to level what is different into the equal or identical. The same gathers what is distinct into an original being-at-one. The equal, on the contrary, disperses them into the dull unity of mere uniformity.[12]

These poets are not equal, though they may be "the same." In each case, I have meant to preserve the difference, between them and *of* them. I have followed their individual poetic statements to "divine a path by which, through what is thought differently, we come nearer to thinking the same as what the poet composes in his poem."

In order to come nearer, closer to what they are saying, my readings have been themselves what we refer to these days as "close." This is very true of my analysis of Char and perhaps even more so of that of Stevens, my commentaries on both "Credences of Summer" and the closing cantos of "Notes" being unarguably dilatory. When the theme of these poets is itself so often closeness, (proximity to the source, the origin, presence, the truth), such an extended meditation is a paradox, one that Stevens neatly sums up at the beginning of "An Ordinary Evening in New Haven," where "The eye's plain version," that "thing apart," provokes an endless, and endlessly prospective, expatiation: "Of this, / A few words, an and yet, and yet, and yet" (*CP* 465). And yet it is only proper perhaps that the "proper" be so scrutinized. There is a poetic justice in it. It is certainly how the poets have brought its law and stricture to task. When, at least, they have not set out to violate its logic outright, they have out-propriated it. They have pressed it close, carried its law away, to that furthest extreme at which it yields up its own paradox and admits the deficiency — the wound — at its very heart. With this deficiency, this dehiscence — this internal distance from itself — they have also discovered a potentially creative opening, the very chance and future of poetry.

Notes to Introduction

1. Paul de Man, *Allegories of Reading: Figural Language in Rousseau, Nietzsche, Rilke, and Proust* (New Haven; Yale Univ. Press, 1979), p. 17.

2. Jacques Derrida, "Structure, Sign, and Play," in *Writing and Difference*, trans. Alan Bass (Chicago: The Univ. of Chicago Press, 1978), p. 292. All further references to this work, henceforth designated by the abbreviation *WD*, appear parenthetically in the text.

3. Martin Heidegger, *What Is Called Thinking*, trans. J. Glen Gray (New York: Harper & Row, 1968), p. 134.

4. Martin Heidegger, ". . .Poetically Man Dwells . . .," in *Poetry, Language, Thought*, trans. Albert Hofstadter (New York: Harper & Row, 1975), pp. 218-19.

5. Heidegger writes in "Language": "But what is pain? Pain rends. It is the rift. But it does not tear apart into dispersive fragments. Pain indeed tears asunder, it separates, yet so that at the same time it draws everything to itself, gathers it to drawing which, like the pen-drawing of a plan or sketch, draws and joins together what is held apart in separation" (*Poetry, Language, Thought*, p. 204).

6. Jacques Derrida, *Margins of Philosophy* (Chicago: The Univ. of Chicago Press, 1982), p. xi. All further references to this work, henceforth designated by the abbreviation *MP*, appear parenthetically in the text.

7. For Mikhail Bakhtin's concept of parody and satire, in relation to "crowning" and "degradation," and to "the material bodily lower stratum," see *Rabelais and His World*, trans. Helene Izwolsky (Bloomington: Indiana Univ. Press, 1984).

8. Paul A. Bové, *Destructive Poetics: Heidegger and Modern American Poetry* (New York: Columbia Univ. Press, 1980), p. 209. For a more affirmative reading of the same poem and of Stevens' deconstruction of the "proper," see J. Hillis Miller's "Stevens' Rock and Criticism as Cure," *Georgia Review*, 30 (1976), 5-31).

9. Jacques Derrida, *Dissemination*, trans. Barbara Johnson (Chicago: The Univ. of Chicago, 1981), pp. 61-177. All further references to this work, henceforth designated by the abbreviation *D*, appear parenthetically in the text. See also Geoffrey H. Hartman, "Words and Wounds," in *Saving the Text* (Baltimore: the Johns Hopkins Univ. Press, 1981), pp. 118-57, and Eleanor Cook's discussion of Stevens' wounding words and fictions in "Riddles, Charms, and Fictions in Wallace Stevens," in *Centre and Labyrinth*, ed. Eleanor Cook et al. (Toronto: Univ. of Toronto Press, 1983), pp. 227-44.

10. I am referring to the title of a recent collection of critical essays, *Identity of the Literary Text*, ed. Mario J. Valdés and Owen Miller (Toronto: Univ. of Toronto Press, 1985).

11. Heidegger calls "willing" "the sober resolution" or *Ent-schlossenheit.* — "unclosedness" — "of that existential self-transcendence which exposes itself to the openness of being as it is set into the work" ("The Origin of the Work of Art," in *Poetry, Language, Thought,* p. 67.

12. Heidegger, *Poetry, Language, Thought,* p. 219.

I

VALLEJO: THE WOUND IN THE VOICE

1. Vallejo and Philosophy

All that philosophers have handled for milennia has been conceptual mummies; nothing actual has escaped from their hands alive. They kill, they stuff, when they worship, these conceptual idolaters — they become a mortal danger to everything when they worship. . . . Be a philosopher, be a mummy, represent monotono-theism by a gravedigger-mimicry!
> Friedrich Nietzsche, *Twilight of the Idols*[1]

The philosopher writes in order to keep himself within the logocentric circle. But also in order to reconstitute the circle, to interiorize a continuous and ideal presence which he knows, consciously or unconsciously — which does not matter since in any event he feels the effect — *already* to have been dispelled within the voice itself.
> Jacques Derrida, "Qual Quelle" (*MP* 291)

Il ne s'agit point de faire passer à Vallejo un examen de philosophie.
> Alain Sicard, "Contradiction et renversement matérialiste dans la poésie de César Vallejo"[2]

The relationship between the poetry of César Vallejo and philosophy is an exceptional one. Nothing is further than his from a poetry of ideas, and yet nothing is more crucial to its appreciation than an understanding of the central role played by Western thought. The particular importance of post-Enlightenment intellectual and scientific upheavals to the writings of Vallejo has by no means been lost on his critics, and has been emphasized perhaps at the expense of much else that is to be found in his poems. Moreover, the ideological drama of his work is only intensified by the striking variance of elements belonging to a post-Darwinian and Marxian world view with what appear to be strong religious and mystical currents. The critic ends up finding what he wants in Vallejo: an imitation of Christ or a prophet of revolution, and this is so true

18

that at times it is hard to believe we are reading the same text.[3]   The allusive difficulty of the verse is in part responsible for such disparate readings, for it is characterized by an irony of voice capable of admitting together seemingly contradictory ideological strands.   In the face of such a potential chaos of interpretations, it is not surprising that one of the most obsessive concerns should be to *identify* the poet, to hold him to himself and insist upon some degree of consistency, even if one has to resort to personal legend, or official belief and intellectual affiliation.[4]   Much of the criticism of the work resembles a jealous struggle among warring parties over the possession of the poet's body, or the body of his writing, an activity that unfortunately tends to treat the poetry itself as a dead letter.   Indeed, this struggle has been reflected, on another front, in the issue of the legal possession and withholding of manu-scripts, making all the more eery the strange seal stamped on each of the original pages of the posthumous poetry: "Propiedad de César Vallejo."[5] Excepting this kind of critical and editorial possessiveness, the concern with Vallejo's intellectual interests, with his ideological alignments and conversions, and with the many references made throughout the poetry to theological, metaphysical, and scientific topics is quite understandable.   Clearly realized by all his readers is the fact that the great questions of belief and knowledge are, in some crucial way, an integral part of his work.

    But what is the role of philosophy in Vallejo's work?   What does the interest in philosophy and in philosophers (in no other poet are there perhaps so many references to the proper names of Western thought) represent in the end? Philosophical theorization on the basis of the poetry is from the very beginning problematic.   Any attempt to derive from the poems an ideological position or the expression of a metaphysical or theological insight is a complicated matter, although this kind of critical approach is common, and not just among Catholic or Marxist partisans.[6]   Such an approach, however, overlooks the extent to which so many of the metaphysical and theological references throughout Vallejo's poetry may, in fact, be indefinitely ironic.   The weighing of irony is, of course, always a difficult task.   The trope is notorious for its slipperiness, and, in seeking to measure and delimit its effect, we can never be sure to what degree we are underestimating or exaggerating its presence.   The difficulty, however, is commensurate only with the critical difference in readings which a more or less ironic ear involves.[7]   Furthermore, there is often a desire to control and reduce the corrosive action of irony, stemming from the anxiety that an identifiable meaning or voice be lost.   An anxiety of this sort appears to be at work in the critical resistance to Vallejo's almost invariable use of the trope (if not of outright parody and satire), whenever certain philosophical topics are introduced and deployed, such as the nature of God, the positing of an absolute, unity and the question of the one and the many, conceptions of space and time, the point and the line, number, etc.   Although much of the studied blasphemy and irreverence of the early writings is in imitation of the decadent posings of the Symbolist poets, even quite early poems such as "Unidad," "Absoluta," or "Linéas," in *Heraldos Negros*, reveal an irony which not only precludes a purely metaphysical or theological point of view, but appears, indeed, to have as its central target metaphysics and theology themselves.   From the very beginning of his career, Vallejo singles out and treats in highly ironic fashion not just certain philosophical ideas or positions, but philosophy as an undertaking, inasmuch as it is the expression of a certain totalizing and unifying aspiration of the human will.

In *Trilce*, the ironic treatment of philosophical topics is even more obsessive; the great themes of Western thought recur from poem to poem, albeit in a rather fragmented form, and come to be one of the most important guiding threads through a work whose overall unity is somewhat uncertain. However, if anything emerges from the reading of that work, it is certainly not a reformulation or even a critical reassessment of the topics in question, but their virtual destruction, since the relentless parody of philosophical pretension and seriousness is hardly containable. The radical subversion of identifications and oppositions regulating the system of rational discourse is reflected in the imperative of XXXVI, "¡Ceded al nuevo impar / potente de orfandad!", and in the invocation of the absurd in XLV:

> Y sí así diéramos las narices
> en el absurdo,
> nos cubriremos con el oro de no tener nada,
> y empollaremos el ala aún no nacida
> de la noche, hermana
> de esta ala huérfana del día,
> que a fuerza de ser una ya no es ala.[8]

The orphan, the absurd, and the odd or unmatched have in common their exclusion from a series of relations, whether it be a family group, signifying system, numerical sequence, or class of objects. Seriality and genus are, in fact, what make "serious" discourse serious and possible in the first place. The significance of the orphan figure in Vallejo's writings is not exhausted by its pathetic or existential connotations, but functions in a more active and productive sense, marking the rupture with a secure network of associations in which the exclusive values of identifiable origin, descent, and genealogy are central. In other words, Vallejo's "orphan complex" may reflect less a romantic case of subjective alienation than an attempt to undercut a predominant system of relations and to write on the margins of the central discourse of our culture.

In the untitled posthumous poetry,[9] Vallejo's relationship to "philosophy" (the word should be cited, since the relationship is, in a sense, one of citation) and, even more so, to the philosophers, emerges as an intensely personal one, or as one that is taken quite personally. Although the interest in philosophy pervades his poetry from the very beginning, it is still lacking a proper name, as it were, and it is this name, or rather these many names that come to represent such an interest in the posthumous poetry. When the poet makes his adieu in "Despedida recordando un adiós," a poem whose redundant title provides an apt rubric for Vallejo's entire work, filled as it is with scene after scene of painfully rehearsed departures, it is from the masters of the *logos* that he takes his leave; it is to those rulers in disorder and chaos ("gobernadores en desorden"), thinkers, theologians, and political theorists, that he addresses himself in his "little note for everyone" ("esta cartita para todos")

> Al cabo, al fin, por último,
> torno, volví y acábome y os gimo, dándoos
> la llave, mi sombrero, esta cartita para todos.
> Al cabo de la llave está el metal en que apprendiéramos
> a desdorar el oro, y está, al fin
> de mi sombrero, este pobre cerebro mal peinado,
> y, último vaso de humo, en su papel dramático,
> yace este sueño práctico del alma.
>
> ¡Adiós, hermanos san pedros,
> heráclitos, erasmos, espinozas!
> ¡Adiós, tristes obispos bolcheviques!
> ¡Adiós, gobernadores en desorden!
> ¡Adiós, vino que está en el agua como vino!
> ¡Adiós, alcohol que está en la lluvia!
>
> (*PC* 635)

What we are left with after such a farewell is a complete unknown, finding ourselves at a threshold of discourse and understanding, in which the reason of the philosopher, nothing more than this "pobre cerebro mal peinado," encounters its unavoidable limit. The soul's "sueño práctico" is said to be "último vaso de humo," while the beautiful play on the turn of phrase which announces a discourse's conclusion or summing up, "Al cabo, al fin, por último," proclaims the end of life as the end of discourse. What lies beyond remains a terribly — and terribly ironic — open question. The effective limits of the logos and of logic ("la lógica, / los linderos del fuego"), of reason and of the rule of identity and difference ("de modo idéntico, / frío del frío y frío del calor"), are now perceived at the vanishing point:

> ¡Adiós, también, me digo a mí mismo,
> adiós, vuelo formal de los milígramos!
> ¡También adiós, de modo idéntico,
> frío del frío e frío del calor!
> Al cabo, al fin, por último, la lógica,
> los linderos del fuego,
> la despedida recordando aquel adiós.
>   (*PC* 635)

The evocation of a liminal state or threshold in which the discourse of the logos is in extremity, faced with what can only be described as an indefinite hiatus, a break or gap beyond which lies an unknown, is remarkably character-istic of the posthumous poetry. In reading one poem after another, one has the impression of an unrelieved process of leave-taking, as though words themselves had been so grievously threatened they were no longer capable of anything but making their own farewell. Given the pleonastic and self-reflexive nature of its title, "Despedida recordando un adiós" is the exemplary poem in this regard. If such a poem pretends to have gotten to the bottom of things, as the obsessively insistent refrain of "Al cabo, al fin, por último" suggests, that which finally remains to be named, revealed, or identified is peculiarly indefinite and uncer-tain. What is disclosed is the very liminality of the threshold state, a condition of perpetual leave-taking in which making one's farewells represents, in its absurd redundancy, a ritualistic and apotropaic gesture that wards off the end as it keeps it constantly in view. If the discourse of philosophy may be defined, in Derrida's words, as "a discourse that has *called itself* philosophy" and which "has always, including its own, meant to say its limit, " then the liminal state evoked by Vallejo must be situated on the margins of that discourse, since it coincides with philosophy's own limit, but as the limit that it cannot master and that unmasters it. In the words of Derrida's essay "Tympan":

> Philosophy has always insisted upon this: thinking its other. Its other: that which limits it, and from which it derives its essence, its definition, its production. To think its other: does this amount solely to *relever (aufheben)* that from which it derives, to head the procession of its method only by passing the limit? Or indeed does the limit, obliquely, by surprise, always reserve one more blow for philosophical knowledge? Limit/passage.
>
> (*MP* x-xi)

It is at this other limit or edge, with its further or one more blow to philosophical knowledge, that so many of Vallejo's poems seem to be written, as they mark dramatically the end, not so much of life, as of the discourse that would master life completely, that is, the discourse held by philosophy:

> Al borde del fondo voy . . . (*PC* 626)
>
> al pie de la mirada; dando voces,
> los límites, dinámicos, feroces . . . (*PC* 639)
>
> Al fondo, es hora . . . (*PC* 629)
>
> Y, en fin, pasando luego al dominio de la muerte . . .
> (*PC* 684)

The ultimate effect of this perspective, taken at the limits of life, is a radical indecision concerning the privilege bestowed upon reason and the word. Vallejo's poetry represents, in a broad sense, an ironic testing or trial of the logos, with the radical hypothesis that the Word, "la palabra," may not in the end survive or be fulfilled; that, contrary to the presupposition on which the tradition of philosophical discourse is based, the letter, as Derrida puts it in "Le facteur de la vérité," may not, in fact, arrive at its destination.[10] This "postal catastrophe" of the Word is the subject of the poem "¡Y si después de tántas palabras," which ironically alludes to the logos in the same terms as the survival of species:

> ¡Y si después de tántas palabras,
> no sobrevive la palabra!
> ¡Si después de las alas de los pájaros
> no sobrevive el pájaro parado!
> Más valdría, en verdad,
> que se lo coman todos y acabemos!
>
> (*PC* 593)

The irony lies here in the fact that the very possibility of such a catastrophe befalling the Word means that the catastrophe has already befallen it; the possibility is itself the catastrophe, since, in the face of it, the security of the logos can no longer be guaranteed in any absolute sense. Thus, the despairing curse "¡Más valdría, en verdad, / que se lo coman todos y acabemos!" is, in such a context, in no way conditional upon the actual event of catastrophe; it refers, on the contrary, to something that has already taken place. The event is actual, has already taken place, as soon as there exists the possibility of it. The logos has already met its downfall in the very possibility that catastrophe might befall it. But if, in one sense, the catastrophe has already happened, in another sense it is still only the speculative object of a horrifying hypothesis: "What if . . . ?" ("Y si después de tàntas palabra . . . !"). The speculative, and yet virtually effective, nature of the catastrophe involves that double focus characteristic of a liminal or threshold state, and it is this spectral focus that gives to so many of Vallejo's poems their *unheimlich* quality, and that makes his posthumous poetry posthumous in a further sense. The poem "Acaba de pasar el que vendrá," ending with the lines "Acaba de pasar sin haber venido," expresses this state in which the future advent is a virtual reality, not yet, but approaching, and at the same time somehow already having occurred. As the opening and closing lines indicate, the Messianic "el" has arrived, and indeed has already, if just, passed by ("Acaba de pasar"), *but*, at the same time, has not in fact, and is yet to, come: "vendrá"; "sin haber venido" (*PC* 667). Similarly, "Piedra negra sobre una piedra blanca" illustrates, in an even more dramatic fashion, the potential paradox of an end which has already taken place, since it is remembered ("tengo ya el recuerdo"), but is still to come, projected into the future ("Me moriré"):

Me moriré en París con aguacero,
un día del cual tengo ya el recuerdo,
Me moriré en París — yo no me corro —
talvez un jueves, como es hoy, de otoño.
(*PC* 579)

The model for such a discourse of the end which, in this case, is primarily the story of the end of discourse, of the catastrophe befalling the logos, lies in the apocalyptic mode itself, whose most obvious source is scriptural. Thus, it is not only apt, but perhaps even compelling, to consider whether the apocalyptic character of so much of Vallejo's writing does not ultimately reflect a religious faith which, far from pointing to the end of the logos, to its catastrophe, points, on the contrary, to the ultimate fulfilment of the Word in revelation. However, the determination of such a hypothesis is extremely uncertain, given the ironic context in which so many of the scriptural allusions in the posthumous poetry are made. Astonishingly enough, the very acuteness of the irony often has the opposite effect, as in Juan Larrea's striking interpretation of the apparently satiric "Lomo de las Sagradas Escrituras" as a profound manifestation of Vallejo's faith, when the pun on *lomo* alone — it can mean either loins or the spine of a book — should be enough to give us pause.[11] Throughout his poetry, Vallejo aims at a parody of the logos and of Scripture, in which, however, the precise relationship between the parodied and the parodying remains in the end somewhat undecidable. Indeed, this is so true that it is hard, if not at times impossible, to tell which is which. In the following lines from the poem "Sermón sobre la muerte," Darwin's human species is set against the human being as governed by the logos, a particular device of juxtaposition that is quite common throughout the posthumous poetry and which, almost like the conflation of two radically variant texts, produces an uneasy and irreducible effect of contradiction or paradox. The undecidability of Vallejo's religiosity is raised once again here, the effect achieved by the poem being, in fact, strongly reminiscent of Pascal's provocative perception of the human being as an enigma, as a paradox or chimera; the human creature is that impossible combination, the contradictory hybrid of the animal and the divine. For Pascal, however, the realization of this absolute state of contradiction that defines humanity is an intuition capable of turning the human being towards God, towards the source of its greatness and away from its baseness. Vallejo, on the other hand, sustains the knot or paradox to the point where it becomes unbearable, but without ever transcending it:

> De esta suerte, cogitabundo, aurífero, brazudo,
> defenderé mi presa en dos momentos,
> con la voz y también con la laringe,
> y del olfato físico con que oro
> y del instinto de immovilidad con que ando,
> me honraré mientras viva — hay que decirlo...
> (*PC* 684)

Two misprisions become possible here: one involves the invention of a Christic Vallejo, martyred champion of a Catholic spirituality, bearing the cross of modernity and fighting the debilitating scientific notion of man; the other looks to the materialist Vallejo, satirist of the false ideology of religious faith, atheist and avid proponent of Darwin and Marx. These mutually exclusive interpretations represent two important poles of the criticism that has treated Vallejo's poetry. In their limited scope, the questions answered by the one are left unasked by the other, as they both find justification in the evidence of contradictory codes at work throughout the poetry: that of the human as ruled by the logos, and that of human species. In each line of the passage from "Sermón," both codes are brought into play at once: "cogitabundo"/"brazudo"; "defenderé," which is used in differing senses — a defence in speech or writing ("en dos momentos") versus the violent physical action of an animal defending its prey ("mi presa"); "la voz" / "la laringe"; "olfato físico" / "oro"; "instinto" / "honraré." The juxtaposition of incompatible codes here is neutral, insofar as no value or privilege is imparted to one code over the other, so that the effect of indefiniteness and irresolvable contradiction is maintained. One might say, to borrow Barthes' play on the two words, that Vallejo takes the conflicting *doxa* of our culture and, joining them together, turns them into paradox ("beyond what is thought"), into an unthinkable and monstrous formulation.[12] The paradox, of course, is not meant to be resolved.[13]

Apocalyptic remains, nevertheless, with all its scriptural connotations in play, the best word to describe the effect of much of Vallejo's poetry, especially in the posthumous works. If elegiac farewells are such a major obsession from poem to poem, just as important is the motif of return and reappropriation. The apocalyptic mode provides a context in which the two movements, of departure and return, come to be somewhat indistinguishable from one another. The confusion or quasi-identity of the two is reflected in the opening lines of "Despedida," a poem which concerns, as we have already discussed, the departure from life and the passing beyond the limits of intelligible discourse: "Al cabo, al fin, por último, / torno, volví y acábome" (*PC* 635). *Volver*, in this context, is almost interchangeable in meaning with the *partir* of the remarkable disappearing act in "París, Octubre, 1936." The poem opens with the lines "De todo esto yo soy el único que parte," where a similar association of departure and, if not return, at least a turning movement ("dar vuelta"; "dase vuelta") is made:

> De los Campos Elíseos o al dar vuelta
> la extraña callejuela de la Luna,
> mi defunción se va, parte mi cuna,
> y, rodeada de gente, sola, suelta,
> mi semejanza humana dase vuelta
> y despacha sus sombras una a una.
> *(PC* 607)

The returning movement active in departure corresponds to the idea of a circular trajectory of reappropriation where fulfilment, totalizing and unifying completion, is confused with the negative finality of life's end, in both senses of end — as both *telos* and close. The potential ambivalence of what Derrida calls the "circle of a restricted economy" (*C* 469) is exploited and drawn out by Vallejo so that the *volver* recurrently mentioned in his poetry is associated not only with a completing return, but also, ironically, with the disastrous emptiness and closure ("torno, volví, y acábome") that mark one's death.[14]

In "Piedra negra sobre una piedra blanca," there is a reference to this catastrophic moment of return which, in this case, amounts to a literal turning-around: "jamás, como hoy, me he vuelto, / con todo mi camino, a verme solo" (*PC* 579). This turning movement is a moment of revelation, but one in which the unredeemable emptiness of the life that has already been lived is disclosed in a single glance and coincides with the poet's prophetic intuition of his own death. This death, or rather murder ("le pegaban / todos sin que él les haga nada; / le daban duro con un palo y duro / también con una soga") only resembles the stoning of a martyr so that it may declare all the more dramatically its difference. The moment of return, which is also the hour of one's death, is not redemptive. The white stone on which one's new and secret name is to be written and revealed (Rev. 2.17) is forever covered over by the black, evil stone of the day of one's death, while the witnesses to the event consist of nothing but a mute and insensible landscape made up of "los días jueves" (the significance of Thursday is, perhaps, that it isn't Friday, that it functions as a kind of anti-Good Friday) and "los huesos húmeros, / la soledad, la lluvia, los caminos."   Similarly, in the poem "Hasta el día en que vuelva," the circular movement of reappropriation is again alluded to in a satiric manner, in this case through the characteristic mixing of codes already referred to, that of the logos and of human species: "Hasta el día en que vuelva y hasta que anda / el animal que soy, entre sus jueces" (*PC* 582) The subject that returns here, at the end of time (the individual's time or the time of human history), as an animal waking among its judges, parodies the dream of both a theological and a metaphysical faith.   The conception of human species denies the Christian vision of a redemptive revelation at the end of human history, as well as its secular counterpart, the positing of a state of absolute knowledge attainable through dialectics, as in Hegel.

The philosopher's dream of a perfect destiny or destination is challenged again and again in Vallejo's poetry, and is offset in poems like "Hasta el día" and "París, Octubre, 1936" by an effect of disorientation comparable to what Derrida, in reference to Lacan's analysis of Poe's "The Purloined Letter," has called "the without-possible-return of the letter, the other scene of its remaining" (*C* 483).   In *The Post Card*, Derrida elaborates upon this postal metaphor, by which he associates the addressing of a "literal" letter with the self-addressed nature of philosophical discourse and its teleo-eschatology. Relating it to one of Heidegger's oracular utterances concerning Being, "Das Schicken im Geschick des Seins" ["the sending in the destiny of Being"], he counters with his own cryptic catchword, *the destinal posts itself*" (*C* 64-65), and later describes the catastrophe attending all philosophical delivery service, that without-possible-arrival or return of the letter, in the following terms: "it is lost for the addressee at the very second when it is inscribed, its destination is immediately multiple, anonymous . . ." (*C* 79). The fact that a letter may not arrive at its destination — which means, in fact, that its destination is always already lost to it — is reflected in the opening lines of a remarkable, although little remarked, poem entitled "Trilce."[15] It speaks of a place where we never arrive, a sort of philosophical dead-letter box: "Hay un lugar que yo me sé / en este mundo, nada menos, / adonde nunca llegaremos." Indeed, the poem contains not only a reference to the complicity of the concept of destiny and destination or address, but an obvious allusion to the postal system as well:

> Más acá de mí mismo y de
> mi par de yemas, lo he entrevisto
> siempre lejos de los destinos.
>
> Ya podéis iros a pie
> o a puro sentimiento en pelo,
> que a él no arriban ni los sellos
>
> . . . .
>
> Mas el lugar que yo me sé,
> en este mundo, nada menos,
> hombreado va con los reversos.
> (*PC* 527)

This spot of which the poet is so certain, as he is assured of its ultimate inaccessibility, is one to which all philosophical correspondence is addressed in vain. In striving futilely "to equal its opposites," it parodies the elusive and ever receding destination of Hegel's negative dialectics.

The circle of a restricted economy, characteristic of the philosopher's self-addressed and self-destined discourse, proves to be the target of another poem "Escarnecido, aclimatado al bien." Gambling ("se juega a copas") here subsumes the economic and postal metaphors, as the idea of a state of absolute chance (inspired perhaps by Mallarmé's famous "Un coup de dés jamais n'abolira le hasard") expresses the catastrophic potential represented by the letter's "without-possible-return."

> Se dobla así la mala causa, vamos
> de tres en tres a la unidad, así
> se juega a copas
> y salen a mi encuentro los que aléjanse,
> acaban los destinos en bacterias
> y se debe todo a todos.
>
> *(PC 629)*

The risk is total, and the loss complete: there is no return, no reappropriation, no final synthetic moment; rather, everything is owed to everyone, as the metaphysical economy collapses, and the destinies end up in bacteria. If there is an avowed destination or goal ("vamos / de tres en tres a la unidad"), it is, in fact, indistinguishable from disaster. The apparent absurdity of the lines "salen a mi encuentro los que aléjanse" reaffirms what we have already identified as the folding into one another, or entanglement, of the contradictory movements of departure and return. The poem "Palmas y guitarra," like "Despedida" an elegiac expression of leave-taking, sets forth this enigmatic entanglement in a refrain consisting of a series of puzzling appositions:

> ¡Hasta cuando volvamos! Hasta la vuelta!
> ¡Hasta cuando leamos, ignorantes!
> ¡Hasta cuando volvamos, despidámonos!
>
> . . . .
>
> ¡Hasta cuando seamos ciegos!
> ¡Hasta
> que lloremos de tánto volver!
>
> . . . .
> ¡Hasta cuando volvamos! Hasta entonces!
> ¡Hasta cuando partamos, despidámonos!
>
> *(CP 662-63)*

This chorus of farewells ironically overturns our normal understanding of the apocalyptic moment as revelation. The moment of return, which in this case, since it coincides with one's death, is also one of parting, is not one of reappropriation, of the final coming into possession of a promised but hitherto inaccessible knowledge. On the contrary, the full irony of the lightly colloquial "Hasta la vuelta" sinks in with the realization that what we are returning to is no state of greater vision. The famous lines from 1 Corinthians 13, "For now we see in a mirror dimly, but then face to face. Now I know in part; then I shall understand fully, even as I have been fully understood,"[16] must be parodically revised. For the knowledge entered into will be impossible to distinguish from blankest ignorance, the depth of vision not to be told from blindness ("¡Hasta cuando seamos ciegos!"). The contradiction and nonsensicalness of the paradox "¡Hasta cuando volvamos, despidámonos.!", "¡Hasta cuando partamos, despidámonos!" are irresolvable. The difference between knowledge and ignorance, blindness and vision, is thus collapsed, just as the concepts of return and departure are almost made meaningless, since they appear to be indistinguishable, and are virtually interchangeable. Revelation, for Vallejo, must be understood as a catastrophic event. Indeed, this is so true that it becomes difficult, in such a context, to perceive a difference between the end of history understood as the attainment of absolute knowledge and that same end understood as an engulfment in death and chaos. This is what makes "Palmas y guitarra" such an ambiguous poem. One may read it according to a tragic or mystical understanding, insofar as it makes reference to a catastrophic event which at the same time takes the form of a spiritual revelation. However, the subject of the poem is the return to a state of what Derrida would call "life without *différance*", where death, in bringing us to the end of life, serves as well as absolute knowledge, since life without *différance* is finally only "another name for death." Derrida writes in *Of Grammatology*:

> The subordination of the trace to the full presence
> summed up in the logos, the humbling of writing
> beneath a speech dreaming its plenitude, such are
> the gestures required by an onto-theology deter-
> mining the archeological and eschatological meaning
> of being as presence, as parousia, as life without
> differance: another name for death, historical
> metonymy where God's name holds death in check.[17]

Indeed, "Palmas y guitarras" indirectly makes an association between the catastrophe of revelation, which here coincides with the hour of one's death, and a kind of execution by firing squad:

> ¿Qué me importan los fusiles,
> escuchame;
> escuchame, ¿qué impórtanme,
> si la bala circula ya en el rango de mi firma?
> ¿Qué te importan a ti las balas,
> si el fusil está humeando ya en tu dolor?
>
> (*PC* 662)

Life without *différance* is thus to be strictly avoided, like death itself, since that is what it amounts to in the end. Accordingly, the poem evokes the escapism of a diversionary "tomorrow we all die" approach to mortality: a dance, a guitar, clapping, and a song ("Ahora, ven contigo, hazme el favor / de cantar algo / y de tocar en tu alma, haciendo palmas"). Death is something from which we can only turn aside and divert ourselves, resigned to the prospect. The urgency of flight and the compelling need for diversion are extremely pressing, when all that remains is the terrible limit between life and death ("huímos en puntillas de nosotros"). Without hope, to hold the threshold and mark time ("marcar el paso de la despedida") become the only hope. On the other hand, the coming together of the two lovers ("ven conmigo . . . ven contigo . . . Ven a mí, sí, y a ti, sí") is not just an escape, but is itself allusively apocalyptic. There is perhaps an echo here of the closing lines of The Book of Revelation: "The Spirit and the Bride say, 'Come.' And let him who hears say, 'Come.' And let him who is thirsty come . . . 'Surely I am coming soon.' Amen. Come, Lord

Jesus!" (Rev. 22:17-21). This coming together of the lovers seems to suggest a return to and reappropriation of themselves which is at the same time a "little death" (before the big one), almost a "death rehearsal." The two lovers, in fleeing and coming out of themselves two by two ("saldremos de nosotros, dos a dos"), may be thought of as dying into one another and, through death, returning to themselves, to their proper selves or state of being. The ominously apocalyptic note is underlined by the insistence on the significance of this very moment, this day: "Ahora . . . Ahora . . . Hoy mismo pesaremos . . . Hoy mismo, hermosa . . . Ahora . . ." But this return to a proper state is only a beautiful illusion; it is only, after all, to death that one returns: "pasemos un instante la vida / a dos vidas y dando una parte a nuestra muerte. . . . ¡Hasta cuando partamos, despidámonos!"

> Hoy mismo pesaremos
> en los brazos de un ciego nuestra estrella
> y, una vez que me cantes, lloraremos,
> Hoy mismo, hermosa, con tu paso par
> y tu confianza a que llegó mi alarma,
> saldremos de nosotros, dos a dos.
> ¡Hasta cuando seamos ciegos!
> ¡Hasta
> que lloremos de tánto volver!
>
>   Ahora
> entre nosotros, trae
> por a la mano a tu dulce personaje
> y cenemos juntos y pasemos un instante la vida
> a dos vidas y dando una parte a nuestra muerte.
> Ahora, ven contigo, hazeme el favor
> de cantar algo
> y de tocar en tu alma, haciendo palmas.
> ¡Hasta cuando volvamos! ¡Hasta entonces!
> ¡Hasta cuando partamos, despidámonos!
>   (*PC* 662-63)

The philosopher's dream of life without *différance*, as presence or *parousia*, is explicitly associated with murder in the poem beginning "Y no me digan nada, / que uno puede matar perfectamente," with its ironic reference to that grand scene portraying the dialectical overcoming of time and history:

> Volveremos, señores, a vernos con manzanas;
> tarde la criatura pasará,
> la expresión de Aristóteles armada
> de grandes corazones de madera,
> la de Heráclito injerta en la de Marx,
> la del suave sonando rudamente . . .
> Es lo que bien narraba mi garganta;
> uno puede matar perfectamente.
> (*PC* 575)

The vision of the return of God's creature to a lost Eden ("Volveremos, señores, a vernos con manzanas; / tarde la criatura pasará") is facetiously couched in the fatuous tones of a serious address. But rather than logos and presence, we have contradiction ("la de Heráclito injerta en la de Marx, / la del suave sonando rudamente"), human species ("Es lo que narraba mi garganta"), and "perfect murder," since the co-existence of incompatible terms is only to be resolved by what is bluntly stated to be an act of assassination ("uno puede matar perfectamente"). The dream of the perfect state of knowledge, or of the politically perfect state, when it implies the collapsing of contraries and differences into unity and identity, is potentially murderous in its desire to bring an end to *différance*. A similar association, in this case reminiscent of Nietzsche's scathing observation, "Wahrheit tödtet — ja tödtet sich selbst,"[18] "the truth kills, it even kills itself," is made in the poem "En el momento en que el tenisto . . . ," where the tennis player's ball also turns out to be the bullet or "bala" of the bestial philosopher's "new truth."

> En el momento en que el tenisto lanza magistralmente
> su bala, le posee una inocencia totalmente animal;
> en el momento
> en que el filósofo sorprende una nueva verdad,
> es una bestia completa. (*PC* 570)

Astonishingly, this poem has been read as a straightforward statement of Vallejo's materialist position. Such a reading does not take into account the irony of certain unavoidable associations. The direct reference to Marx and Feuerbach which concludes the poem ("¡Oh alma! ¡Oh pensamiento! ¡Oh Marx! ¡Oh Feuerbach!") is difficult to read as anything but a mocking apostrophe. Nevertheless, Alain Sicard, an otherwise astute critic of Vallejo's verse, sees the comparison with the tennis player as serving "de référence à l'ensemble de la démonstration qui veut prouver l'absolue primauté chez l'homme de la vie organique sur la vie spirituelle."[19] But if the philosopher is a beast in surprising his new truth, the truth in this case is materialism itself, that brutal truth of the philosopher-brute. And what, then, does the absurdity of the poem's paradoxical syllogism (with its reference to Anatole France's affirmation of a religious feeling which would be the function of a special bodily organ) say about the quest for (this kind of) truth? What is at stake here is a presupposition common to both materialism and idealism: the very presupposition of truth, that faith by which the philosopher lives and dies and, in all his innocence, kills (even more, kills himself).

Vallejo's extensive use of philosophical ideas and concepts does not aim at the demonstration of a coherent theoretical position, but represents a strategy which would turn philosophy against itself, hoist it on its own petard, as it were, fragment and explode the context in which its discourse is possible. Far from being the expression or statement of an ideological strand or *parti pris*, it is, in its grim irony, a rigorous way of keeping silent, of clamming up. If philosophy or the history of metaphysics can be said to be, in Derrida's terms, *"the unfolding of the structure or schema of an absolute will-to-hear-oneself-speak,"*[20] then Vallejo resembles nothing so much as the philosopher's uncanny "dummy," in whose voice every word will ring hollow, diverted from its origin, and unmastered by that which it would master and name. This is a way of saying that the disparate languages of species and the logos, of the biologist and the philosopher, of death and presence, never resolve their contradiction. As Americo Ferrari has indicated, for Vallejo there is no *Aufhebung* in Hegel's sense, in which the antithetical movement of thought would pass into the synthetic. Vallejo's poetry remains an *agnosis*, on the threshold of, but never passing into, a dialectical process and progress of knowledge; it is a motionless dialectic, like Pascal's "Renversement continuel du pour au contre."[21] Even more, for Ferrari:

> La dialéctica es, en Vallejo, *regresiva*, hacia una unidad anterior. Lo que hay es perplejidad de Vallejo frente a los contrarios, no dialéctica . . . . Lo importante est la atmósfera, y la actitud vital de la persona que adhiere una visión dialéctica, que es forzosamente progresista y optimista . . . Por ejemplo, la Muerte, en la dialéctica no es sino un momento del proceso, y el hombre se queda muy tranquilo frente a su muerte . . . . En Vallejo, no se trata de materialismo o de idealismo, sino de una profunda perplejidad frente a lost contrarios.[22]

If anything is absolute in Vallejo's poetry, it is precisely this perplexity and not its resolution in self-knowledge. But the faith in an ultimate presence is not simply done away with. It remains as a powerful element of contradiction. In the poem "A lo mejor soy otro," the poet is able to say "a lo mejor . . . mas allá no hay nada," perceiving himself in all his finitude as nothing but "una aguja prendida en el gran átomo," a creature only capable any long of a "No" saying ("¡No! ¡Nunca! ¡Nunca ayer! ¡Nunca después!") At the same time, the last verse of the same poem is undecidable in its final meaning, with its mention of "sospechas póstumas":

> Y de ahí este tubérculo satánico,
> esta muela moral de plesiosaurio

> y estas sospechas póstumas,
> este índice, esta cama, estos boletos.
>   (*PC* 636)

Posthumous suspicions, of course, may point either to a vestigial belief in the presence of life after death, or to the prospect of its absence; either way, they remain suspicions, and suggest a state of Hamlet-like uncertainty. But another kind of posthumous life is alluded to here: not that of the individual subject, but that of the species. The human, like any other animal, only survives as a species by virtue of its reproductive organ, "este tubérculo satánico," but the very nature of that survival hands down its death sentence as an individual. Chances are, at the best, then, that the human being is a mere animal, and thus "otro," in the sense of being alienated from itself by the very contradiction of its own discourse and reason. This is, in a way, a modern rewriting of Hamlet's famous speech: "What is a man, / If his chief good and market of his time / Be but to sleep and feed? A beast no more" (III.viii.34-35).[23] In Vallejo's case, however, the state is more absurd than tragic, and differs from the tragic hero's dilemma in this: the logos, that "large discourse, / Looking before and after" (III.viii.36), is itself made impotent, not merely the individual speaking subject. And yet in spite of this compromising view, the persistance of the belief in a posthumous life, in a principle of permanence beyond death, is not simply scientifically rejected. What Ferrari refers to as the perplexity at the heart of Vallejo's work points to an excess or irreducible remainder that the discourse common to science, metaphysics, and theology, to both logic and the logos, cannot subsume. The question as to whether the human is species, reason, or spirit is never posed by Vallejo in such a way that it can be answered; the human is ultimately identical with none of these, but is the threshold or limit at which the question itself becomes otiose. The terms of such an alternative collapse precisely at that point where the human loses its name and emerges as a nameless enigma. Like the Sphinx's question to Oedipus, the question is posed in the posthumous poetry as a riddle, but one that must remain unanswerable, except in the form of an irresolvable paradox. For it is posed in such a way that it cannot be understood or "heard" in the philosophical sense, by the philosophical "ear." Maurice Blanchot addresses this question of the human in the following way:

> Evoquons un instant le Sphinx comme question, l'homme come réponse. L'être qui questionne est nécessairement ambigu: l'ambiguité même questionne. L'homme, lorsqu'il s'interroge, se sent interrogé par quelque chose d'inhumain, et il se sent aux prises avec quelque chose qui n'interroge pas. Oedipe devant le Sphinx, c'est en première apparence l'homme devant le non-homme. Tout le travail de la question est de conduire l'homme à la reconnaissance que, devant le Sphinx, le non-homme, il est déjà devant lui-même. . . . La question profonde, c'est l'homme comme Sphinx, la part dangereuse, inhumaine et scarée, qui arrête et tient arrêté devant elle, dans la face d'un instant, l'homme qui avec simplicité et avec suffisance se dit simplement homme.[24]

A different hearing is demanded of a different ear in the poem "Oye a tu masa, a tu cometa" (*PC* 644), as the human being, that most serious cetacean ("gravísimo cetáceo"), is asked to envision itself revealed at last in all its nakedness: "*oye* a la túnica en que estás dormido, / *oye* a tu desnudez, dueña del sueño" (emphasis added). The new description of the human must not only exceed the categories of Western metaphysics and theology, but those of a scientific scrutiny as well. For if this creature is to be understood, from one point of view, as a moment of evolution, as simply a particular mammal whose ultimate origins and end are lost to it in the ocean of time, there is, on the other hand, an undeniably apocalyptic and Messianic character to Vallejo's humanism — one which, if it can be interpreted to some extent as religiously inspired, is first of all anti-theological. The body of poetry known as *Poemas Humanos*, for all its obsessive reference to the human and for all its moving expression of humanity and compassion, remains a remarkably "inhuman" work. Whatever the authenticity of such a title, "Human Poems," quite contrary to Larrea's dogmatic insistence that it is "un pegote en grave desacuerdo con su contenido lírico y con el modo de expresarse de la imaginación Vallejiana, siempre tan sobrada y imprevisible en sus concepciónes,"[25] seems indeed to be a thoroughly, if ironically, appropriate title for a work which might equally be called "Inhuman Poems." Concerning this opposition of the human and the inhuman, we might consider the following passage from Derrida's essay "White Mythology":

> Each time that polysemia is irreducible, when no unity of meaning is even promised to it, one is outside language. And consequently, outside human-ity. What is proper to man is doubtless the capacity to make metaphors, but in order to mean some thing, and only one. In this sense, the philosopher, who ever has but one thing to say, is the man of man.   (*MP* 248)

If the word "human" is eternally at the tip of Vallejo's tongue, its meaning is never voiced as it is for the philosopher, that most human of humans, that is, as a unity, as one meaning. Rather, it is declined stammeringly, in an endless stutter, as an irreducible and discordant plural. The human creature who makes his appearance throughout the pages of the posthumous poetry is a creature completely foreign to himself, an alien being of agonizing contradiction, a thing made up of and primarily defined by things, resembling Foucault's description of man, that perhaps already vanishing species of modern invention ("like a face drawn in sand at the edge of the sea"), as "a finite, determined being, trapped in the density of what he does not think, and subject, in his very being, to the dispersion of times."[26] In "Oye a tu masa," the imperatives aimed at the revelation of this still unknown, and perhaps unknowable, creature are presented according to an oppositional logic that remains unresolved, and whose resolution is open only to the future. This is the Messianic future, outside of history, and unfathomable, as the poem suggests with its allusion to a process of stripping and clothing, which points to that apocalyptic reclothing which will take place at the end of time. However, the Scriptural version of a reclothing in immortality is grimly and ironically rewritten by Vallejo. The change that will take place is not one, as Paul would have it, in which "this imperishable nature must put on the imperishable, and this mortal nature must put on immortality," in which "Death will be swallowed up in victory" (1 Cor.15:53-56). On the contrary, the human being is to be described in all its nakedness, as "atmosférico, sér de humo, / a paso redoblado de esqueleto." The nature of human nakedness's naked truth is a finally undecidable one; it is one in which death and life, the bestial and the divine, are indefinitely opposed, each one countering and contradicting the other. The human being proves to be the neutral and nameless place where the contradiction itself is both unendurably real and irresolvable: death is countered by life, life by death, the happy beast is asked to think, and the unhappy god to stop thinking.

> Oye a tu masa, a tu cometa, escúchalos; no gimas
> de memoria, gravísimo cetáceo;
> oye a la túnica en que estás dormido,
> oye a tu desnudez, dueña del sueño.
>
> . . . .
>
>
> ¿La muerte? ¡Opónle todo tu vestido!
> ¿La vida? ¡Opónle parte de tu muerte!
> Bestia dichosa, piensa;
> dios desgraciado, quítate la frente.
> Luego, hablaremos. (*PC* 644)

Vallejo's vision of the human dilemma here is a conscious reworking of Pascal's radical perception of the human, with the added element of Darwinian science. The closing stanza of "Oye a tu masa" contains, indeed, an explicit reference to the following passage in Pascal's *Pensées*:

> Quelle chimère est-ce donc que l'homme? Quelle nouveauté, quel monstre, quel chaos, quel sujet de contradiction, quel prodige! Juge de toutes choses, imbécile ver de terre; dépositaire du vrai, cloaque d'incertitude et d'erreur; gloire et rebut de l'univers.
>
> Que démêlera cet embrouillement? La nature confond les pyrrhoniens, et la raison confond les dogmatiques. Que deviendrez-vous donc, ô hommes qui cherchez quelle est votre véritable condition, par votre raison naturelle? Vous ne pouvez fuir une de ces sectes, ni subsister dans aucune.
>
> Connaissez donc, superbe, quel paradoxe vous êtes à vous-méme. Humiliez-vous, raison impuissante; taisez-vous, nature imbécile: apprenez que l'homme passe infiniment l'homme, et entendez de votre maître votre condition véritable que vous ignorez. Ecoutez Dieu.[27]

For Vallejo as well "l'homme passe l'homme" and all "philosophie humaine."[28] Like Pascal, he mercilessly attacks philosophy by exposing the extraordinary force of contradiction that is located in human existence. Whether this implies in Vallejo's case a corresponding religious solution, which for Pascal is all determining, is uncertain. It does point, at any rate, to an extreme humanization of the religious, but a humanization opposed to all philosophical humanism.

Playing on the differing senses of the word *fin*, Derrida writes in "les fins de l'homme":

> The *relève* or *relevance* of man is his *telos* or *eskhaton*. The unity of these two *ends* of man, the unity of his death, his completion, his accomplishment, is enveloped in the Greek thinking of *telos*, in the discourse on *telos*, which is also a discourse on *eidos*, on *ousia*, and on *aletheia*. Such a discourse, in Hegel as in the entirety of metaphysics, indissociably corodinates teleology with an eschatology, a theology, and an ontology. *The thinking of*

> *the end of man, therefore, is always already*
> *prescribed in metaphysics, in the thinking of the*
> *truth of man.* What is difficult to think today is an
> end of man which would not be organized by a
> dialectics of truth and negativity, an end of man
> which would not be a teleology in the first person
> plural. (*MP* 121)

The difficulty of thinking of an end of the human that is not organized by a dialectic of truth and negativity is perhaps one of the lessons of the posthumous poetry. The critical need for such an alternative is made explicit in a poem like "Quiere y no quiere su color mi pecho," where the absolute contradiction expressed in the poem's opening line reflects the very impossibility of being human. In the poem, both ends of man are expressed in terms of the individual's death, which is both the end of him and that moment when he completes himself, becoming unified and identical with himself. But this end, pointing as it does to the stasis of death and not to life, is in no way desirable; it is, indeed, a consummation devoutly *not* to be wished for. For in it, with diabolic horns at one's temples in place of reason, ambidextrous and ambivalent, one lies down dead in one's soul. The human is both the extreme animal and the extreme philosopher, the brute's brute and the most human of humans, but the *end* of this creature is finally only one: death.

> Quiero su rojo el mal, el bien su rojo enrojecido
> por el hacha suspensa,
> por el trote del ala a pie volando,
> y no quiere y sensiblemente
> no quiero acquesto el hombre;
> no quiere estar en su alma
> acostado, en la sien latidos de asta,
> el bimano, el muy bruto, el muy filósofo.
> (*PC* 619)

Vallejo is preoccupied with philosophy, and above all with its succession of proper names: Heraclitus, Aristotle, Erasmus, Spinoza, Bacon, Descartes, Pascal, Locke, Kant, Rousseau, Hegel, Darwin, and Marx. But this preoccupation is not, in the final account, a philosophical one. It represents, rather, the struggle with that which can only be made to show itself, or which can only be indicated — pointed to, but never expressed, eluding as it does the ambitious "*absolute-will-to-hear-oneself-speak*" (*SP* 102) — by the *lesion* of that discourse which would master it, to allude to those lines from one of Vallejo's most powerful poems, "Panteón": "Y si ví en la lesión de la respuesta, / claramente, / la lesión mentalmente de la incógnita" (*PC* 647). Ferrari suggests that we relate these lines to the closing moments of Hegel's *Phenomenology of Spirit*, where the procession of the Spirit's triumph in absolute knowledge is finally staged:

> Podemos recordar las últimas frases de la "Fenomenología del Espíritu": "las heridas del Espíritu no dejan cicatrices . . ." Marx piensa lo mismo. La Historia borra las cicatrices, las resorbe. En cambio, en Vallejo, queda la cicatriz. La cicatriz es lo importante. No hay en Vallejo visión progresiva del tiempo, del hombre y de la Historia . . .[29]

In Vallejo, indeed, not only is the scar ineradicable, but the wound itself never heals. For this "lesion of the unknown" seen in the "lesion of the response" points to a context in which neither dialectics nor dialogue is possible anymore. Wound within a wound, doubly, redundantly catastrophic, it stems from a grave blow to discourse, like Derrida's "further" or "one more blow to philosophical knowledge," by which philosophy itself is perhaps no more: "Or indeed does the limit, obliquely, by surprise, always reserve one more blow for philosophical knowledge?" (*MP* xi). In a parody of Christ — if, as Larrea insists, there must be such an imitation — the lesion in humanity is opened again and again, in an unarrestable bleeding of the logos or Word, in an irreparable division and dispersal of any unity of voice. For how can one give voice to the unknown without engulfing the voice itself in an abyss? "Se estremeció la incógnita en

mi amígdala" (*PC* 622), the poet writes in "Quedéme a calentar en la tinta en
que me ahogo." The significance of this "unknown" is reminiscent of Nietzsche's
rejection, in *The Gay Science*, of a potentially monotonotheistic "Unknown One"
in favour of the unknown's infinite and inexhaustible perspectival horizon:

> Rather has the world become "infinite" for us all
> over again, inasmuch as we cannot reject the
> possibility that *it may include infinite interpreta-
> tions*. Once more we are seized by a great shudder;
> but who would feel inclined immediately to deify
> again after the old manner this monster of an
> unknown world? And to worship the unknown
> henceforth as "the Uknown One"? [30]

The traumatic perspective of the unknown, for Vallejo as for Nietzsche, cannot
be limited, its power of dissemination anchored or mastered, by the imposition of
any commanding unity of voice.

Philosophy's *"absolute-will-to-hear-oneself-speak,"* in such a context, is
shown to be vain and impotent. The poem "Quiere y no quiere" renounces as a
futile act even the project of articulating one's suffering, of giving it a coherent
voice and embodying it in a signification. Suffering, precisely as that which has
no reason or goal, and consequently evades signification, confounds the ideal of
discourse or self-expression as an instrument of knowledge and understanding or,
in the poet's cryptic words, as a way of knowing "por qué tiene la vida esta
perazzo."

> Que saber por qué tiene la vida esta perazzo
> por qué lloro, por qué,
> cejón, inhábil, veleidoso, hube nacido
> gritando;
> saberlo, comprenderlo
> al son de un alfabete competente,
> sería padecer por un ingrato.
>
> ¡Y no! ¡No! ¡No! ¡Qué ardid, ni paramento!
> Congoja, sí, con sí firme y frenético
> coriáceo, rapaz, quiere y no quiere, cielo y pájaro;
> congoja, sí, con toda la bragueta. (*PC* 619)

Philosophy knows its limit at that point where the ideal of a human discourse governed by the logos can no longer hold. In Vallejo's poetry, indeed, we never get beyond the agonizing stutter which, according to legend, gave *Trilce* its unintelligible title: "Vallejo felt mortified. Several times he repeated *tres, tres, tres,* with that insistence he had for repeating words and deforming them, *tresss, trisss, trieesss, tril, trilsss.* He stammered and in the lisp *trilssce* came out . . . trilce? trilce?"[31] Crying and shouting or, as it is put in "Esto / sucedió entre dos párpados," "Comprendiéndolo y todo . . . / . . . en el sentido llorante de esta voz" (*PC* 621), are perhaps the only way of ever giving voice (broken voice to a truthless truth) to life's reason for being "such an utter bitch." Translating this into language means the inarticulate breaking up of all vocal unity. No speech can ever encompass or contain the absolute contradiction of what it is to be human. Any such pretension can be regarded only as a travesty ("¡Y no! ¡No! ¡No! ¡Qué ardid, ni paramento!") or at best as a superfluous artifice or ornament. To say that the expression of suffering is to suffer for an ingrate ("sería padecer por un ingrato") means that one cannot bridge the abyss between the mute act of suffering and the language that purports to represent it. In language, one's suffering can take place only by proxy, alienated and estranged from itself in a form that betrays that suffering and falsely represents it, just in representing it at all, robbing it of its inaccessible truth: a truth that, in the end, is utterly truthless, since it is spiritually indigestible and barred discourse, never successfully to be absorbed by the logos.

The possibility of a counter-language is the subject of the poem "La punta del hombre," with its indirect allusion to a kind of apocalyptic rending of the veil. The veil, in this case, is discourse itself, the "ardid" and "aparamento" that characterize the logos's great cover-up of suffering and death's truthless truth. That which pierces and tears it, like a sharp point, is human reality at its limit, its edge. On the other side of this edge, a different, alternative writing emerges, one that is described as barely writing, as a writing on the fringes or margins of speech and discourse: "apenas / escribir y escribir con un palito / o con el filo de la oreja inquieta" (*PC* 615). The hearing of Vallejo's "restless ear" implies an understanding quite distinct from that of philosophy's own desire for mastery, its desire to hear itself speaking in an absolute voice. The point of "La punta del hombre," which is the point of man himself, is irreducibly multiple: points, not point.[32] Like the punctured ear of Derrida's "Tympan" which, in contrast with the Hegelian wound which "always *appears* sewn up again," may "give birth, from the lesion without suture, to some unheard-of partition" (*MP* xxvi), Vallejo's ear points to a fundamental rupture or wound, and not to the healing of an ultimate consolation in philosophy, nor to a reassuring discursive synthesis:

> La punta del hombre,
> el ludibrio pequeño de encojerse
> tras de fumar su universal ceniza;
> punta al darse en secretos caracoles,
> punta donde se agarra uno con guantes,
> punta el lunes sujeto por seis frenos,
> punta saliendo de escuchar a su alma.
> (*PC* 615)

Man's point is at once his destiny, but also his end, the cigar stub's trace of ash, that barest and barren essence burned up and left after his purgation. It is that point made and heard only in the winding and secret staircases of the cochleas,[33] lost at last to a philosophical hearing, the soul's salient point ("punta salendo") listened to and stuttered in a speech which, spurring itself on, strains and tears the philosopher's vocal chords. The pencil-tip, which here writes and puns on "punta" itself, makes a point with which, poinard-like, it pricks and punctures the metaphysical eardrum or tympany. In

Trilce XL a similar counter-writing is alluded to, one which will make use of "lustrales plumas terceras, puñales, / nuevos pasajes de papel de oriente" (*PC* 464).   Man's point, his limit, his end, his death, are no longer to be sung to sleep by a logos dreaming its plentitude.   They are to be rewritten, "de otra manera," the pen in the other hand now, writing in another way.   Indeed, what is indicated is a writing which deafens as well as plays dumb, as suggested by the pun on "tímpano" in the final stanza: "tímpano sordísimo."   This broken instrument and deafest eardrum, and its companion "Acorde de lápiz," refer to the rupture of a radical disharmony and disunity, in which the philosopher's straining vocal chords are supplanted by the writer's dissonant and discordant pencil-chord.

> De otra manera,
> fueran lluvia menuda los soldados
> . . . .
> De otra manera, caminantes suegros,
> . . . .
>
>   ¡Oh pensar geométrico al trasluz!
> ¡Oh no morir bajamente
> de majestad tan rauda y tan fragrante!
> ¡Oh no cantar; apenas
> escribir y escribir con un palito
> o con el filo de la oreja inquieta!
>
>   Acorde de lápiz, tímpano sordísimo,
> dondoneo en mitades robustas . . .
>   (*PC* 615)

A marginal writing that would disrupt any unity of voice and elude all philosophical hearing in the secret windings of an auricular labyrinth is, of course, the possibility entertained by Derrida in "Tympan":

> Can one violently penetrate philosophy's field of listening without its immediately — even pretending in advance, by hearing what is said of it, by decoding the statement — making the penetration resonate within itself, appropriating the emission for itself, familiarly communicating it to itself between the inner and middle ear, following the path of a

tube or inner opening, be it round or oval? In other words, can one puncture the tympanum of a philosopher and still be heard and understood by him?

To philosophize with a hammer. Zarathustra begins by asking himself if he will have to puncture them, batter their ears . . . with the sound of cymbals or tympani, the instruments, always, of some Dionysianism. In order to teach them "to hear with their eyes," too.

But we will analyze the metaphysical exchange, the circular complicity of the metaphors of the eye and the ear.   (*MP* xii-xiii)

The poem "Panteón" (*PC* 647) ironically plays on this metaphysical exchange, this circular complicity of metaphors of sight and hearing. The title suggests a tomb inhabited by the host of philosophy's illustrious dead, by all those proper names, from Heraclitus on, with which Vallejo is so obsessed in the posthumous poetry, all those unmastered masters of the logos, the "gobernadores en desorden" (*PC* 635) already met in the elegiac "Despedida recordando un adiós."   The poem's climax is reached when the poet takes in (with all his senses, in a kind of Baudelairean synesthesia) the ineluctable nature of the catastrophe his vision reveals to him.   The vision itself is that of a loss of vision, and of voice.   The poet asks at last that he be piously thrown to the philosophers ("piadosamente echadme a los filósofos"), so as to end up with all the other pathetic heroes of thought in the metaphysical charnel house.   The title "Panteón" may be related to an aphorism in *Contra el secreta profesional*: "Crucificados en vanas camisas de duerza avanzan así las diferencias de hojas alternas hacia el panteón de los grandes acordes."[34]   The complexity of the mixed metaphor here is quite suggestive.   It identifies, in a way reminiscent of Hegel, the final synthetic moment of absolute knowledge ("el panteón de los grandes acordes") with Christ's passion ("Crucificados").   At the end of the *Phenomenology*, Hegel writes of History and the Science of Knowing: ". . . the two together, comprehended History, form alike the inwardizing and the Calvary of absolute Spirit, the actuality, truth, and certainty of his throne, without which he would be lifeless and alone."[35]   There is also a reference to a "pantheon" in the *Phenomenology*, in the section "The spiritual work of art": "Thus it is that the separate beautiful national Spirits unite into a single pantheon, the element and habitation of which is language."[36]   Vallejo's "Panteón" represents the philosopher's Calvary or Golgotha, in another sense than Hegel's.   It is a place of suffering and a burial ground, in this case marked by a skull emptied of reason.   The aphorism indicates, moreover, that the unity assured by a teleo-eschatological destiny or end is one which may be violently imposed ("Crucificados en vanas camisas de fuerza").   The pantheon of grand harmonies collapses and absorbs all difference — and *différance* — only by force, and only at the sacrifice of movement and life.   It is not just a place where the gods, heroes, and idols set up their club-house and hierarchies; it is also, like Golgotha, a place of death.   The unity it secures proves to be one in which the pages of writing and difference ("las diferencias de hojas alternas") are brought to an end in a voice that is, as Derrida has put it, "at once absolutely alive and absolutely dead" (*MP* 102).   Life without *différance*, since it is properly inconceivable, always turns out to be death without *différance*, in which the grand harmonies are funeral marches, and the figure of absolute knowledge lies in state, asleep in his pantheon-like tomb.

"Panteón" represents, in many ways, a parody of vision, but what makes it such a powerful poem is that it is also, at the same time, truly apocalyptic.   It is precisely this tension between travesty and authentic revelation that gives the poem its enormous power, as the final object of vision turns out to be utterly catastrophic, and the truth it unveils utterly truthless.   The apocalyptic nature of the vision is underlined by the insistence on the poet's role as witness and the poem's status as a testimonial, as well as by the obsessively repetitive use of the past tense of verbs of vision and hearing ("He visto . . . ví . . . y si ví . . . y si vó"; "oí . . . si escuché"), and by the timeless focus on the hour in which the vision unfolds, that "swollen" — if not fulfilled — hour of revelation: "pues que estaba la hora / suavamente, / premiosamente henchida de dos horas." In the first stanza, the separation of a rainbow from the sunset is an omen only ironically to be identified, given the poem's relentless revelation of life's horror, with a sign promising the restoration of a lost presence. If the vision here concerns the end of life, it is also one in which any posthumous life, or principle of permanence beyond death, is indefinitely suspended. But there is no third day in Vallejo's revelation. The apocalyptic associations of the opening stanza are all very allusive, but Eshleman and Barcia, in translating this loosing ("desprenderse") of a rainbow, choose to use the expression "rip loose," which suggests not only the release of a shaft from a bow ("arco"), but also a ripping apart. This violent action is, however, only implicit in Vallejo's "cuando oí desprenderse del ocaso/ tristemente / exactemente un arco, un arcoíris." But it is all the more significant when we consider, in the same stanza, the adverb "puntualmente," which modifies the verb "alejarse" and is in apposition to "mortuoriamente." For "puntualmente" evokes a point or tip like that of "La punta del hombre," like the tip of an arrow let loose from a bow, which might prick, pierce, or puncture, and serve for example, to rend a curtain or veil.[37]

> He visto ayer sonidos generales,
>   mortuoriamente,
>   puntualmente alejarse
> cuando oí desprenderse del ocaso
>   tristemente
>   exactemente un arco, un arcoíris (*PC* 647)

The second stanza outlines this apocalyptic moment in terms of a potential temporal catastrophe. Time and history are not fulfilled in revelation; rather, the fulfilment is excessive, too much for the hour in which it takes place. The hour swells to a point of acute dilation: "estaba la hora / suavamente / premiosamente henchida de dos horas." The notion of eternity intersecting with the moment is carried to its mad extreme. The momentary swiftness of the *Augenblick* is drawn out and made to drag, the minute expanded into an hour, the hour into two. The instant dilates with the expanding pupil of the visionary eye, as the generous time of the minute is said to be seen infinitely, "tied insanely to large time." The filling hour, stuffed with eternity, turgid and distended, threatens to burst apart, and to ejaculate catastrophically, in a fatal dissemination.

> Ví el tiempo generoso del minuto,
> infinitamente
> atado locamente al tiempo grande
> pues que estaba la hora
> suavamente
> premiosamente henchida de dos horas.
> (*PC* 647)

This visionary catastrophe is further brought on by the crossing of visual and auditory perceptions which opens the poem, a parody of what Derrida refers to as "the circular complicity of the metaphors of the eye and of the ear" (*MP* xiii). Maurice Blanchot discusses this complicity in *L'Entretien infini*, where Heidegger's notion of "une saisie par l'ouie qui saisit par le regard," as Blanchot puts it, is set against the perspective of a writing whose activity subverts the circular, unitary implications of precisely this kind of metaphysical formulation: "Ecrire, ce n'est pas parler; ce qui nous ramène à l'autre exclusion: parler, ce n'est pas voir, et ainsi à rejeter tout ce qui — entente ou vision — définirait l'acte en jeu dans l'écriture comme la saisie immédiate d'une présence, que celui-ci soit d'intériorité ou d'extériorité."[38]   Philosophical discourse, according to Derrida, has always insisted upon sight and hearing as the special metaphors implicated in "knowledge of the presence of the object, as the being-before-oneself of knowledge in consciousness" (*SP* 115).   The securing or assurance of this knowledge is parodied in the opening stanza of "Panteón" by a translation of the two modes of sense perception into one another: "He visto . . . sonidos . . . oí desprenderse del ocaso . . . un arco . . . ."   Powerful ironic elements break down, from the beginning, the hierarchy of the senses protecting, and projecting, the unity of philosophical discourse.   The subversion becomes flagrant as the poem progresses — perhaps it would be better to say regresses — and the lesser senses, such as touch and smell, invade and disturb the clarity and certainty of a reflective understanding.   This more primitive, physical, "earthy" level markedly contrasts with what amounts to an obsessive use of verbs of sight and hearing, associated with understanding, dialogue, and perceptual, as well as conceptual, clarity:

> He visto sonidos generales . . .
>
> . . . oí desprenderse . . .
>
> Ví el tiempo generoso del minuto . . .
>
> Dejóse comprender, llamar . . .
>
> Y si ví, que me escuchen . . . que vean . . .
>
> Y si ví en la lesión de la respuesta
> claramente
> la lesión mentalmente de la incógnita,
> si escuché, si pensé . . .
>
> (*PC* 647)

The network of associations characteristic of philosophical discourse loses its coherence as, with the introduction of troubling alien elements, the crossing of senses becomes increasingly confused, and confusing.   The confusion reaches its critical limit with the ironic use of the word "claramente," since at this point everything has become completely dim: "Y si ví en la lesión de la respuesta, / claramente, / la lesión mentalmente de la incógnita." Hearing and thought have now been taken over by the nostrils, or by an organ which is said to be at once nasal, funereal, and temporal: "mis ventanillas nasales, funerales, temporales." The object of perception, in this case, is indeed a literal stink, the notoriously unphilosophical "bad smell" raised by the ineluctable fact of death, that limit of limits set against philosophy's overweening dream of absolute knowledge's self-presence.

> Y si ví, que me escuchen, pues, en bloque,
> si toqué esta mecánica . . .
>
> si escuché, si pensé en mis ventanillas
> nasales, funerales, temporales . . .
> *(PC* 647)

The lesser senses serve to convey those aspects of experience which, in the final analysis, must be purged, refined, and redeemed by the work of the logos, and until then can have no proper place in metaphysical discourse. For example, death must be converted into negativity, the irremediable discontinuity and dispersal of temporal experience into the teleology of history, the unknown and the unknowable into the antithetical movement of dialectical thought. However, it is precisely these sorts of conversions that Vallejo ironically undercuts, as in the idea of the earth's "earthly" letting "itself be understood, and called."

> Dejóse comprender, llamar, la tierra
> terrenalmente;
> negóse brutalmente así a mi historia . . .
> *(PC* 647)

The earth's understanding or naming itself with the intelligence and language of the earth is as great a tautological catastrophe, in one sense, as philosophy's own madly self-addressed monologue. For the earth is that which, in letting itself be understood, means the very catastrophe of understanding. Understanding is not conceivable outside of history; it takes place only in the context of a process of signification which, although it cannot perhaps be strictly described as teleological, is at least temporal and purposive, and to this extent involves a *telos*. The catastrophe befalling the understanding and destroying the very possibility of a discourse that unfolds historically and significantly, suggests that what we are left with now is simply an anti-logos, a discourse of death, of finitude and species. Indeed, after the poet has asked to be "piously thrown to the philosophers," he refuses even the last consolation of the logos, the language of self-expression, as in the poem "Quiere y no quiere" (*PC* 619), where he forswears, as a debilitating exercise in alienation and self-estrangement ("padecer por un ingrato"), the romantic quest for an alphabet of suffering ("alfabeto competente"). With the allusion to "canto llano" ("plain song") and the "son del alma / tristemente / erguida ecuestramente en mi espinazo" ("the sound of the soul / sadly / straightened equestrianly in my spine"), the power of the Word, from which stems the power of the poet's words, is now seen as a mere vestige or ghost of itself. The temptation of poetic self-expression — the only lure of discourse that remains at all in force — is finally abjured ("no más . . . no más"), while all that is left of the certainty of reflective understanding is the grimly stoic "estoy seguro" which follows hard upon the final pronouncement: "la vida es implacablemente, / imparcialmente horrible. . . ." The final irony, of course, lies in the poem "Panteón" itself, which as a dramatic portrayal of the refusal of the word, as a representation of the limits placed on discourse and on a belief in the ambitions and power of the logos, remains itself in the very success of its linguistic expression, such a remarkable vindication of the power of words.

> Mas no más inflexión precipitada
> en canto llano, y no más
> el hueso colorado, el son del alma
> tristemente
> erguida ecuestramente en mi espinazo,
> ya que, en suma, la vida es
> implacablemente,
> imparcialmente horrible, estoy seguro
> (*PC* 647)

2. Suffering and the Neuter

L'inconnu est toujours pensé au neutre.
Maurice Blanchot, *L'Entretien infini*[40]

I lie stretched out, inactive; the only thing I see is emptiness, the only thing I move about is emptiness. I do not even suffer pain. . . . Even pain has lost its refreshment for me. If I were offered all the glories of the world, or all its pain, the one would move me as little as the other, I would not turn over on the other side either to obtain them or to escape them. I die the death. . . . My soul is like the Dead Sea, over which no bird can fly; when it has flown midway, then it sinks down to death and destruction.

. . . .

But for those who can follow me, although I do not make any progress, I shall now unfold the eternal truth, by virtue of which this philosophy remains within itself, and admits of no higher philosophy. For if I preceded from my principle, I should find it impossible to stop; for if I stopped, I should regret it, and if I did not stop, I should also regret that, and so forth. But since I never start, so can I never stop; my eternal departure is identical with my eternal cessation.

Sören Kierkegaard, *Either/Or*[41]

In Vallejo's posthumous poetry, philosophy is put to the test, put on trial, and condemned, sentenced to be itself, to speak only to itself, to whisper its (one) truth (of the one) only to itself. In the end, the enemy or accuser of philosophy, its adversary, is simply life, "la vida que tiene tres potencias" (*PC* 638) spoken of in the poem "Tengo un miedo terrible." Life, for Vallejo, represents that polytropic power which is by its very nature finally unrepresentable, and which, if it can be seen to a large extent as the invention of a scientific break with a world conceived of as informed by the logos, has become, in a frighteningly real sense, a Frankenstein's monster. It dramatically exceeds the mastery of analysis, measure, and rule. The categories belonging to logic and science cannot exhaust its *polytropoi*. Vallejo and Nietzsche are, indeed, very close here:

> It is no different with the faith with which so many materialistic natural scientists rest content nowadays, the faith in a world that is supposed to have its equivalent and its measure in human thought and human valuations — a "world of truth" that can be mastered completely and forever with the aid of our square little reason. What? Do we really want to permit existence to be degraded for us like this — reduced to a mere exercise for a calculator and an indoor diversion for mathematicians? Above all, one should not wish to divest existence of its *rich ambiguity* . . .[42]

The nature of this "vieldeutigen Charakters" may itself be ambiguous, or ambivalent.[43] In Vallejo's case, life often verges on outright horror, as in "Panteón": " . . . la vida es implacablemente, / imparcialmente horrible, estoy seuguro" (*PC* 647). It is then interpreted as an affliction, as a catastrophe which has befallen the unity of the logos. Life's inherent *polytropoi* are experienced as a deadly dissemination in which the human destiny has lost its historical destination, as exemplified in the poem "Escarnecido, aclimatado al bien," where the destinies end up in flies and bacteria ("acaban en moscas los destinos," "acaban los destinos en bacterias," *PC* 629). In that same poem, life is named and identified as the source of such a catastrophe, as the source of death itself, being a force "behind the infinite" ("detrás / del infinito"), and unfolding "spontaneously" ("espontáneamente") before the philosopher's and scientist's "legislative temple" ("la sien legislativa"). The administrations of a reasoning and moralizing forehead — however large its span — can do nothing to comprehend or redeem the apocalyptic hour of one's own death, that "century of hard breathing" ("el siglo del resuello") against which neither logic nor the logos has any effective power:

> Al fondo, es hora,
> entonces, de gemir con toda el hacha
> y es entonces el año del sollozo,
> el día del tobillo,
> la noche del costado, el siglo del resuello,
> . . . .
> Así es la vida, tal
> como es la vida, allá, detrás
> del infinito; así, espontáneamente,
> delante de la sien legislativa.
>
> Yace la cuerda así al pie del violín . . .
> (*PC* 629)

Life means — although how can it mean anything, since it is the very possibility of signification that collapses in the face of it — the irremediable dispersal of presence. It completely diverts and destroys any teleo-eschatological conception of time and history, whether it be the movement of Hegel's Absolute Spirit, Marx's dialectical materialism, or, more crucial for Vallejo in its mythic power, the religious Messianic vision of a human redemption and of the return to a restored paradise. Moreover, life mocks even that calculative science that claims it as its specific object. Behind the infinite. which we must imagine as a veil or curtain behind which life hides its truthless truth, and yet just over there, in all its seeming innocuousness, life sits, speechless and monstrous, something which can only be indicated, pointed to ("Así es la vida, tal / como es . . . allá . . . así"), but without meaning, refusing to speak up before the legislative temple, before reason's tribunal, effectively eluding the metaphysical will, philosophy's imperious *"absolute will-to-hear-oneself-speak"* (*SP* 102).

Learning to live with life, then, proves to be the problem, an enormous problem. This is articulated in terms not so much of living life, which implies a form of active mastery, but of being lived by life, according to a passive position that imitates and, in imitating, parodies the attitude of Christ's passion and suffering. To be lived by life means — if we may deform the syntax to project the odd passivity of this condition — that one is also "died" by life. In "Epístola a los transeúntes," one dies of life, and not of time: "Pero cuando yo muera / de vida y no de tiempa" (*PC* 574). This ineluctably passive relationship to life (and death) characterizes the new dispensation that emerges in the wake of that catastrophe befalling the Word contemplated in "Y si después de tantas palabras."

> ¡Y si después de tánta historia, sucumbimos,
> no ya de eternidad,
> sino de esas cosas sencillas, como estar
> en la casa o ponerse a cavilar!
> (*PC* 593)

Reflection, for Vallejo, always means a "reflecting on life," which is how Eshleman and Barcia translate the phrase "ponerse a cavilar." This is a very different thing, of course, from thinking about God, essences, Platonic ideas, or the categorical imperative. The poem "Al cavilar en la vida, al cavilar," with its mocking use of the same word *cavilar* ("to quibble"), mocks philosophical thought's great ambition: the total discursive mastery of life. The caricature of thought as a captious splitting of hairs is simply a way of saying that philosophical reflection has no empire over existence's slow, inscrutable, and unarrestable flow ("el esfuerzo del torrente," *PC* 612). It is to the force of this mute and deaf flow, and not to eternity, that the philosopher's self-addressed and monological thought must finally succumb ("no ya de eternidad / sino de esas cosas sencillas"), and in this submission another kind of reflection takes over, one which, in its uncertain passivity, takes in and assents to existence's verdict, listens for and hears, without even the possibility of quibbling, without a hope of reasoning, its own death sentence.

> Al cavilar en la vida, al cavilar
> despacio en el esfuerzo del torrente,
> alivia, ofrece asiento el existir,
> condena a muerte . . . (*PC* 612)

The best word, perhaps, to describe Vallejo's uncertain and passive relationship to life is neutrality. The word is not to be understood here as pointing to some kind of scientific objectivity, nor as connoting any lack of involvement or engagement. On the contrary, one completely undergoes life, to the point where, as in the poem "Does niño anhelantes," one is "thought" by life ("es la que piensa y marcha, es la finita"), whereas one's own reasoning about its nature is that of the philosopher-animal, the philosopher-machine, robot-like and automatic: "Lo sé, lo intuyo cartesiano, autómata" (*PC* 651). It is the very fact that one is "lived by life" in so thorough and total a way, without, however, ever getting at its essence or comprehending what it in fact means to be alive, that makes one's relationship to life a necessarily neutral one. There is no perspective from which to judge life, except life itself, and that perspective involves an infinite displacement. This neutrality, which is very close to ambivalence at times, stems from the necessity of seeing life as being neither this nor that, as being simply inscrutable, inexpressive, and inexpressible. For the poet, the quandary is reflected in the struggle to express the fact of life in a language characterized by an uncertainty of reference and fundamental lack of definition. Not to be contained or made intelligible in words, life's "presence" is such that in order for it to be expressed, language first must attain a simple indicative condition: ". . . en suma, la vida es . . . horrible" (*PC* 647); "Es la vida no más . . . Es la vida no más; sólo la vida . . . Es la vida y no más" (*PC* 651). Or its syntax must be deprived even further, and reduced to the stammering of inane demonstratives and exclamations: "Sólo la vida; así: cosa bravísima" (*PC* 651); "Así es la vida, tal / como es la vida, allá . . . así" (*PC* 629); "Es un ojo éste, aquél; una frente ésta, aquélla . . . Y repetiendo: / ¡Tánta vida y jamás . . . / Tantos años y siempre, siempre, siempre!" (*PC* 586); "La vida, esta vida . . . Vida! Vida! Esta es la vida!" (*PC* 584). The translation of one's relationship to life into language is thus threatened with catastrophe, as though words had been condemned to a strictly autistic or aphasiac use. The most dramatic example of this is the poem "La paz, la avispa, el taco . . . , " which consists of a series of paratactic groupings of different parts of speech, without any syntax beyond that of simple apposition. All that one can say about life is that it is "horrible," or that it is "thus," "like that," "this," "there." Life, in the end, is simply life.

The uncertainty of the pleasure derived from life is the story told in "La vida, esta vida," with its elegiac farewell to a sympathetic band of "troping" doves. This troop of troubadour birds ("Zurear su tradición rojo les era"); "advenían . . . a contarme sus cosas fosoforosas, / pajaros de contar"), red-blooded, inexhaustibly productive and protean, performing "según sus afflicciones, sus dianas de animales," embodies the polytropic character of life itself, being indeed "su instrumento," both the agent, means, or organ of its power, and its inventive musical voice, telling life's untranslatable story: "Vida! Vida! Esta es la vida" (*PC* 584). But, as "La vida, esta vida" says farewell to life's pleasures, so the poem which immediately follows it in Larrea's edition, "Hoy me gusta la vida mucho menos" (*PC* 586-87), carries the burden, also a refrain in this case ("¡Tánta vida y jamás! . . . Tánta vida y jamás . . . tánta vida y jamás!"), of life's terrible anguish. What is truly terrible about this anguish is that it cannot even definitely decide about its own anguish, an indecision reflected in the blunt and understated phrasing of the neutral opening lines: "Hoy me gusta la vida mucho menos, / pero siempre me gusta vivir." Thus, in either poem, we can never be certain where the pleasure ends and the pain begins. The clear borders of strict conceptual and emotional categories are blurred and run into one another. In "Hoy me gusta la vida," the use of the adverbs "tánto," "jamás," and "siempre," confuses the distinctions between the meanings of "never" and "always," "so much" and "so little," so that the words themselves seem to be almost interchangeable. It is as though "always" were now to be taken for "never," "so much" for "so little."

> Tánta vida y jamás!
> Tántos años y siempre mis semanas! . . .
> . . . .
>
> ¡Tánta vida y jamás! ¡Y tántos años,
> y siempre, mucho siempre, siempre, siempre!
> (*PC* 587)

In a similar way, the fundamental terms of the poem, the extremes of life and death, rigorously neutralize one another, as they do in that aphorism from a section entitled "La muerte de la muerte" in *Contra el secreto profesional*: "No hay nada que temer. No hay nada que esperar. Siempre se está más o menos vivo. Siempre se está más o memos muerto."[44] One likes life much less, but still likes to live anyway; one likes life enormously ("Me gusta la vida enormemente"), but without ever forgetting one's "beloved death" ("pero, desde luego, / con mi muerte querida y mi café"); one desires always to be alive, and yet one has never known life, has never lived ("Me gustará vivir siempre, así fuese de barriga . . . tánta vida y jamás!"); in life one is always somehow already dead, since one is always in the process of dying, and in death one goes on living, since one can never quite manage to die completely, once and for all ("Mis padres enterrados con su piedra / Y su triste estirón que no ha acabado"); and at the close of one's life, one is, paradoxically, somehow fully alive, erect and dressed up in one's being at last, oneself at last: "de cuerpo entero hermanos, mis hermanos, / y, en fin, mi sér parado y en chaleco." It is worth noting Eshleman and Barcia's not entirely accurate translation of these lines as "full length brothers, my brothers, / and, finally, by Being standing and in a vest." "Being," capital *B*, with its metaphysical and ontological connotations — one cannot help but think of Heidegger — is beautifully suggestive here, especially when set against Derrida's cryptic formulation concerning Husserl's theory of signs: "*A voice without differance, a voice without writing, is at once absolutely alive and absolutely dead*" (*SP* 115). What *is* at last, in this case, what has come to be in such a full and absolute way, is completely dead, or at least dead enough for a coffin, since the very idea of being completely dead or live is precisely what has been complicated by the poem.[45]

The passivity of Vallejo's neutral relationship to life has much in common with the Christian passion, the most consistent expression of that relationship being suffering, "El placer de sufrir" (*PC* 642) as Vallejo calls it in "Guitarra." In the posthumous poetry, the fact of suffering stands as a radical limit to the administrative power of reason and the word. Nor is it surprising, in light of this, that for so many critics it represents a limit only insofar as it becomes at the same time the supreme instance and, indeed, veritable means of the redemptive and synthetic unity of Vallejo's poetry. Clayton Eshleman formulates this paradoxical understanding in succinct dramatic terms: *"In Vallejo the amount of physical suffering is the alteration it seeks"*; relating it to the kind of romantic Messianism we find in Blake, he asks: "Is there a point at which the true poet is no longer a literary man but resumes his place as primal Adam?"[46] This is much more interesting, although not essentially different, from the view of Larrea, for whom the suffering represented by Vallejo's life and work is a version of the redemptive suffering of the Word:

> Nada sería más opuesto a su espíritu iconoclasta que su propia idolización. Es el Ser de todos que en Vallejo ha sufrido las miserias del mundo feneciente y que nos da un ejemplo de entrega a la redención de lo humano en la que todos hemos de particpar con nuestro espíritu de Amor y de sacrificio.[47]

But what if suffering for Vallejo were not in the end redeemable, were, indeed, precisely that which could not be recovered and reclaimed as meaning, and which is never to make its way into a symbolic economy, being in fact that which divides, breaks up, and disperses the organization of such an economy? What if the limit suffering would then represent — if it could be said to represent anything at all — stemmed from its very limitlessness? Suffering would have to bear at its heart's core the truthless truth of the following paradox: a suffering that can be placed, whose end can be conceived, whose origin has a visible horizon, a suffering not strictly rootless, displaced, endless and without cause, is no suffering at all. In other words, a suffering in possession of the truth, in possession of its own meaning and truth, would not be true suffering. True suffering has no truth.

Two of Vallejo's prose poems, "Las ventanas se han estremecido . . ." and "Voy a hablar de la esperanza," clearly bear out this case of a suffering that, in its limitlessness, is irredeemable. "Las ventanas" may be thought of as a wild rewriting of Mallarmé's "Les Fenêtres." However, the Symbolist sickness with life, with the sickness that is identified with life ("Las du triste hôpital"), is extended in Vallejo's poem well beyond the context of an esthetic or artistic salvation ("Je me mire et me vois ange! et je meurs . . . A renaître . . . Au ciel antérieur où fleurit la Beauté"), where the self would be translated out of this world's corruption into the narcissistic and imperishable realm of art. This movement could itself be interpreted as a revision of the Christian spiritualization of suffering. Instead, in "Las ventanas," an extreme test is staged, as religion and science take their turns in an attempt to absolve human suffering, while the world of perfect health ("el mundo de la salud perfecta," *PC* 551) becomes a metaphor for a Hegelian state of perfected Spirit. Religion and Science, of course, are the two forms of knowing — and in that order — which close the *Phenomenology*; Science, for Hegel, is the systematic Science of the Spirit, that is, the most highly developed form of philosophy. We might keep in mind as well the following passage from *The Gay Science*:

> No doubt, those who are truthful in that audacious and ultimate sense that is presupposed by the faith in science *thus affirm another world* than the world of life, nature, and history; and insofar as they affirm this "other world" — look, must they not by the same token negate its counterpart, this world, *our* world? — But you will have gathered what I am driving at, namely, that it is still a *metaphysical faith* upon which our faith in science rests — that even we seekers after knowledge today, we godless anti-metaphysicians still take our fire, too, from the flame lit by a faith that is thousands of years old, that Christian faith which was also the faith of Plato, that God is the truth, that truth is divine. — But what if this should become more and more incredible, if nothing should prove to be divine any more unless it were error, blindness, the lie — if God himself should prove to be our most enduring lie?[48]

Like Nietzsche, Vallejo dramatically identifies these three different discourses of the truth — science, metaphysics, and religion — with a single condition of faith. In "Las ventanas," both surgeon and priest show themselves incapable of recognizing in the extremity of human agony a suffering whose limitless nature strikes an irremediable blow to their dream of an absolute, and an absolving, knowledge. It is difficult in the context to distinguish between these two functionaries or custodians of mortality. Religion becomes just another rationalizing science ("¡Ciencia de Dios, Teodicea!", *PC* 551), whose dirty job is to vindicate not only moral but physical evil. On the other hand, the scientist's probing instruments are forsaken in the end for an unfolding love or *caritas*, that greatest of the three Christian virtues in Corinthians: ". . . sus párpados científicos vibran, tocados por la indocta, por la humana flaqueza del amor. Y he visto a esos enfermos morir precisamente del amor desdoblado del cirujano, de los largos diagnósticos, de las dosis exactas, del riguroso análisis de orinas y excrementos" (*PC* 550). That the sick die of love, rather than being cured by it, is devastating testimony to the radical and utterly human character of suffering and death. In rhetorical terms, "Las ventanas" is a madly extended hyperbole of pain, dramatically portraying the illimitable nature of suffering in face of the oppressiveness of its theological and scientific denial. At stake in the incurability and bottomlessness of the suffering is, in fact, the entire edifice of Western thought and belief. The human faith in the logos shows its stupefaction in a frenzied questioning of love's failure to fulfil its implicit promise of defeating death. The underlying question seems to be: if one can do nothing of worth without the power of love ("and if I have all faith . . . but have not love . . . and if I deliver my body to be burned, but have not love, I gain nothing," 1 Cor. 13:3-4), what good then is love if it cannot do this uttermost? The terrible letdown involved in witnessing death's victory over love is, ironically enough, experienced as a kind of counter-miracle, or anti-miracle, as though what were astonishing and awesome were not the miraculous, but the very non-event of the miracle, the incredible fact that it does not take place. What is truly awesome and miraculous is death itself, not the miracle of its overcoming — death swallowing us up, not itself being swallowed up in victory. This is because suffering and death stand as an insurmountable, ineradicable limit to the promise of Scripture, to a complete faith in the power of love and the Word.

> Ignoro lo que será del enfermo esta mujer, que le besa y no puede sanarle con el beso, le mira y no puede sanarle con los ojos, le habla y no puede sanarle con el verbo. ¿Es su madre? ¿Y cómo, pues, no puede sanarle? ¿Es su amada? ¿Y cómo, pues, no puede sanarle? ¿Es su hermana? ¿Y cómo, pues, no puede sanarle? ¿Es, simplemente, una mujer? ¿Y cómo, pues, no puede sanarle? ¿Por que esta mujer le ha besado, le ha mirado, le ha hablado y hasta le ha cubierto mejor el cuello el enfermo y, ¡cosa verdaderamente asombrosa! no le ha sanado.   (PC 549)

The child-like faith in a cure based on the Word makes death much more surprising and wondrous a thing here than in the preceding passage where it only seems to elude, in its horribly banal fortuitousness, the doctors, who quibble endlessly only to pronounce at last "sus llanas palabras de hombres" (PC 548). The word "llanas" ("simple" or "plain"), which modifies "palabras," is the same as that which modifies the song renounced at the end of "Panteón" ("Mas no más inflexión precipitada / en canto llano") in the face of life's unmitigated horror ("la vida es . . . horrible, estoy seguro," PC 647). The use of "cavilar," as in the poem "Al cavilar en la vida," mocks the vanity and impotence of a merely analytic relation to life and death, to be viewed in the end as nothing but a petty "quibbling" over what is an insurmountable limit posed to the understanding. The surgeons must finally give up their vain and ponderous debate, and are finally left with nothing but simple, human words: humans confronted with the inhuman, like Blanchot's Oedipus, "l'homme qui avec simplicité et avec suffisance se dit simplement homme," faced with "La question profonde . . . l'homme comme Sphinx, la part dangereuse, inhumaine et sacrée. . . ."[49] Both these simple, human words and the passionate and faithful words of mother and lover prove to be, in the final account, equally incapable, implicating in their failure the dramatic failure of the logos itself. This word robbed of its power is graphically reflected in the suffering man's own utterance which opens the poem. His speech is violently divided between opposed and competing bodily orifices: mouth and anus.

> Las ventanas se han estremecido, elaborando una metafísica del universo. Vidrios han caído. Un enfermo lanza su queja: la mitad por su boca lenguada y sobrante, y toda entera, por el ano de su espalda.
> Es el huracán. Un castaño del jardín de la Tullerías habráse abatido, al soplo del viento, que mide ochenta metros por segundo. Capiteles de los barrios antiguos, habrán caído, hendiendo, matando.
> ¿De qué punto interrogo, oyendo a ambas riberas de los océanos, de qué punto viene este huracán, tan digno de crédito, tan honrado de deuda, derecho a las ventanas del hospital? ¡Ay las direcciones inmutables, que oscillan entre el huracán y esta pena directa de toser o defecar! ¡Ay las direcciones inmutables, que así prenden muerte en las entrañas del hospital y despiertan células clandestinas, a deshora, en los cadáveres!
> *(PC 548)*

The use of the word "metafísica" in the first line suggests an etymological conceit. However, if the windows are shaken by a force which violently thrusts us beyond (*meta*) the limits of the physical universe, it also thrusts us beyond the metaphysical universe as well, into a limitless region where human understanding and the power of self-expression have become otiose. The hurricane of the sick man's cry breaks the limits of the conceivable world and extends indefinitely beyond. In the falling glass of the hospital windows there may be an allusion to an event already contemplated in Mallarmé's "Les Fenêtres": "Est-il moyen . . . / D'enfoncer le cristal . . . / Et de m'enfuir . . . / Au risque de tomber pendant l'éternité?" But we are well beyond the context of an esthetic consciousness in "Las ventanas." The terrible force of the complaint wrenched from the suffering man, who has fallen into the hands of the living death, is linked to the winds blowing out the windows by what the poet calls "las dirrecciones inmutables." For all their so-called immutability the directions are changeless, inalterable only in their oscillation and in the radical state of uncertainty they provoke. Indeed, one is incapable of telling from what direction the hurricane comes, or for that matter from what point one is even questioning ("¿De qué punto interrogo?") in the attempt to ascertain the direction. The unrelenting directions pull the suffering man *between* two poles. In so doing they literally pull him apart, tear him in two: between the hurricane and the difficulty of coughing or defecating, between the death that takes root in the hospital's entrails and the life that is awakened in the clandestine cells of the corpses. The dying man, torn between life and death, expresses himself in a complaint that is similarly divided, his utterance being split between the mouth and the anus. His condition is best described by the term used in the closing passages of the poem: "espantosa incertidumbre" (*PC* 551).

The trial by suffering staged in "Las ventanas" represents an extreme ordeal of the Word. If a language that not only reasons but loves as well cannot effect the cure, cannot absolve the agony of the dying, then the Word or logos, which remains the final court of appeal for a critic like Larrea ("Este Verbo, que . . . se identifica precisamente con la figura de Cristo en que se funda el ser de la cultura cristiana"),[50] must be seen as nothing but a mockery and lie. The belief in the logos only serves the end of passing over or covering up suffering, not of overcoming it, or of finally absolving it in some form of redemption:

> ¿Cuánto tiempo ha durado la anestesia, que
> llaman los hombres? ¡Ciencia de Dios, Teodicea! si
> se me echa a vivir en tales condiciones, anestesiado
> totalmente, volteada mi sensibilidad para adentro!
> ¡Ah doctores de las sales, hombres de las esencias,
> prójimos de las bases! Pido se me deje con mi
> tumor de conciencia, con mi irritada lepra sensitiva,
> ocurra lo que ocurra, aunque me muera. Dejadme
> dolerme, si lo queréis, mas dejadme despierto de
> sueño, con todo el universo metido, aunque fuese a
> las malas, en mi temperatura polvorosa. (*PC* 551)

The care or concern that comes to bear on the event of suffering, under the auspices of God and knowledge, ironically resembles nothing so much as a form of persecution and harassment that deliberately keeps suffering from awakening fully and refuses to allow the human being to die. Priest and surgeon ultimately serve the same cause. They provide suffering with the opium to put it to sleep and to keep it out of the picture, keep it from talking, from testifying — paradoxically, by the very incapacity to voice itself — to the conspiracy of silence that attempts to shut it up. Indeed, what truly becomes oppressive in the poem is not suffering, nor the terrible event of death, but the elaborate systems of denial and anesthetization. They stifle actual suffering and death, not by silence, but by the fact that they seek to bring them into discourse, endow them with an essence and a base, an origin and an end. But the true tumour of conscience, the irritated, sensitive leprosy that belongs to man, and that cannot be taken from him, even at the hands of his relentless inquisitors, is that which has no voice, and has no truth to speak. Truthless and speechless, it allows man to die ("aunque me muera") and to feel pain ("Dejadme dolerme"), and awakens him in his pain with all the universe embedded: ". . . dejadme despierto de sueño, con todo el universo metido. . . ." What the suffering voice of the poem so desperately seeks is that, speechless and incomprehensible, it be left for dead, so that it may suffer and die on its own at last.

This demand would seem to stem from a great hopelessness. But what is asked by the poet is that suffering be allowed not to take place as a metaphysical or theological event, or for that matter as a phenomenon of scientific knowledge and scrutiny. This is what makes the nature of such a suffering so hard to conceive. For it would have no place in which to take place, no longer controlled or consoled by religion and philosophy, no longer absorbed by the logos, nor rationalized by logic, no longer falling within the jurisdiction of thought or analysis, no longer administered by surgeon or priest, no longer comprehended by the science of God, or by systematic science, or by science itself. Indeed, in its "espantosa incertidumbre," such a suffering would no longer even be an event in the rigorous sense of the word. "Las ventanas" is Vallejo's revision of the Book of Job. In both cases, the subject of suffering grows well aware of the futility involved in all rationalization of suffering, in all mere attempts to "explain it away." However, what Job possesses is the power of utterance, as well as the faith in the ultimate justice of morality and religion which accompanies that power in the relentless demand for a hearing. This is, of course, precisely what we find lacking in Vallejo. It is as though God had not in the end intervened, but kept silent and withdrawn, so that the book itself were left unfinished, and Job were left suspended in the abyss of a suffering without the ministry of either faith or reason. But what would be the nature of this suffering that has finally eluded the alert and tireless vigilance of God, thought, and science? If such a question were to be posed by the philosopher, it would, indeed, have to be asked in terms of its essence, and this is precisely the question that has been precluded.

For Vallejo, fully awakened suffering is "essentially" inessential, without essence. It is not anything; rather, it can no longer be placed in the context of a discourse where the opposition essential/inessential, indeed, where the mode of oppositional logic itself, is operative. The seemingly unanswerable question of this suffering is posed with disturbing directness in the closing moments of the poem: "¿Dónde está, pues, el otro flanco de esta queja de dolor, si, a estimarla en conjunto, parte ahora del lecho de un hombre?" (*PC* 551). In one sense, "Las ventanas" indefinitely suspends even the possibility of an answer, as it is suspended in the poem "El alma que sufrió de ser su cuerpo," where the equation of reflection with navel-gazing is taken quite literally in the line "a tu ombligo interrogas: ¿dónde? ¿cómo?" (*PC* 664). To pose such questions about the human destination and destiny to one's belly-button, the ineradicable mark of one's subjection to life as a generative process that has no traceable origin or conceivable end, is an ironic way of saying that the answer is nowhere or the question elsewhere. The irony of the title, as well as of the specific nature of the opening line's diagnosis, "tu sufres de una glándula endocrína, se ve," does not lie solely in the opposition soul/body or man/animal. It points to a suffering that is precisely unlocatable, without cause or meaning, that cannot be placed or summed up in any rational way. The toast that closes "El alma" expresses the irreducible contradiction of the human being in the face of suffering: "¡Salud! ¡Y sufre!" The imperative "Suffer!", in such a context, is the same thing as saying "Live!"

If suffering draws a limit to the power of the logos, it is not simply as a moment of negativity. Suffering opens up an illimitable region, and in that region the straining voice of the philosopher and of all his fellow "rulers in chaos" can no longer be heard. With the fading of this dying voice what *is* heard is philosophy's limit, but expropriated and spoken in *another* voice, not its own. That which Derrida refers to as "its own limit" (*"Its own limit* had not to remain foreign to it. Therefore it has appropriated the concept for itself; it has believed that it controls the margin of its volume and that it thinks its other," *MP* x) is invaded by the illimitable, by that which philosophy is incapable of reclaiming and making its property. In "Las ventanas," that other limit to philosophy, which is never to be made proper to it, is heard by a different ear in a certain kind of laughter ("otra risa de contrapunto"), another laughter, a counter-laughter bursting out in a parody of reason's own mocking laughter. The latter would make a travesty of suffering, incapable of recognizing in it anything but an eradicable absurdity, a tumour to be removed, or a leprosy to cure: "En el mundo de la salud perfecta, se reirá por esta perspectiva en que padezco, pero, en el mismo plano y cortando la baraja del juego, percute aquí otra risa de contrapunto" (*PC* 551). Georges Bataille tells of the discovery of a hilarity quite similar to this other laugh, which percusses here in counterpoint to the perspective taken by philosophy. Indeed, the discovery itself is explicitly related in terms of a counter-example that eludes or exceeds the philosophical definition and appreciation of laughter:

> Je dirai l'occasion d'où ce rire est sorti: j'étais à Londres (en 1920) et devais me trouver à table avec Bergson; je n'avais alors rien lu de lui (ni d'ailleurs, peu s'en faut, d'autres philosophes); j'eus cette curiosité, me trouvant au British Museum je demandai le *Rire* (le plus court de ses livres); la lecture m'irrita, la théorie me sembla courte (là-dessus le personnage me déçut: ce petit homme prudent, philosophe!) mais la question, le sens demeuré caché du rire, fut dès lors à mes yeux la question clé.[51]

Of this hidden meaning of laughter, not the philosopher's, Bataille writes: "le rire était révélation, ouvrait le fond des choses."

In the illimitable region of suffering portrayed in "Las ventanas," a similar revelatory and exuberant laughter bursts out against the serious and labouring discourse that belongs to an anesthetic metaphysics. This laughter accompanies the intuition of life as absolute risk and play: ". . . en el mismo plano y cortando la baraja del juego." Earlier in the poem the surgeon ausculates the patients for hours on end, until the labour has become too much for him and his hands begin to drift and "play": "Hasta donde sus manos cesan de trabajar y empiezan a jugar, las lleva a tientas, rozando la piel de los pacientes, en tanto sus párpados científicos vibran tocados por la indocta, por la humana flaqueza del amor" (PC 550). It is not, in the end, from death that human beings die, but from the "amor desdoblado del cirujano, de los largos diagnósticos, de las dosis exactas, del rigoroso análisis de orinas y excrementos." We die from the labour of knowledge, the deliberation of analysis, the terrible and ponderous exactness of science. The world of perfect health is not the world in which humans live and suffer. It is the image of a Hegelian state, or stasis, of absolute knowledge, where the tumour of consciousness is relentlessly *aufgehoben*. But it is the very removal of the tumour that proves fatal. In a paradoxical way, human beings suffer from having their suffering put to sleep and their "irritada lepra sensitiva" stripped from them. They die from the tremendous work that goes into taking their death away from them, that work of the negative against which, from the abyss of suffering, a countering laughter heroically bursts forth.

The point of this "otra risa de contrapunto" we have already met elsewhere: in the limit and sharp point of "La punta del hombre." In its countering action this laugh does not simply oppose philosophical understanding, answering in a strictly negative way the philosopher's empty mockery. It pits itself against it, counters it by parrying it — kicks against the metaphysical pricks, as it were — pricks against it and pierces it, or hits it hard and gives it that "one more blow for philosophical knowledge" of which Derrida speaks in the opening passages of "Tympan." "Counterpoint," of course, is first of all a musical term, and in the context points to a radical dissonance, as in the moans of the succeeding passage, which "En la casa del dolor" are dealt like harsh blows to the "síncopes de gran compositor" and, counter to any harmony, accord, or resolution, "freeze us in terrifying uncertainty" ("nos hielan de espantosa incertidumbre").

> En la casa del dolor, la queja asalta síncopes de
> gran compositor, golletes de carácter, que nos hacen
> cosquillas de verdad, atroces, arduas, y, cumpliendo
> lo prometido, nos hielan de espantosa incertidumbre.
>
> (*PC* 551)

"La queja," which in the opening passage of the poem is described as part mouth and completely anus, is just as inexpressive here. The complaint is not heard, but felt intensely, like "real, arduous, atrocious tickles." Tickling is the perfect word to depict that extraordinary state of uncertainty in which one cannot be sure whether to scream or to break out laughing. In a similar way, the dying man of the opening lines is torn between the desire to defecate and the compulsion to cough. The word "síncope" is another word for "counterpoint." But it also refers to a brief loss of consciousness, brought on by a drop in blood pressure, for example, or, more pertinent here, by a certain threshold or excess of pain:

> En la casa del dolor, la queja arranca frontera
> excesiva. No se reconoce en esta queja de dolor, a
> la propia queja de la dicha en éxtasis, cuando el

> amor y la carne se eximen de azor y cuando al
> regresar, hay discordia bastante para el diálogo.
>
> (*PC* 551)

This passage concerns the excessive nature of suffering: that "tanto" ("so much") of the litany of pain in Vallejo's deliriously apocalyptic "Los nueve monstruos," which is supplanted by the "muchísimo" ("too much") of the poem's last line, "hay, hermanos, muchísimo que hacer" (*PC* 655). The region opened up by suffering is one in which the line can no longer be drawn between tickling and torture, between an ecstatic hilarity and complete agony. Indeed, this uncertainty is an obstacle to the decipherment of the passage itself. First of all, it is not certain or decidable who the subject or source of the complaint is: whether the subject which hears the cry is also the one who cries out, or whether the effect of the complaint is being felt only by those who are listening but from whom the agonizing cry does not stem. The open-endedness of the syntax does not allow us to make these kinds of identifications and distinctions. Secondly, it is impossible to tell — again because of the syntax — if the fact that we do not recognize ("no se reconoce") in this cry of pain "la propia queja de la dicha en éxtasis" ("one's own moan of happiness in ecstasy"), means that this is because it is not present, or because it is simply unrecognizable, but nevertheless there. This moan uproots excessive frontier ("arranca frontera excesiva"), and in so doing produces a moment of suspension, a threshold state, a state reflected in the very undecidability of the syntax, and in which the subject of suffering is frozen by a terrifying uncertainty, held, without hope of release — except in death — between two poles. The uncertainty is one in which a radical discord precludes even the possibility of dialogue, not to mention dialectics, although the ambiguity of the syntax leaves us once again unsure. To say that in this region of suffering there is not "discordia bastante para el diálogo," may mean that there is not enough discord or that there is too much; it may point to either a lack or an excess, and suggests in the final account that this region is one where the difference or line drawn between too much or too little is no longer clear.

The unanswerable question of suffering is then asked: "¿Dónde está, pues, el otro flanco de esta queja de dolor, si, a estimarla en conjunto, parte ahora del lecho de un hombre?"   What is asked here concerns the generative power of suffering, and, in a startling reversal, it is no longer the ineluctable eventuality of death that pain announces, but the life it is in the midst of giving birth to out of "el otro flanco de esta queja de dolor."   This other side of suffering turns away from the intent gaze and listening of the philosophers and theologians, from the recuperative operations of the surgeons and metaphysicians; it turns away from the Hegelian labours of reason and the spirit to labour elsewhere, in another sense of labour.   The excessive and immeasurable character of suffering finally *gives birth* to an ineffable plenitude, to an overflowing not only beyond words, but beyond even emotive expression:

> De la casa del dolor parten quejas tan sordas e inefables y tan colmadas de tánta plenitud, que llorar por ellas sería poco, y sería ya mucho sonreír.

> Se atumulta la sangre en el termómetro.
> (*PC* 551-52)

Pain never ceases to be pain, and yet it has turned into something else, in relation to which our response is always too little or too much, deficient or excessive.   The concept of pain opposed to ecstasy is utterly inadequate.   This "something else" that pain verges on and whose abundance overflows the borders beyond which human suffering must go nameless, is both a limiting and a limitless sphere.   For as a limit it opens onto the limitless.   Thus the poem closes with a liturgical prayer that states in a contradictory way the impossible nature of this limit, by which we are made to face, in the cessation of life in death, the incomprehensible event of life itself:

> ¡No es grato morir, señor, si en la vida nada se
> deja y si en la muerte nada es posible, sino sobre
> lo que se deja en la vida!

> ¡No es grato morir, señor, si en la vida nada se
> deja y si en la muerte nada es posible, sino sobre
> lo que se deja en la vida!

> ¡No es grato morir, señor, si en la vida nada se
> deja y si en la muerte nada es posible, sino sobre
> lo que pudo dejarse en la vida!
>
> (*PC* 552)

In another prose poem, "Voy a hablar de la esperanza," which immediately follows "Las ventanas" in Larrea's edition, Vallejo addresses the same question of suffering in different terms. Suffering now emerges as that which, to the extent to which it can be called personal, throws personhood itself into question, and suspends the very possibility of ever making suffering one's own, of ever being able to reclaim one's suffering in the name of the self, or even of being in the position to say "I suffer" without at the same time utterly draining of content and meaning the idea of a unique and proper self. The Marxist critic Alain Sicard's reading of the poem is quite interesting in this regard. The very aspects of the poem he focuses on, far from depicting, as he attempts to show, suffering as an "expérience de l'objectivité" or "expérience de l'objectivité d'un type très particulier dans la mesure où c'est le corps humain qui en est le siège,"[52] render, indeed, precisely such terms as these — as well as the opposing concepts such as "subjectivity" or "ideality" — no longer adequate to conceive of suffering on its own, in its proper terms. The paradox is, in fact, that there is absolutely nothing "proper" about suffering.

> Yo no sufro este dolor como César Vallejo. Yo
> no me duelo ahora como artista, como hombre ni
> como simple ser vivo siquiera. Yo no sufro este
> dolor como católico, como mahmetano ni como ateo.
> Hoy sufro solamente. Si no me llamase César
> Vallejo, también sufriría este mismo dolor. Si no
> fuese artista, también lo sufriría. Si no fuese
> hombre ni ser vivo siquiera, también lo sufriría. Si
> no fuese católico, ateo ni mahometano, también lo
> sufriría. Hoy sufro desde más abajo. Hoy sufro
> solamente.   (*PC* 553)

The dark irony of the phrase "I am going to speak of hope" finds an
echo in Blanchot's paradoxical words: "L'espoir est le plus profound, lorsque lui-
même se retire et se destitue de tout espoir manifeste."[53] The paradox of such
a hope is that it is as bottomless or abysmal as the pain from which it is born.
This pain exceeds the objective as it does the subjective, the material as well as
the ideal, the collective as well as the personal. Indeed, it exceeds antithetical
thought in its most general as in its most specific form; like the suffering in
"Las ventanas," which drastically uproots "frontera excesiva," it leaves us in a
region out of reach of even negative dialectics. The point of the poem is that
suffering does not allow itself to be summed up in an identifying or unifying
discourse, even if it be one of negativity. Suffering is always in excess, or in
deficiency, of that which would hope to name it. The opening passage, contrary
to the implications of Sicard's analysis, performs a sort of anti-phenomenological
"epoche" of the subject, in which the subject here becomes, indeed, a literal
sub-ject ("thrown under"), the empty, abysmal core lying at the bottomless
bottom of suffering, which no amount of unlayering can discover. The subject
of suffering is caught up in a relentless process of displacement which undoes it
and leaves it utterly destitute of any identity. Far from indicating the truly
material and collective nature of suffering, the poem unveils a suffering so
hyperbolic that it is no longer dependent on consciousness as such, no longer

dependent even on "living being": "Si no fuese hombre ni ser vivo siquiera, también lo sufriría." As Blanchot writes concerning a suffering of equally abysmal proportions: "Il s'agit . . . d'une souffrance comme indifférente, et non soufferte, et neutre (un fantôme de souffrance), si celui qui y est exposé est privé, justement par la souffrance, de ce 'Je' qui la lui ferait souffrir."[54] The truth of suffering has been cast into the bottomless well of suffering itself. The "I" who suffers can no longer even say "I" except as a pure subject of suffering, and therefore as a being no longer even a subject, since its subjectivity coincides in an absolute way with the act and passion of suffering. Suffering is thus left adrift without its subject and without its truth. The logic of suffering "solamente" ("only" or "merely," but also "alone") means one's suffering must always be "further below" ("más abajo") and/or "further above" ("más arriba") all possible categorization, attribution, identification, or denomination.

> Me duelo ahora sin explicaciones. Mi dolor es
> tan hondo, que no tuvo ya causa ni carece de causa.
> ¿Qué sería su causa? ¿Dónde está aquello tan
> importante, que dejase de ser su causa? Nada es su
> causa; nada ha podido dejar de ser su causa.
> (PC 553)

Unidentifiable and nameless, the act or event of suffering can hardly be graced by the words "act" or "event." In its utter neutrality and feature-lessness, pain has become purely generic, "no-name." Being not only without cause but without an absence of cause as well ("no tuvo ya causa ni carece de causa"), it is an event that, in rigorous terms, does not even take place. From this derives the contradictory irony of the active Spanish "Yo sufro," as opposed to Eshleman and Barcia's translation "I am in pain." Devoid of all activity, the subject of this suffering approaches a point of such inert passivity that it is as thought pain itself were an entity that suffered through the human subject in a completely absorbing way. "Neutral" is a word which comes close to describing the bad infinity of this suffering which suffers through man, or which man actively undergoes, and whose neutrality actively neutralizes the attempt to impose a discourse made up of what Derrida calls "philosophemes": those of cause and effect, origin and end, absence and presence, etc.[55] However, the disadvantage of the word is that it is in fact too neutral; that is, it carries with it certain unavoidable connotations of disengagement and non-involvement. To designate Vallejo's intuition of suffering a better word may substitute, a cognate of the word "neutral" itself, which carries over from another sphere associations that allow it to translate what is most actively — if it can be put that way, since suffering, in Vallejo's sense, renders precisely such concepts as active and passive questionable — neutral in the passion of suffering: what Blanchot calls "le neutre." The neuter is that which, being "une menace et un scandale pour la pensée,"

> ne se distribue dans aucun genre: le non-général, le non-générique, comme le non-particulier. Il refuse l'appartenance aussi bien à la catégorie de l'objet qu'à celle du sujet. Et cela ne veut pas seulement dire qu'il est encore indéterminé et comme hésitant entre les deux, cela veut dire qu'il suppose une relation autre, ne relevant ni des conditions objectives, ni des dispositions subjectives.[56]

Since it is not simply a negation or absence, but indeed indicates a relation, the neuter can be recognized as the effect of a disjunction or "neither/nor" (*neuter*, "neither one of the two") that undercuts the mode of discourse governed by binary opposition. In Blanchot's use of the word, the neuter proves to be both grammatically and philosophically corrupt, as it exploits and at the same time exceeds the various meanings attached to it: the syntactic neither/nor, the grammatical gender, the third person singular "it," and the verbal intransitive, as well as the zoological and botanical categories it denotes and by which the entire network of problems of gender and the generic are brought into play.

In "Voy a hablar de la esperanza," the neuter is strongly suggested by the use of a disjunction which governs the phrasal patterns of the poem:

> Y no me duelo ahora como artista . . . ni como simple ser vivo siquiera.
>
> Si no fuese hombre ni ser vivo . . .
>
> Si no fuese católico, ateo, ni mahometano . . .
>
> Mi dolor es tan hondo, que no tuvo ya causa ni carece de causa.
>
> . . . mi dolor de hoy no es padre ni es hijo.
>
> Le falta espalda para anochecher, tanto como le sobra pecho para amanecer.
>
> . . . si lo pusiesen . . . no daría luz . . . y si lo pusiesen . . . no echaría sombra.   (*PC* 553-54)

But the neuter, as we have said, exceeds a merely grammatical disjunctiveness. It draws us into an irresistible process of displacement that Derrida has called, in another context, "la loi du genre," a law which rigorously demands its own transgression, so that it turns out to be at the same time the law of its own contamination or "la loi de *débordement*."[57]   Vallejo's suffering is inexorably caught up in this law, commanded by it to transgress it, and unfolding in such a way that, like Blanchot's neuter, it is always somewhere else than where one has located it, "toujours ailleurs qu'on ne le situe, non seulement toujours au-délà et toujours en déça du neutre, non seulement dépourvue de sens propre et même d'aucune forme de positivité et de négativité, mais ne laissant ni la présence ni l'absence le proposer avec certitude à quelque expérience que ce soit, fût-ce celle de la pensée."[58]

> ¿A qué ha nacido este dolor, por sí mismo? Mi dolor es del viento del norte y del viento del sur, como esos huevos neutros que algunas aves raras

ponen del viento. Si hubiese muerto mi novia, mi
dolor sería igual. Si me hubieran cortado el cuello
de raiz, mi dolor sería igual. Si la vida fuese, en
fin, do otro modo, mi dolor sería igual. Hoy sufro
desde más arriba. Hoy sufro solamente.

Miro el dolor del hambriento y veo que su
hambre anda tan lejos de mi sufrimiento, que de
quedarme ayuno hasta morir, saldría siempre de mi
tumba una brizna de yerba al menos. Lo mismo el
enamorado. ¡Que sangre la suya más engendrada,
para la mía sin fuente ni consumo!

Yo creía hasta ahora que todas las cosas del
universo eran, inevitablemente, padres e hijos. Pero
he aquí que mi dolor de hoy no es padre ni es hijo.
Le falta espalda para anochecer, tanto como le
sobra pecho para amanecer y si lo pusiesen en una
estancia oscura, no daría luz y si lo pusiesen en
una estancia luminosa, no echaría sombra. Hoy
sufro suceda lo que suceda. Hoy sufro solamente.

(*PC* 553-54)

This pain does not simply lack an origin, for, as with its cause, just as nothing could be its origin, nothing could ever stop being its origin. Indeed, in a twist on Blake's cryptic aphorism, "Joys impregnate, sorrows bring forth,"[59] it would be that which gives birth to itself, which brings itself forth self-generatively, if only genus as birth and generation were not precisely that which this suffering disrupts and transgresses. This pain "comes from" ("es del . . ."), is generated from the very image of the nongenerative and the unborn, since it is figured as a literal inheritance of the wind — sown by the winds from the north and south, whose opposed directions "neutralize" one another, and laid "como esos huevos neutros que algunas aves raras ponen del viento" ("like those neuter eggs certain rare birds lay in the wind"). The origin of this pain is not simply indeterminate, but is undecidable in an even more radical way, and this undecidability extends not only to its place of non-birth and non-origin, but to its own sex or gender and to its power of engenderment. Its power of engenderment, even beyond death, is in one sense infinite or boundless: "saldría siempre de mi tumba una brizna de yerba al menos." But as such it represents the engenderment of death as much as of life, of life and death in their "double invagination,"[60] to borrow Derrida's suggestive term; of the life beyond death, and of the death that is always already part of life; of the life that contains death as part of its process, and of the death that enfolds all of life. This double invagination of life and death characterizes a pain which, at its ultimate limit, is purely neuter, without source or use, sexless and sterile, without gender or the power of engenderment: "Lo mismo al enamorado. ¡Que sangre la suya más engendrada, para la mía sin fuente ni consumo!" Moreover, pain and suffering are strictly para-generic, and para-genealogical: "Yo creía hasta ahora que todas las cosas del universo eran, inevitablemente, padres e hijos. Pero he aquí que mi dolor de hoy no es padre ni es hijo." Indeed, by dint of the relentless transgression of the law of genus, according to that "loi du genre" which commands that its own law be broken, the pain suffered by the subject of Vallejo's poem turns out to be that which takes place, and is made to take place inexorably, by the very inconsequentiality, the utter lack of consequence it represents as an "event": "Hoy sufro suceda lo que suceda." Whatever happens, no matter what happens, I suffer, which means that in one sense nothing happens when I suffer, or indeed that what does not happen in the end — that is, what does not take place as an event — is my suffering.

The pervasive effect of this neuter relation throughout Vallejo's poetry is remarkable. This is the effect at work in the poem "Lomo de las Sagradas Escrituras," where it undercuts and neutralizes the terms necessary to the kind of theological and metaphysical reading that Larrea insists upon. Vallejo's astonishing status as a version of the Incarnated Word, to which Larrea raises the poet in his interpretation of the lines "Escucha, / Hombre, en verdad te digo que eres el HIJO ETERNO," is not only out of all proportion, but this very disproportion tells us that something else entirely, something *other* may be at stake in the poem. The fact that Larrea collapses Christ and Oedipus into one in the mythic figure of Vallejo is, however, for all its extravagance and fantasy, quite suggestive.[61] A Vallejo-Oedipus — whose significance, however, may not be strictly "Oedipal" — might well be uncovered in the poet's dramatic refusal of the normal genealogical relation to the father in the name of an eternalization of sonhood and its all absorbing maternal relation.

> Sin haberlo advertido jamás exceso por turismo
> y sin agencias
> de pecho en pecho hacia la madre unánime.
>
> Hasta París ahora vengo a ser hijo. Escucha,
> Hombre, en verdad te digo que eres el HIJO ETERNO,
> pues para ser hermano tus brazos son escasamente iguales
> y tu malicia para ser padre, es mucha.
> (*PC* 566)

To interpret this eternalization of sonhood as Christ-like is to ignore the tone of mockery and irony with which "el HIJO ETERNO" is introduced; it is because of one's incapacity to be a true brother in the sharing of a common humanity and because of one's abundant "malice to be a father" that one can only settle for the arrested maturity of being a son forever. But at the same time the desire to be an eternal son is a premonition of *another* relation, which is the sense as well behind Vallejo's celebrated "orphan complex." This other relation would be with "la madre unanime," who is a unique figure in being excluded from the law of genus: that is, from the law of generation and genealogy, from the restrictive economy of life and death, and even from that fundamental category of identity, gender.

In his essay on Freud's *Beyond the Pleasure Principle* ("Speculate — on 'Freud'") Derrida refers to the figure of the mother as "the figureless figure" or "face without face": "All speculation . . . implies the terrifying possibility of this *usteron* *proteron* of the generations. When the face without face, name without name, of the mother returns, in the end, one has what I called in *Glas* the logic of obsequence. The mother buries all her own. She assists whoever calls herself her mother, and follows all burials" (*C* 333). The face without face of the mother is a presence in a number of Vallejo's poems. In "El buen sentido," the self distinctly portrays itself in an Oedipal role, as it relates to a powerful maternal figure who holds the keys of life and death:

> La mujer de mi padre está enamorada de mí, viniendo y avanzando de espaldas a mi nacimiento y de pecho a mi muerte. Que soy dos veces suyo: por el adiós y por el regreso. La cierro, al retornar....
> ....
>
> Mi adiós partió de un punto de su ser, más externo que el punto de su sér al que retorno.
>
> (*PC* 545-46)

A darker figure, almost that of an anti-mother — perhaps closest to what Derrida intends by "la figure sans figure" — emerges and displaces the domestic figure of the mother in the poem "Tendríamos ya una edad misericordiosa." An old hen ("una gallina"), "no ajena, ni pondedora, sino brutal y negra" ("neither alien nor egg-laying, but brutal and black"), is said to have clucked ("Cloqueaba") "en mi garganta" and to be "maternalmente viuda de unos pollos que no llegaron a incubarse" (*PC* 556). The paternal word is said in the poem to be the law of life: "Y tal, la ley, la causa de la ley. Y tal también la vida." This law of genus, of generation and genealogy, is disrupted and displaced by a sinister maternal figure who steals away or "castrates" the speech of the father, and supplants his word in the throats of his sons: "En los labios del padre cupo, para salir rompiéndose, una fina cuchara que conozco. En las fraternas bocas, la absorta amargura del hijo, quedó atravesada." The supplanting of the father by a violent theft of his speech entails, along with the loss of the power to signify, the short-circuiting of a generative economy of life and death:

> Cloqueaba en mi garganta. Fue una gallina vieja,
> maternalmente viuda de unos pollos que no llegaron
> a incubarse. Origen olvidado de ese instante, la
> gallina era viuda de sus hijos. Fueron hallados
> vacíos todos los huevos. La clueca después tuvo el
> verbo. (*PC* 556)

The obsessive concern with genus, evident from the very beginnings of Vallejo's poetry, is curiously linked in the posthumous poems with the motif of writing. In "Quedéme a calentar la tinta," mention is made of a female genealogy ("digiero sacratísimas constancias, / noches de madre, días de biznieta"), while the act of writing is undertaken by a subject metaphorically related to the earth, sun, and moon, but with the gender of *tierra* and *luna* inverted by an apparent *slip of the pen*, we have "tierro" and "luno" to accord with a masculine sun, "sol," a word which is significantly without a vowel ending:

> he aquí que caliente, oyente, tierro, sol y luno,
> incógnito atravieso el cementerio,
> tomo a la izquierda, hiendo
> la yerba con un par de endecasílabos,
> años de tumba, litros de infinito,
> tinta, pluma, ladrillos y perdones.
> (*PC* 622)

Along the same lines, writing is associated, in "La punta del hombre," with a puzzling network of associations: life, death, memory, writing, and — in the grotesque closing lines — the eating of "un pedazo de queso con gusanos hembras, / gusanos machos y gusanos muertos":

> Acorde de lápiz, tímpano sordísimo,
> dondoneo en mitades robustas
> y comer de memoria buena carne,
> jamón, si falta carne,
> y un pedazo de queso con gusanos hembras,
> gusanos machos y gusanos muertos.
> (*PC* 615)

The final mention of "dead worms" in a series that opens with a differentiation of the worms by their sex seems to imply that the category "dead" may be thought of as a third gender, a neuter. The concern with genus is already evident in the genealogy of the second stanza of the poem, where reference is made to "caminantes suegros," "cuñados en misión sonora," and "yernos por la via ingratísima del jebe." If life is either male or female, then perhaps death, or that which is dead, is neuter. The dead as neuter — although the neuter itself can be categorized as neither living nor dead — may be linked to the idea of writing and memory as sarcophagus activities ("comer de memoria buena carne") that bring into play the ghost of an absent presence.

Similar associations are to be found in the closing tercets of "Intensidad y altura," a poem which opens with the complaint: "Quiero escribir, pero me sale espuma."

> Vámonos, pues, por eso, a comer yerba,
> carne de llanto, fruta de gemido,
> nuestra alma melancólica en conserva.
>
> ¡Vámonos! ¡Vámonos! Estoy herido;
> vámonos a beber lo ya bebido,
> vámonos, cuervo, a fecundar tu cuerva.
>
> (*PC* 641)

With the references throughout the poem to questions of genus — generation, engenderment, genetics, gender — one might begin to suspect that the "generator" of such a poem is the problem of genus itself. The subject is, moreover, the impossibility of generating a poem, of expressing oneself in words. Genus, in all its ramifications, has the irreducible peculiarity, in Vallejo's poetry, of disrupting any unity of voice governed by the logos as word, reason, knowledge, science. This peculiarity — the law of genre or genus as a kind of anti-logos — is reflected in another ingenious slip of the pen, as Vallejo combines *voz* ("voice") and *tos* ("cough") in the expression "toz hablada." The closing line, "vámonos, cuervo, a fecundar tu cuerva," crudely sums up this singular interest in gender and generation. Nor should we overlook the sonnet form of the poem, its *genre*, especially notable in the work of a poet whose use of classical forms is very infrequent. Paradoxically, in this case, the turn to a classical genre coincides with the theme of the impossibility of self-expression in poetry.[62]

Vallejo's obsessive concern with genus, however, reflects finally a fascination with that which in fact transgresses genus and its logic, escapes the stricture of its economy, its law of the proper: what Blanchot calls the "neuter." The word itself makes a conspicuous appearance in one of the late prose poems, "Algo te identifica":

> Algo típicamente neutro, de inexorablemente neutro, interpónese entre el ladrón y su víctima. Esto, asimismo, puede discernirse tratándose del cirujano y del paciente. Horrible medialuna, convexa y solar, cobija a unos y otros. Porque el objeto hurtado tiene también su peso indiferente, y el órgano intervenido, también su grasa triste.
>
> (*PC* 677)

The pair of relations referred to in these lines — thief and victim, surgeon and patient — suggests a comparison with Hegel's celebrated opponents of the section on "Independence and dependence of self-consciousness: Lordship and Bondage" in the *Phenomenology*. Vallejo's two duos seem to be mock versions of Hegel's master and slave, in a way that is elucidated by a section in Bataille's *L'Expérience intérieure*, where a hypothetical project is outlined whose end is to "out-Hegel Hegel" and which would consist in a miming of absolute knowledge:

> Si je 'mime' le savoir absolu, me voici par nécessité Dieu moi-même . . . *La Phénomenologie de l'Esprit* compose deux mouvements essentiels achevant un cercle: c'est achèvement par degrés de la conscience de soi (de l'*ipse* humain), et devenir tout (devenir Dieu) de cet *ipse* achevant de savoir . . . Mais si de cette façon, comme par contagion et par mime, j'accomplis en moi le mouvement circulaire de Hegel, je définis, par-délà les limites

> atteintes, non plus un inconnu mais un
> inconnaissable. Inconnaissable non du fait de
> l'insuffisance de la raison mais par sa nature . . .[63]

This unknowable, which is unknowable by its very nature and not by a deficiency of reason, is reminiscent of that "lesión de la incógnita" heard in "la lesión de la respuesta" (*PC* 647) of Vallejo's "Panteón," as well as of that unknown and unknowable referred to in "Quedéme a calentar la tinta": "Se estremeció la incógnita en mi amígdala" (*PC* 622). The analysis of Vallejo's poetry on dialectical lines is, of course, a favorite and familiar one. Enric Miret and Alain Sicard apply a dialectical understanding to individual poems as well as to the trajectory of the entire body of writings; both allude to a negative movement of thought at work throughout his poetic career, and see an eventual synthetic overcoming of contradiction in the later poetry.[64] Juan Larrea just as clearly aims at comprehending Vallejo's entire body of work on the model of a total dialectical coherence which, however distant it may be from the ideological presuppositions of Sicard's reading, for example, nevertheless claims for the work a similar unity and synthesis.[65] In this case, it is the number three — not the Marxist triangle this time, but the symbol of the Christian trinity — which symbolically reflects the harmonious resolution in which the poetry is seen as finally reposing. But it is precisely the security and the ground of this kind of dialectical movement that "Algo te identifica" throws into question.

In a note in *del carnet de 1936/37 (1938?)* (a collection of posthumous notes and fragments published by Georgette Vallejo) Vallejo addresses the question of dialectics in disarmingly personal terms.[66] The discussion is apropos of a conversation held between Vallejo and his wife during a visit to the cemetery: "Una visita al cementario del domingo 7 de Novembre 1937, con Georgette." The locale of the conversation is in no way indifferent. It places the topic in a certain context: that of a contemplation of death and, moreover, of that figureless figure, that face without face of the mother, that vaginal tomb in which life and death are inextricably entangled and enfolded in one another, or "doubly invaginated"; "La tumba de su madre. La contemplación de la muerte, desde el punto de vista biológico y vital (madre, amante, los nueve meses y madre después, fuera del vientre)." This figureless figure is pondered only after a wild synopsis of the dialectical tradition and its central importance in Western thought. The overview seems expressly designed to make the specialist in philosophy wince. Hegel and Marx are said to have done little more than discover the rudimentary law of dialectics: "Me refiero a Hegel y Marx, que no hicieron sino descubrir la ley dialéctica." Vallejo claims to have perceived the fundamental inadequacy of that law in its present form, and recognizes the necessity of taking "una actitud crítica y revolucionaria delante de este deter-minismo dialéctico," noting at the same time that the overcoming of this vulgar dialectics has already been achieved. This achievement is the work of none other than Pascal, "cuyo pensamiento figura, sin duda, entre los que animó una velocidad dialéctica más grande, pasando del materialismo o cientifismo (su física), a la filosofía, luego a la metafísica, luego a la religión, luego al cris-tianismo y, por último al catolicismo." The velocity of the dialectical changes rung by Pascal's "Renversement continuel de pour au contre" may, indeed, be even more unarrestable and revolutionary than Vallejo himself suggests. As one dialectic "dialectically" displaces and supersedes another, we may end up without any motion at all. We may end up "por ultimo," and before very long, with that face without face of the mother who would now follow the funeral procession of catholicism itself — the latter having gone the way of all the rest — and even pick up after the incarnated Word and the Father who return to her at last, and whom she buries in the end. She would inherit all that is left of their life, which is all that is left of life, or which might have been left of life, that is, their mortality. As it is put in "Las ventanas"; "No es grato morir, señor, si en la vida nada se deja y si en la muerte nada es posible, sino sobre lo que pudo dejarse en la vida!" (*PC* 552).

The final passage of this fragment concerns again the contemplation of a tomb and, in the face of the ineluctable eventuality of death, the "'esperanza'" — Vallejo significantly quotes the word — "cristiana, en el mas allá." The Christian hope in the beyond is not referred to in terms of an ultimate reality in which one's faith rests assured, but as the "creación formidable de Jesús, que nace de lo más hondo del dolor humano," that is, as a human creation born from human suffering, and therefore as more of a consoling fiction than a divine truth. The creative power of this hope is almost to be conceived of as the result of a revulsion. The faith of the Christian is not affirmed here, or rather it is only affirmed as something cited, quoted ("Después de la guerra, debería haberse producido un renacimiento enorme de la concepcion cristiana del destino del hombre. Etc."). For in the final account, all human life must return to the face without face, the "unanimous mother," from which it has departed. The power of this figure and its obsequent logic is, like Blanchot's neuter, such that it exceeds and eludes, while providing the abysmal background for, the merely apparent dialectical coherence and purpose of human life.

If that background is abysmal, then the unity of life is itself a façade, for which the only cure or remedy is a groundless faith. In this sense the two opening stanzas of "Algo te identifica" are a deceiving *trompe l'oeil*. They merely mime the antithetical movement of dialectics by a symmetrical series of oppositions: identity/separation; leaving/remaining; slavery/power; returning/departing; sorrow/rejoicing. These oppositions do not unfold dialectically. In their mirror-like symmetry, they fold and collapse into each other so that the signification of one sentence simply cancels out the other, just as each sentence on its own is formulated to negate or undo the meaning that it only appears to have. The result of this merely apparent dialectical movement is a neutral state of suspended motion:

> Algo te identifica con el que se aleja de tí, y es la
> facultad común de volver: de ahí tu más grande pesadumbre.
> Algo te separa del que se queda contigo, y es la esclavitud
> común de partir: de ahí tu más nimios regocijos.
>
> (*PC* 677)

The poem's indeterminate, indefinite "Algo" may be identified as that element in excess of the dialectical process, which as such is without identity, which cannot in fact be identified. In evading all oppositional logic it turns out to be, indeed, the groundless ground against which contraries and opposites are neutralized. This neutralization only gives the appearance of a synthesis, being a sort of sham *Aufhebung*. The overcoming of contradiction is purely feigned; it is the effect of a non-dialectical excess that undercuts the antithetical movement of the dialectical. This neuter "something" is the unassimilable unknown of all thought, the residue left over as unabsorbable when the labours of reason and the spirit are completed or have reached, at least, their ever receding limit, the limit they can never appropriate. In the next passage of the poem it is depicted in terms of a margin, border, or frontier.

> Me dirijo, en esta forma, a las individualidades
> colectivas, tanto como a las colectivades individuales
> y a los que, entre unas y otras, yacen marchando al
> son de las fronteras o, simplemente, marcan el paso
> inmóvil en el borde del mundo.   (*PC* 677)

As in the mock dialectic of the first two stanzas, and in the spirit of Bataille's "mime du savoir absolu," the frontier or border skirted by those who lie between "individualidades colectivas" and "las colectividades individuales" indicates a limit which is only deceptively Hegelian. At the end of the *Phenomenology*, Hegel writes: "The self-knowing Spirit knows not only itself but also the negative of itself, or its limit: to know one's limit is to know how to sacrifice oneself"[67] Thus, the movement of the Spirit is summed up as that consciousness that steps out of itself or alienates itself, in order that it may know and absorb the limit and return to itself in the form of knowledge, ultimately absolute knowledge. The limit depicted by Vallejo differs crucially in that those who skirt the margins paradoxically "yacen marchando al son de las fronteras o, simplemente, marcan el paso inmóvil en el borde del mundo." The phrase "marcan el paso inmóvil" suggests a literal "stepping motionlessly," which brings to mind that effect of motionlessness characterizing Pascal's perpetual reversal of the pro and the con. Like the phrase "yacen marchando" ("lie marching"), it evokes the neutralization that we have already encountered in the opening two stanzas of the poem. The limit represented is completely inert, in one sense. On the other hand, it is actively, dynamically inert; it is an impossible *coincidentia oppositorum* of activity and passivity. This, then, is not a negative limit, but a neutral one or, in Blanchot's words, a "Limite qui est peut-être le neutre."[68]

This neuter limit is not to be commanded or mastered even by the negative. Resembling the marginal limit of Derrida's "Tympan," it has at its reserve "always one more blow for philosophical knowledge." Derrida plays on the cognateness of the word *marge* with the words *marche* and *marque* (*MP* xxiv), an etymology also exploited by Vallejo in "Algo te identifica." Those who are addressed on the margins, who attend on the borders of discourse to the poet's straining voice, are said to "march" ("marchan") to the sound of the frontiers, and to "mark" ("marcan") time at the edge of the world. They march along and mark out the frontiers that disrupt the coherence and unity of metaphysical discourse, borders that verge on the limitless and open onto that which is *other* than philosophy's always already mastered reflection of itself. Those addressed on the margins are said to lie *between* ("entre unas y otras") collective individualities and individual collectivities, incestuous twins who, in their verbal inversion, are merely the mirror transposition of one another. If those who lie *between* these narcissistic twins can be called a third term, insofar as they are the final term of a triadic structure, they do not represent a moment of mediation or synthesis. Indeed, the moment is itself explicitly disjunctive, since the use of the word "or" presents an unresolved alternative: "los que yacen marchando . . . o, simplemente . . ." Indeed, the number three throughout Vallejo's work, contrary to what Larrea asserts, may not be the number of a stabilizing and unifying moment, but a radically marginal number, a neuter number almost illegible and written always on the margins of discourse. It may be an orphan number, an excess number which does not count, which is not counted, which is not taken into account, a number inscribed on "neuvos pasajes de papel de oriente" by the "lustrales plumas, terceras, puñales" of *Trilce* XL. For these dwellers on the margin lie *between* the two ghost images of the individual and the collective, and not as a middle term, but askant and askew of a self-reflective reason's dialectical and oppositional logic. Marginal and oblique, they are not picked up in the glass, and what they listen to is spoken by a different voice, heard by another ear than that of the philosopher. As Derrida writes concerning a passage from Hegel:

> To philosophize *à corps perdu*. How did Hegel understand that?
> Can this text become the margin of a margin?
> Where has the body of the text gone when the

margin is no longer a secondary virginity but an inexhaustible reserve, the stereographic activity of an entirely other ear?

Overflows and cracks: that is, on the one hand compels us to count in its margin more and less than one believes is said or read, an unfolding due to the structure of the mark (which is the same word as *marche*, as limit, and as *margin*); and on the other hand, luxates the very body of statements in the pretensions to univocal rigidity or regulated polysemia. A lock opened to a double understanding no longer forming a single system. (*MP* xxiii-iv)

The relation between the thief and the victim, between the surgeon and the patient, escapes the dialectical movement of thought in the irreducible contingency that characterizes human interaction. The violence of such a relation is part of that contingency. What we face is a situation in which the possibility of the progress of knowledge through dialogical self-consciousness is precluded from the very beginning. An irrecoverable loss lies at the heart of the relation: something is stolen; an organ is operated upon and removed. This dispossession knows no redemption, no moment of reappropriation. The relation is traversed throughout with a "peso indiferente" or "grasa triste" which, speechless and without significance, makes its "presence" felt as that which rigorously resists the work of the negative, and is lost, irrevocably, to the movement of history. This is the mere refuse, dross, or excrement that the Spirit on its way to its triumph at the end of time cannot assimilate or digest. "Something typically neuter, inexorably neuter" actively intervenes and disrupts the mastery of metaphysics; it closes its ears to the march of thought and history, and marches without moving on the margins to the sound of a different drummer, a different tympany, one that deafeningly percusses and punctures the eardrum of philosophy itself, typically and inexorably. It is typically neuter because it is both nameless and generic, generic to the point of extreme neutrality, and inexorably so because in its unrelentingly inert resistance, in its radical passivity, it is infinitely more compelling and active than that which would make it a part of its proper apparatus, a part of its apparatus of the "proper."

The poem closes with an ironic reversal of the dream that extends from Plato to Hegel and on: the dream of a progress and perfectability of knowledge and of a happy ending promised in history to be brought about by the labours of thought and reason. It closes on the paradoxical reformulation of the encouraging question: "What is more hopeful on earth, than the possibility that the unhappy man become happy and the evil man become good?"

> ¿Qué hay de más desesperante en la tierra, que
> la imposibilidad en que se halla el hombre feliz de
> ser infortunado y el hombre bueno, de ser malvado?
> ¡Alejarse! ¡Quedarse! ¡Volver! ¡Partir! Toda
> la mecánica social cabe en estas palabras.
> (*PC* 677)

To readdress the question of human perfectability in the form of its direct contradiction is, of course, simply to state the opposite: that this hope is a desperate and disturbingly uncertain one. If to distance oneself is only to remain ("¡Alejarse! ¡Quedarse!"), and if to return is only to depart ("¡Volver! ¡Partir!"), then the dialectical process is neutralized from the very beginning. Philosophy cannot even begin to begin, can never even get started, and it cannot begin only because it can never stop, can never end, can never be completed. More than anything else, it is with this sense of a perpetual motionlessness, of an endless neutralization of movement, that we are left in Vallejo's posthumous poetry. We are reminded of the following passage in Kierkegaard's *Either/Or* which, as a parodic assessment of philosophy and of the ever optimistic philosopher, Vallejo's work would seem to confirm so exhaustively.

> . . . since I never start, so can I never stop; my
> eternal departure is identical with my eternal
> cessation. Experience has shown that it is by no

means difficult for philosophy to begin. Far from it. It begins with nothing, and consequently can always begin. But the difficulty, both for philosophy and for philosophers, is to stop. This difficulty is obviated in my philosophy; for if anyone believes that when I stop now, I really stop, he proves himself lacking in the speculative insight. For I do not stop now, I stopped at the time when I began. Hence my philosophy has the advantage of brevity, and it is also impossible to refute; for if anyone were to contradict me, I should undoubtedly have the right to call him mad. Thus it is seen that the philosopher lives continuously *aeterno modo*, and has not, like Sintenis of blessed memory, only certain hours which are lived for eternity.[69]

Notes to Chapter 1

1. Friedrich Nietzsche, *Twilight of the Idols* and *The Anti Christ*, trans. R. J. Hollingdale (Harmondworth: Penguin, 1968), p. 35.

2. Alain Sicard, "Contradiction et renversement matérialiste dans la poésie de César Vallejo, " in *Séminaire César Vallejo* (Poitiers: Centre de Recherches Latino-Américaines, 1973), p. 75n: "Il ne s'agit point de faire passer à Vallejo un examen de philosophie. Mais il n'est pas non plus déplacé de poser cette question du choix idéologique chez le poète, dans la mesure oú il est aisé de suivre l'itinéraire qui le conduit de la crise religieuse à l'adhésion philosophique et politique."

3. Juan Larrea's work on Vallejo is the best example of a Catholic interpretation of the poetry, first of all because of its complexity and sophistication, and secondly because of its many excesses. See, for example, "Significado conjunto de la vida y de la obra de César Vallejo," in *César Vallejo, poeta transcendental de Hispanoamerica: Su vida, su obra, su significado*, Actas del simposium celebrado por la Facultad de Filosofía y Humanidades de la Universidad Nacional de Córdoba, *Aula Vallejo*, Nos. 2, 3, 4 (1962), pp. 221-63.
   One of the finest Marxist critics writing on Vallejo is Alain Sicard, who makes an interesting case for a 'scientific' Marxist reading of the poetry. See "Dos principios de contradicción," and "Los desgraciados," in *Approximaciones a César Vallejo*, ed. Angel Flores, 2 vols. (New York: L. A. Publishing Co., 1971); and, especially, "Contradiction et renversement," in *Séminaire César Vallejo*, pp. 59-86.

4. As John Deredita puts it in his perceptive view of the early and more recent critical work on Vallejo in "Vallejo Interpreted, Vallejo Traduced," *Diacritics*, 8 (Dec. 1978), 16-27: "The biographical curiosity usually surrounding a poet thought to be major was compounded in Vallejo's case by the relatively isolated life he had led, at least in Europe, and the early state of *vallejismo* consisted primarily in memoirs, biographical studies and explications pointed toward

discovering the poet behind the text. When the approach was not directly biographical, the other ideological options available to the early critics — Spitzerian stylistics, varieties of existential humanism — tended to reinforce Vallejo's proprietary hold on 'his' texts" (17-18).

5. Vallejo's widow, Georgette Vallejo, née Phillipart, plays a somewhat infamous role in this history of manuscripts, though one certainly never approaching the kind of damaging interference with a writer's legacy that we associate with someone like Nietzsche's sister, for example. Looming on the horizon as well is that other ambitious proprietor of Vallejo and his text, Jan Larrea. Georgette Vallejo rightly objects to Larrea's invention of a fantastic Christlike Vallejo. For her side of the story, see *Apuntes biográficos sobre "Poemas en prosa" y "Poemas humanos"* (Lima: Moncloa, 1968). The battle for the ownership of Vallejo is strategically centred for Larrea on the question of the entitlement, in both senses of the word, of and to the posthumous work. See "Impropiedad del titulo 'Poemas humanos,'" in *Al amor de Vallejo* (Valencia: Pre-Textos, 1980), pp. 184-85; also, the preface written by Larrea to "Poemas postumos" in his edition of Vallejo's work, *Poesía completa*, pp. 531-40. Deredita resumes this proprietary conflict, as follows: "Proprietary rights or rights of the inheritance therefore hampered the reading of this key text for three decades. Finally, the widow authorized and oversaw the publication of the *Obra poética completa* (Lima: Moncloa, 1968), including photo facsimiles of the typescripts corrected in the poet's hand. Despite some debatable criteria — such as the continuing use of the title *Poemas humanos*, only one of these the poet had considered for the larger share of the late poems — the 1968 volume came closer to being a proper edition. 'Proper,' of course is related to 'proprietary,' and as if to commemorate the long proprietary phase of the Vallejo canon, each of the originals photographed had visibly stamped on it (by Vallejo? by Georgette? by the editor?) the legend *Propiedad de César Vallejo*" ("Vallejo Interpreted," 17).

6. Saul Yurkievich stresses the complex nature of the epistemological status of Vallejo's poetry in "El salto por el ojo de la aguja (Conocimiento de y por la poesía)," in *Séminaire César Vallejo*, pp. 97-108. The tendency to read Vallejo for his 'ideas,' that is, philosophically and ideologically, is one that we ourselves will not have escaped, and is perhaps a necessary one. Perhaps the thing is not to avoid reading Vallejo philosophically, but to read him philosophically not in the name of, but against or *contra* philosophy, in a counter-reading akin to that which is suggested by the titles of two of Vallejo's works: *Moscú contra Moscú* and *Contra el secreto profesional*. Relevant here are Yurkievich's comments in the discussion following Sicard's "Contradiction et renversement," in *Séminaire César Vallejo*: "Habría que saber en qué medida la forma es portadora de ideología . . . . Y luego está el problema de la plurivalencia en Vallejo . . . . Usa una pluralidad de discursos. Y sus distintas instancias discursivas son portadores de ideologías distintas en conflicto. Hay como un discurso polifónico, donde las ideologías conviven, mantenidas en la contradicción en suspensión, y que no se resuelve nunca . . ." (93).

7. As Yurkievich rightly observes in *Séminaire César Vallejo*, "no hay que olvidar el caràcter a menudo paródico, o irónico que cobra a menudo la sistematización de los contrarios en *Poemas humanos*. Vallejo, muchas veces, toma protocolos preestablecidos, modelos de discurso oratorio, por ejemplo, expositivo. Pero si el poema *externamente* tiene esta forma, internamente es

plurivalente. Hay una tensión disonante" (94).

8. César Vallejo, *Poesía completa*, pp. 460, 470. As stated in the prefatory note to the thesis, this edition will be used for all further references to Vallejo's poetry. All translations of the posthumous poetry are based on Clayton Eshleman and José Rubia Barcia, *César Vallejo: The Complete Posthumous Poetry* (Berkeley: Univ. of California Press, 1978).

9. The body of posthumous verse to which I refer here does not include *España, aparte de mí este cáliz*, which was prepared for publication before Vallejo's death. The posthumous verse has, until recently, been universally known as *Poemas humanos*, with the exception of a number of poems which Georgette Vallejo collected under the title of *Poemas en prosa*. Juan Larrea has violently objected to the title "Poemas humanos" and, in the expensive edition of the complete poems, *Poesía completa*, has taken things into his own hands, dividing the poems into two volumes with the titles *Nómina de huesos* and *Sermón de la barbarie*. Larrea's insistence on the bipartite nature of the work, along the lines he suggests, is certainly not without valid criteria, but his choice of titles is curiously no less grounded and arbitrary than the violation of which he accuses Georgette Vallejo in her choice of "Poemas humanos." We have it on Larrea's word alone that one of the titles was suggested by Vallejo himself, and even then at a date long before his death, and therefore before the final revision of the poems. The other title is simply Larrea's own invention based on a line from "Sermón sobre la muerte" (see *PC*, 531-40). The violent objections to the 'original' title of the poems undoubtedly has to do with its connotations of Marxist humanism. Clayton Eshleman resumes the logic and pertinence of Larrea's choice of titles in his introduction to *César Vallejo: The Complete Posthumous Poetry*, p. xxxvi: "As for the dated poems, no title can be found. Larrea makes a plausible, if not convincing, case for *Sermón de la barbarie*, arguing that it is the key phrase in the last dated poem . . . and suggests that 'la barbarie' was a metaphor for 'Babel,' the Word (*bab-ilu*), the 'Gate of God' that Vallejo engaged in the central book of his career."
    What is in a name? One might innocently ask, rather too innocently, since the answer here is — everything. Why, then, this obsessive need to establish the real title of the posthumous poetry, especially when it becomes increasingly clear that the 'proper name' of this body of poetry is irrevocably lost, or rather, has never existed? Larrea's focus on the word 'Babel,' with its quite obvious desire to conceive of Vallejo's poetry as a heroic struggle, in the name of the logos, to rescue the word from the threat of an engulfing babble, begs the question of the work's ultimate self-possession and unity. The purpose of naming the poems is twofold: it entitles one to them or takes possession of them, and it wards off the anxiety of a confusion of tongues by reducing all polysemy to a proper name or identity.

10. Jacques Derrida, "Le facteur de la vérité," reprinted in *The Post Card: From Socrates to Freud and Beyond*, trans. Alan Bass (Chicago: The Univ. of Chicago Press, 1987), p. 489: "The divisibility of the letter — this is why we have insisted on this key or theoretical safety lock of the Seminar — is what chances and sets off course, without guarantee of return, the remaining [*restance*] of anything whatsoever: a letter does *not always* arrive at its destination, and from the moment that this possibility belongs to its structure one can say that it never truly arrives, that when it does arrive its capacity not to arrive torments

it with an internal drifting." All subsequent references to *The Post Card*, henceforth designated by the abbreviation *C*, appear parenthetically in the text.

11. See Juan Larrea, "Un poema singular e ignorado de Vallejo," in *Al Amor de Vallejo*, pp. 151-58. "A nadie parece serle lícito desde ahora dudar del carácter de los valores metafísicos subjacentes en la personalidad vallejiana. Quien se expresa por sun pluma pretende ser el Hijo Eterno, revelando la autenticad del arquetipo que en el planteo de eas su personalidad había ya descubierto nuestra exégesis. Y hasta se las da de Verbo encarnado, corrobando por su boca y a posteriori — como si lo hiciese desde fuera del tiempo y de espacio — algunas de las proposiciones al parecer más imprudentes que se oyeron en el Simpósium y que se recogen en sus Actas" (156). This is a good example of the sort of heavy-handed reading of which Larrea is capable.

12. See Roland Barthes, *Roland Barthes* (Paris: Editions du Seuil, 1975), p. 75.

13. Jean Franco's analysis of this kind of juxtaposition of the spiritual code and the code of human species is enormously helpful in understanding the contradictory effects of Vallejo's poetry. See *César Vallejo: The Dialectics of Poetry and Silence* (New York: Cambridge Univ. Press, 1976) and *Poetry and Silence: César Vallejo's Sermon upon Death*, The Seventeenth Annual Canning House Lecture, London, 1973.

14. Sicard examines this play of departure and return in "Contradiction et renversement," pp. 71-72, 78-79. Characteristically enough, he uses the concept of "une dialectique," but it is precisely a dialectical understanding of beginning and end, departure and return, that Vallejo undercuts and throws into question.

15. The poem bears the same title as Vallejo's second collection of poems; curiously, it is included in no volume itself. Larrea has placed it just before the posthumous poems in *Poesía completa*.

16. All Biblical references are to *The New Oxford Annotated Bible with the Apocrypha: Revised Standard Version*, ed. Herbert G. May and Bruce M. Metzger (New York: Oxford Univ. Press, 1973).

17. Jacques Derrida, *Of Grammatology*, trans. Gayatri Chakravorty Spivak (Baltimore: The Johns Hopkins University Press, 1974), p. 71. All further references to this work, henceforth designated by the abbreviation *G*, appear parenthetically in the text.

18. Philippe Lacoue-Labarthe cites this phrase (in French) as an epigraph to his essay, "Le détour (Nietzsche et la rhétorique)," *Poétique*, 5 (1971), 53. The phrase is to be found in Friedrich Nietzsche, *Nachgelassene Fragmente (Sommer 1872 bis Ende 1874)*, Vol. IV of *Werke*, eds. Giorgio Colli and Mazzino Montinari (Berlin: Walter de Gruytere, 1978), p. 231.

19. Sicard, "Contradiction et renversement," p. 84.

20. Jacques Derrida, *Speech and Phenomena* and *Other Essays on Husserl's Theory of Signs*, trans. David B. Allison (Evanston: Northwestern Univ. Press, 1973), p. 102: "The history of being as presence, as self-presence in absolute knowledge,

as consciousness of self in the infinity of *parousia* — this history is closed. The history of presence is closed, for "history" has never meant anything but the presentation (*Gegenwärtigung*) of Being, the production and recollection of beings in presence, as knowledge and mastery. Since absolute self-presence in consciousness is the infinite *vocation* of full presence, the achievement of absolute knowledge is the end of the infinite, which could only be the unity of the concept, logos, and consciousness in a voice without *differance. The history of metaphysics therefore can be expressed as the unfolding of the structure or schema of an absolute will-to hear-oneself-speak.* This history is closed when this infinite absolute appears to itself as its own death. *A voice without differance, a voice without writing, is at once absolutely alive and absolutely dead.*" All further references to this work, henceforth designated by the abbreviation S*P*, appear parenthetically in the text.

21. Blaise Pascal, *Pensées*, in *Oeuvres complètes*, ed. Jacques Chevalier (Paris: Gallimard, 1954), p. 1166: "*Raison des effets.* — Renversement continuel du pour au contre.

Nous avons montré que l'homme est vain, par l'estime qu'il fait des choses qui ne sont point essentielles; et toutes ces opinions sont détruites. Nous avons montré ensuite que toutes ces opinions sont très bien fondées, le peuple n'est pas si vain qu'on dit; et ainsi nous avons détruit l'opinion qui détruisait celle du peuple.

Mais il faut détruire maintenant cette dernière proposition, et montrer qu'il demeure toujours vrai que le peuple est vain, quoique ses opinions soient saines: parce qu'ils n'en sent pas la vérité oú elle n'est pas, ses opinions sont toujours très fausses et très mal saines."

22. These are comments made by Americo Ferrari in the discussion following Sicard's "Contradiction et renversement," in *Séminaire César Vallejo*, pp. 86-87. For an analysis of Vallejo's work in terms of a radical *agnosis*, see the same author's *El Universo poético de César Vallejo* (Caracas: Monte Avila Editores, 1972).

23. William Shakespeare, *The Tragedy of Hamlet Prince of Denmark*, ed. Tucker Brooke and Jack Randall Crawford (1917; rpt. New Haven: Yale Univ. Press, 1947).

24. Maurice Blanchot, *L'Entretien infini* (Paris: Gallimard, 1969), pp. 21-22. For a discussion of the Marxist roots of Vallejo's intense concern with the question of the human, see Noël Salomon, "Algunos aspectos de lo 'humano' en *Poemas humanos*," *Approximaciones*, II, 191-230.

25. Larrea, preface to "Poemas postumos," *Poesía completa*, pp. 537-38.

26. Michel Foucault, *The Order of Things* (New York: Random House, 1970), p. 387, p. 338.

27. Pascal, pp. 1206-07.

28. Pascal, p. 1206.

29. *Séminaire César Vallejo*, p. 87.

30. Friedrich Nietzsche, *The Gay Science*, trans. Walter Kaufmann (New York: Vintage, 1974), p. 336.

31. As cited by Clayton Eshleman, translator's introduction to César Vallejo, *Poemas humanos/Human Poems* (New York: Grove Press, 1969), p. viii.

32. In Spanish there are two 'points': *punto* and *punta*. Their different meanings overlap, and may easily be confused, as in my copy of Eshleman's bilingual edition of *Human Poems*, where "La punta" is misprinted as "La punto del hombre" (156). This provides an interesting inversion of gender in no way out of place in the context of Vallejo's poetry, as we shall see later.

33. Eshleman and Barcia have translated "caracoles" as "snails," and the entire line as "tip on yielding in secret snails" (in Eshleman's *Human Poems*, as "point striking into secret snails"), which is as surprising a line as it is incomprehensible. Although the series of puns on "puntas" are obscure, to a point of incomprehensibility, "caracoles" may in fact make more sense, however allusively, if translated as a play on two of its other meanings: 1) a spiral or winding staircase; 2) a spiral-shaped cavity forming a division in the internal ear of man and other mammals. One might then read the line as suggesting both knifings that happen in secret staircases, since *punta* has this sense of knife-tip, and the puncturing of eardrums by a pointed instrument.

34. César Vallejo, *Contra el secreto profesional* (Lima: Mosca Azul Editores, 1973), p. 39. The English translation of these lines would run something like this: "Crucified in empty straitjackets, the differences advance on alternate pages unto the pantheon of grand harmonies."

35. Georg Wilhelm Friedrich Hegel, *Phenomenology of Spirit*, trans. A. V. Miller (Oxford: Oxford Univ. Press, 1977), p. 493.

36. Hegel, p. 439.

37. For a discussion of the very complex play on the relations between 'apocalyptic' truth, veils, woman, and the prick or point of the pen, see Jacques Derrida, *Eperons: Les styles de Nietzsche* (Paris: Flammarion, 1978).

38. Blanchot, *L'Entretien infini*, p. 390.

40. Blanchot, *L'Entretien infini*, p. 440.

41. Sören Kierkegaard, *Either/Or*, trans. David F. Swenson and Lillian Marvin Swenson (Garden City, N.Y.: Doubleday & Company, 1959), I, 36-38.

42. Nietzsche, *The Gay Science*, p. 335.

43. Nietzsche is, of course, much more positive about life's inherently deceptive power of dissemination than is Vallejo: ". . . For you only have to ask yourself carefully, "Why do you not want to deceive?" especially if it should seem — and it does seem! — as if life aimed at semblance, meaning error, deception, simulation, delusion, self-delusion, and when the great sweep of life has actually always show itself to be on the side of the most unscrupulous *polytropoi*." (*The

Gay Science, p. 282)

44. Vallejo, *Contra el secreto profesional,* p. 22

45. This state of Being which is at the same time a being dead allows us to read the following assertion made by Juan Larrea — an assertion whose pretensions are enormous — with a certain, antidotal irony: "Su [Vallejo's] proceso existencial, de substancia mística, es equivalente al la historia que es también . un proceso que proviene del ser y proyecta al Ser" ("Significado," 263).

46. Eshleman, introduction to *Human Poems,* p. xv.   Eshleman follows Larrea's lead in the invention of a Christ-Vallejo, as in another passage: "Vallejo speaks very naturally in the tone and compassion of Jesus in *Poemas humanos;* there is almost nothing literary about his Christianity — he lived it, dreadfully, died on Good Friday and a few months before his death called his last sheaf of poems *Spain, Let this Cup pass from Me.*   There is no satisfactory explanation of his death" (xiii-xiv).

47. Larrea, "Significado," p. 263.   John Deredita comments on this bizarre critical passion for the passion of a Christ-Vallejo: "A suffering persona may indeed be read throughout the Vallejo text, but the critics' move from that code and the facts or legends of the Vallejo life to interpretations founded on the archetype of martyrdom seems now an unenlightening manifestation of Hispanic Christian atavism" ("Vallejo Interpreted," 18).

48. Nietzsche, *The Gay Science,* p. 283.

49. Blanchot, *L'Entretien infini,* p. 22.

50. Larrea, "Significado," p. 257.

51. Georges Bataille, *L'Expérience intérieure* (Paris: Gallimard, 1954), p. 80.

52. Sicard, "Contradiction et renversement," pp. 76-77.

53. Blanchot, *L'Entretien infini,* p. 58.

54. Blanchot, *L'Entretien infini,* p. 63.

55. This neutralizing effect is noted by Sicard, who understands it essentially as a failure, on Vallejo's part, to achieve a *"dépassement des contradictions":*   "Ces conditions très particulières dans lesquelles s'opère le dèpassement peuvent sembler le 'neutraliser' d'une certaine façon: à travers son corps, le poète rejoint l'Universel, mais un universel qui ne se situe pas au-délà de l'individuel" ("Contradiction et renversement," 84).

56. Blanchot, *L'Entretien infini,* p. 440.

57. Jacques Derrida, "La Loi du genre"/"The Law of Genre," *Glyph 7* (Baltimore: The Johns Hopkins Univ. Press, 1980), p. 184.

58. Blanchot, *L'Entretien infini,* p. 450.

59. William Blake, *The Marriage of Heaven and Hell*, in *The Poetry and Prose of William Blake*, ed. David V. Erdman with commentary by Harold Bloom (Garden City, N.Y.: Doubleday & Company, 1965), p. 36.

60. Derrida, "La Loi du genre," p. 191.

61. Larrea, "Significado," pp. 250-57.

62. Compare Michèle Bernu, "L'écriture sur l'écriture dans la poésie de César Vallejo," in *Séminaire César Vallejo*, pp. 24-27. See also Philippe Lacoue-Labarthe and Jean-Luc Nancy, "Genre," in *Glyph*, pp. 1-14.

63. Bataille, *L'Expérience intérieure*, p. 127.

64. See Enric Miret, "Conflicto y contradicción en la obra de César Vallejo," in *Séminaire César Vallejo*, pp. 41-53, and Sicard, "Contradiction et renversement."

65. Larrea is the prototype of a certain critical approach to Vallejo, which would convert the polysemy of the work into a definitive unity of voice, and make the stuttering Vallejo, always at a loss for words, speak at last and say one thing. Larrea's critical astuteness and his own eloquence serve to make the poet speak even when he is silent and, even in such a stammering title as *Trilce*, to speak long, and to speak Hegel: "Trátase de un desarollo cuya triplicidad responde, según parece, al titulo de *Trilce*; desde luego al hecho de que al escribirlo contaba cuarenta y cinco años que en otro poema triparte: 'habiendo atravesado quince años, después quince, y, antes quince' — 'por la vida que tiene tres potencias' —; y al concepto de que 'no hay Dios ni hijo de Dios sin desarrollo,' que define a su ser mismo, a todas luces trinitario. Es evidente que ha rebasado el estado social de antítesis para proyectarse simbolicamente a la situación tercera o de síntesis, más allá de tiempo y de espacio; a una 'masa' o entidad más vasta, poética, espiritual, puesto que el Amor en que se disuelve el ego es la potencia característica del Espíritu" ("Significado," 250).

66. Vallejo, *Contra el secreto profesional*, pp. 99-101.

67. Hegel, *Phenomenology*, p. 492.

68. Blanchot, *L'Entretien infini*, p. 558.

69. Kierkegaard, *Either/Or*, I, pp. 38-39

II

STEVENS: THAT SAVING SUPPLEMENT

1. The Quest for Satisfaction/The Question of Enough

> Without the possibility of differance, the desire
> of presence as such would not find its
> breathing-space. This means by the same token
> that this desire carries in itself the destiny of
> its non-satisfaction. Differance produces what it
> forbids, makes possible the very thing that it
> makes impossible.
>
> Jacques Derrida (*G* 143)

The question of enough, of the possibility of "a satisfaction in the irremediable poverty of life" (*OP* 167), or of the successful effort on the part of "a dissatisfied man to find satisfaction through words, occasionally of the dissatisfied thinker to find satisfaction through his emotions" (*OP* 165), is one that is posed again and again throughout Wallace Stevens' poetry. If the question is more than rhetorical, it is, for Stevens, above all a question of rhetoric, having to do with the inexhaustible figures and fictions, "The poses of speech, of paint, / Of music" (*CP* 199) in which language so delights. The imperative "Add this. It is to add," which closes "Add This to Rhetoric," affirms an irreducible rhetorical factor in language, always in excess of any "proper" state of expression. The title of the poem "The Lack of Repose" depicts a condition inherent in Stevens' quest for satisfaction in words. If "in nature it merely grows," in language, "It is posed and it is posed" (*CP* 198), re-posed and re-puzzled, without any final repose in sight. However, the quest itself presupposes, in theory at least, the possibility of satisfaction, a moment in which there would be at last enough, and therefore the operation of a certain economy of desire, working according to what Derrida calls "the law of proper" or "the law of the house" (*oiko-nomia*).[1] Of course, that the possibility of an *absolute* satisfaction can never be seriously entertained anyway would seem self-

107

evident.   But this very self-evidence makes it all the more remarkable that in Stevens' poetry precisely such a possibility is, however speculatively, constantly entertained.   "To find the real, / To be stripped of every fiction except one, / The fiction of an absolute" (*CP* 404) is the ultimate desire underlying his work. Indeed, it is because such a desire for an absolute, for a speech of unconditional propriety ("the luminous melody of proper sound"), is so insistent, that its intermittence with the affirmation of language's most obvious improprieties, which belong to its figurative nature, proves to be so provocative.   In the act of both posing and withdrawing the possibility of an absolute satisfaction in words, Stevens complicates any simple understanding of poetry as a quest for presence and truth.   In its place a certain logic of the supplement, an effect of language's endless *différance*, is brought into play.[2]

      This alternation of the desire for the "proper" with the affirmation of language's unavoidable impropriety is the subject of the much discussed "The Poems of our Climate."

> Pink and white carnations — one desires
> So much more than that. The day itself
> Is simplified: a bowl of white,
> Cold, a cold porcelain, low and round,
> With nothing more than the carnations there.
>
>   (*CP* 193)

Differing desires are encountered here: the one seeks to be at the end of desire, in a state of completion and simplicity; the other seeks to renew desire and to throw off this propriety "like a thing of another time," knowing "that what it has is what is not" (*CP* 382).   "The Poems" thus anticipates the difference in "Notes" between the demand for a purified "first idea" and the desire to escape from an "ennui of the first idea" (*CP* 381).   The alternate comparatives "So much more than" and "nothing more than" point to both a lack and an excess of desire countering the possibility in principle — but only in principle —

of a proper economy of desire and a moment in which there would be at last enough. The scene composed by "Clear water in a brilliant bowl, / Pink and white carnations" proves to be primarily negative, induced as it is by a reduction of all excess, by the process of exclusion and repression that has brought us to such a simplified scene. And thus it turns out to be a "nothing more than," a lack in which the desire for "So much more than" is inevitably revived. This is not so much a conflict of opposing desires as an alternation. The desire for "So much more than" the "nothing more than" the carnations in their bowl points to a vitality abiding in complexity, change, and difference, which now reverses the drive toward simplicity, unity, and identity, the latter serving only to whitewash or cover up "the evilly compounded, vital I." But the excess, eliminated but now returning as the need for *more*, is of course the original cause for the negative drive toward propriety. This propriety, paradoxically, is now itself to be purged, in the recognition that "Still one would want more, one would need more, / More than a world of white and snowy scents." The once desired purity, in which the "proper" colour *par excellence*, white, so dominates, is now perceived as a betrayal of the life of the self and of language. One would now spatter and soil this purity and whiteness with words restored again to their vital defectiveness:

> There would still remain the never-resting mind,
> So that one would want to escape, come back
> To what had been so long composed.
> The imperfect is our paradise.
> Note that, in this bitterness, delight,
> Since the imperfect is so hot in us,
> Lies in flawed words and stubborn sounds.
> (*CP* 194)

Language's ultimate resistance to a strict propriety is not seen as a negative tendency. It is clearly affirmed as springing from the source of its life: the figurative energy of words. But this is by no means simply to reject the desire for such a propriety. The two drives are interdependent. An energy arises from the tension between the desire for an inalterable state that would satisfy once and for all and the opposing affirmation of an excess inherent in language. One wants not only to escape from such a perfect scene but "to escape, come back / To what had been so long composed," most obviously to the "evilly compounded, vital I," but at the same time — as these lines might also be read — to the composition of the very scene just rejected, which is indeed "composed" in a painterly sense. To escape, come back: to escape from the scene is to return to the complexity and imperfection of a vital self but also only to awaken again into the dream of composing "this complete simplicity", in the endlessly renewed project of "the never-resting mind." This tension is syntactically expressed by the apposition of "escape, come back" and, four lines down at the end of the line as well, by the parallel placing of "bitterness, delight": that which makes life bitter, the flawed nature of our language and consciousness, is also the provider of delight, the delight in fiction and the figurative, in the imagination's feigning which "lies" — in both senses of the word — "in flawed words and stubborn sounds."[3]

"The Creations of Sound," in developing a fundamental distinction between two conceptions of proper speech, reaches a related understanding. First, there is X, "an obstruction, a man / Too exactly himself" (*CP* 310), whose desire for propriety adheres to a classical esthetics. T. S. Eliot, as Harold Bloom suggests, may well be the target here (see *The Poems* 151-52). But it is just as plausibly Stevens himself, that Stevens who wants to make language say what it means purely and simply, without evasive rhetoric, so that there is no longer any gap between meaning and expression in a speech aptly described as "dirty silence clarified." This poetry of things as they are, this desire to expunge the improprieties of words, is certainly one aspect of Stevens' poetic economy. Opposed to it is a speech inclusive of a metaphoric straying from proper meaning. In this case what is proper derives from a rhetorical understanding of words, which affirms the power of eloquence beyond the demand for a strict significance.[4] Such an alternative form of speech would come to one "of its own," unconsciously perhaps, or at least "without understanding," from a power beyond oneself, "in sounds not chosen, / Or chosen quickly, in a freedom / That was their element." The subject doing the speaking is no longer the lyrical subject, nor the impersonal, authoritative subject associated with the classicism of Eliot. Indeed, the words of this speech would be

> Better without an author, without a poet,
>
> Or having a separate author, a different poet,
> An accretion from ourselves, intelligent
> Beyond intelligence, an artificial man
>
> At a distance, a secondary expositor,
> A being of sound, whom one does not approach
> Through any exaggeration.   (*CP* 310-11)

This inhuman author is not a source but an effect of language, and as such the propriety of "A being of sound, whom one does not approach / Through any exaggeration" involves at the same time an estrangement, since he is "At a distance," "secondary," "artificial." What is proper here is language's very impropriety: "silence made still dirtier," not "dirty silence clarified." One *approaches* — in the metaphysics of presence, the *proper* is that which is absolutely near (to itself) — this "accretion from ourselves" only through the propriety (in the sense of decorum) of a certain eloquence, a certain verbal elegance, through a supplement or excess of speech, not through a reduction of the same. We approach, in other words, that which is most proper, the rightness of this being of sound, only by means which we normally think of as *de-*

propriating, as removing and distancing us from a literal meaning or proper state of things as they are. Being the effect of "more than an imitation for the ear," this "separate author" is never exactly himself. In being most himself, he is always in excess of himself, secondary, artificial, incremental. To say that "From him, we collect" is to say that the collected works of such an author are never final, never authoritative. Caught up in an interminable supplementation, the text of his speech is nothing but the series of additions to itself, at the core, at the end of which no proper text is to be found. Nevertheless, its secondary nature, artificial and accretive, has a definitive priority, for it is X's poetry that suffers from a critical lack — a lack of supplement. "He lacks this venerable complication. / His poems are not of the second part of life." X is reduced to himself, nothing but himself. It is the "second part of life" that has priority, must come first; in the end, it is what is most proper to life.

We are beginning to outline here the operation of a peculiar economy, a logic of the supplement that betrays the regulative oppositions belonging to a restricted economy of desire and law of the proper.[5] The possibility of satisfying the need this logic seems to presuppose, and indeed provokes or gives rise to — for if there is a supplement, there would seem to be a deficiency to supply — is precluded, made impossible by the illimitable supplementation it brings into play. What Derrida calls, in the context of a similar logic he locates in Rousseau's writings, "the structural necessity of the abyss" is equally pertinent here. This abyss or *mise en abyme* reflects the "indefinite process" by which the supplement is always already the supplement of a supplement, for

> the indefinite process of supplementarity has always already *infiltrated* presence, always already inscribed there the space of repetition and the splitting of the self. Representation *in the abyss* of presence is not an accident of presence; the desire of presence is, on the

contrary, born from the abyss (the indefinite multiplication) of representation, from the representation of representation, etc. The supplement itself is quite exorbitant, in every sense of the word. (*G* 163)

"Of Modern Poetry," indeed, projects the possibility of satisfaction upon a form of speech whose proper nature is undecidable, whose ground is uncertain, or is the abyss itself. It is impossible to separate the conditions of satisfaction outlined in the poem from a context in which the quest for "What will suffice" would be limitless. The ground of modern poetry's speech could be said, then, to possess a false bottom, one which opens onto the bottomless, the abyss, but which at the same time entails a unique satisfaction, what Derrida calls in "Parergon" "the comic effect" of the "satire of the abyss," which "is never missing if the abyss never is enough, if it has to remain — undecided — between the groundless and the grounding of the ground."[6]

> It has to be on the stage
> And, like an insatiable actor, slowly and
> With meditation, speak words that in the ear,
> In the delicatest ear of the mind, repeat,
> Exactly, that which it wants to hear, at the sound
> Of which, an invisible audience listens,
> Not to the play, but to itself, expressed
> In an emotion as of two people, as of two
> Emotions becoming one.   (*CP* 240)

The finding of what will suffice may seem to be a project of the minimal, but at the same time the propriety sought by modern poetry in the speech which it would speak, "wholly containing the mind," is both exact and total in its ambition, predicated as it is on the reaching of a double limit "below which it cannot descend, / Beyond which it has no will to rise." Its "sudden rightness" arises from a sound twanged on an instrument by "A metaphysician in the dark," bringing to mind the "Abysmal instruments" (*CP* 384) in canto IV of "It Must be Abstract" in "Notes," as well as the "abysmal melody" (*CP* 433) in canto II of

"The Owl in the Sarcophagus." As proper and abysmal at once, the bottom ground of this proper sound remains undecided. The speech of poetry totters precariously, hilariously on the verge of the comic, the satirical, the satire of the abyss if, in Derrida's words, "the abyss never is enough" — and, of course, the abyss never is — not even, especially, when it is filled with itself.

> The actor is
> A metaphysician in the dark, twanging
> An instrument, twanging a wiry string that gives
> Sounds passing through sudden rightness, wholly
> Containing the mind, below which it cannot descend,
> Beyond which it has no will to rise. (*CP* 240)

What is remarkable, then, about the speech in "Of Modern Poetry," about this "poem of the mind in the act of finding / What will suffice," is its precarious and — to make an unavoidable pun — *fundamentally abysmal* structure. Founding itself on the new ground that it clears for itself, divested of the old theatre, scene and script, and forced "To construct a new stage," it is still without any foundation. The limits set to "What will suffice" remain uncertain. No wonder that modern poetry is figured as "insatiable" and "in the dark." In speaking only to itself, and listening only to itself speak what it would hear, it circles and rejoins itself, but according to a circuit in which, being self-grounded, it runs aground on its own tautological groundlessness. It both completes itself and remains limitless in its quest for satisfaction. "In the act of finding/ What will suffice," modern poetry fulfils itself, but without ever satisfying itself. The circular and abysmal nature of this proper sound or speech resembles what Heidegger, in his lectures on Nietzsche, describes as philosophy's ultimate ambition, which involves above all the question of its self-grounding. Indeed, in the following passage one could, without forcing the analogy, replace the word "philosophy" with Stevens' "modern poetry" or with his proper sound or speech:

> It concerns the fact that, whatever philosophy is, and however it may exist at any given time, it defines itself solely on its own terms; but also that such self determination is possible only inasmuch as philosophy always has already grounded itself. Its proper essence turns ever toward itself, and the more original a philosophy is, the more purely it soars in turning about itself, and therefore the farther the circumference of its circle presses outward to the brink of nothingness.[7]

The idea of a self-grounding for poetry touches on the inexhaustible belief in fiction, so much a part of Stevens' poetry. It finds its extreme formulation in one of his *Adagia*: "The final belief is to believe in a fiction, which you know to be a fiction, there being nothing else. The exquisite truth is to know that it is a fiction and that you believe in it willingly" (*OP* 163). This aphorism, doubtless an extension of "willing suspension of disbelief," is, however, more than just that. It constitutes, in fact, the opening up of a new perspective on the nature of fiction. The need for poetic fiction is not for something simply lacking. It should not be understood strictly in economic terms, according to what Derrida calls the law of the proper or of the house. The best expression of this need is "The Well Dressed Man with a Beard," that great poem of affirmation, so Nietzschean in its import, in which "what will suffice" is a fictional extra, in excess of the truth, a remainder left over after an exhaustion and diminishment of the store of fiction. It is both a *no more than* and *more than nothing*, and therefore enough.

Truth, in "The Well Dressed Man," plays a negative role, that of the demystifier and nay-sayer, cleaning away all fictions, counter to which the one thing saved would be a saving fiction, which would happily save us from the truth. The world literally hangs in the balance here, for "After the final no there comes a yes / And on that yes the future world depends" (*CP* 247), and what it depends on is the fictive, the affirmation of fiction over and above the truth. If "No was the night," the labour of the negative in pursuit of truth, "Yes is the present sun," a new project of the sun, whose power lies all in its seeming, in its power to *lie*, or at least to affirm a feigning over the truth. Truth and fiction do not so much oppose each other here as alternate, like night and day, in a close alliance. In fact, the "Yes" of "this present sun" depends on the "final no," which clears the world of its clutter and refuse, its used-up language and exhausted descriptions, its heap of dead letters and dead metaphors — all the "yeses" that have already seen their day, all the fictions that have been taken for the truth. When this ground is cleared, in the very midst of poverty, an almost impossible affirmation is made possible, one that must will itself into being on the groundless ground of truth-less fiction, not on the basis of truth. It is not the affirmation of something's truth, but a truth-less affirmation.[8] This may be why the affirmation itself remains purely speculative ("If the rejected things . . ."), and why the object of belief must be diminished and inconsequential ("one, one only," "No greater than a cricket's horn, no more / Than a thought to be rehearsed all day"). The object of belief must not be a basis for belief. A firm "yes" may be said to "one thing that was firm," but that thing is almost no-thing, and its firmness depends entirely on its af-*firm*ation and not on itself.

> If the rejected things, the things denied,
> Slid over the western cataract, yet one,
> One only, one thing that was firm, even
> No greater than a cricket's horn, no more
>
> Than a thought to be rehearsed all day, a speech
> Of the self that must sustain itself on speech,
> One thing remaining, infallible, would be
> Enough.   (*CP* 247)

If nothing will come of nothing, a great deal can nevertheless be made of almost nothing, of something "No greater than a cricket's horn." If it must be as "a thing believed," belief should not be understood as belief in the truth of the thing believed. This is a case, rather, of that final belief of which Stevens speaks in his *Adagia*. It is not the truth of something we believe in, but the fiction of it. We suspend the relation to truth, making it indeterminate and indefinite. This placing of the truth in the abyss of fiction is not a provisory or temporary move; it is not attendant upon the return of truth, as in our ordinary understanding of willing suspension of disbelief. On the contrary, this move reflects a belief in the fictional value, and not the truth-value, of its object. As Stevens himself poses the paradox in a letter to Henry Church (8 Dec. 1942):

> I said that I thought we had reached a point at which we could no longer really believe in anything else unless we recognized that it was a fiction. The student said that this was an impossibility, that there was no such thing as believing in something that one knew was not true. It is obvious, however, that we are doing that all the time. There are things with respect to which we willingly suspend disbelief; if there is instinctive in us a will to believe, or if there is a will to believe, whether or not it is instinctive, it seems to me we can suspend disbelief with reference to a fiction as easily as we can suspend it with reference to anything else.[9]

If truth is attained, as it is for Hegel, by the negation of negation, then a belief in fiction could be said to involve the affirmation of affirmation. In "The Well Dressed Man," fulfilment comes from "out of a petty phrase, / Out of a thing believed, a thing affirmed," where the firmness of the thing in question is entirely owing to its affirmation. Belief here may be contrasted with the less groundless belief in an enduringly firm truth portrayed in canto VI of

"Credences of Summer." There, as we shall see when we look at that poem, if we encounter a truth that is allegedly unshakable as a rock ("The rock cannot be broken. It is the truth," [*CP* 375]), we are by the same token threatened with a more petrifying sustenance in such "things certain sustaining us in certainty." A stone-like stasis is the risk of excessive certainty, whereas "a speech / Of the self that must sustain itself on speech" implies perhaps the opposite danger: the instability of "a world of words," "In which nothing solid is its solid self" (*CP* 345). Confronted with the final "no," what Stevens' well dressed man affirms, and which only confirms the abyss he faces and the insatiability of his need for "yes," is affirmation itself: a saying "yes" to "yes," the present sun. This resembles what Derrida calls, in characterizing the Nietzschean *Ja*, "the joyous affirmation of the play of the world and of the innocence of becoming, the affirmation of a world of signs without fault, without truth, and without origin which is offered to an active interpretation. *This affirmation then determines the noncenter otherwise than as a loss of the center*" (*WD* 292). It is a case of what Derrida similarly poses in a reading of Blanchot's *L'arrêt de mort* as the gaiety of "an act or instance of living on, the levity of its affirmation, of the *yes, yes, yes* to *yes* . . . *saying and describing nothing, performing only this affirmation of the yes* saying yes to yes."[10] This "performative" comprises a staging like that of the "insatiable actor" in "Of Modern Poetry," involving an active mastery in the form of a Nietzschean will to power as art.

In *The Collected Poems*, "The Well Dressed Man" and "Mrs Alfred Uruguay" are separated, significantly, by "Of Bright & Blue Birds & The Gala Sun," a poem in which the poet seconds Nietzsche's *The Gay Science* in speaking of

> a bright *scienza* outside of ourselves,
>
> A gaiety that is being, not merely knowing,
> The will to be and to be total in belief,
> Provoking a laughter, an agreement, by surprise
> (*CP* 248)

The gaiety of a world affirmed as "there, being imperfect" recalls the paradise of the imperfect in "The Poems of Our Climate," with its affirmation of language's irreducible errancy and of the delight "in flawed words and stubborn sounds" (*CP* 194), an attitude best summed up by the motto in canto XI of "Esthétique du Mal": "Natives of poverty, children of malheur, / The gaiety of language is our seigneur" (*CP* 322). A "gay science" is, indeed, a reversal of an "esthetics of evil," which is converted into an art of innocent becoming, "no longer satanic mimicry" (*CP* 316) but the negation and surpassing of a negative poetics hitherto giving birth to nothing but "fleurs de mal," nothing but "firm stanzas" hanging "like hives in hell / Or what hell was" (*CP* 315). What now takes the place of absolute knowledge is this new knowledge and affirmation of the joyous relativity of all things, of all belief and being.[11]

To a large extent this affirmation can be understood as primarily rhetorical, as celebrating that ideal of life which Richard Lanham describes in *The Motives of Eloquence*:

> The rhetorical view of life, then, begins with the centrality of language. It conceives reality as fundamentally dramatic, man as fundamentally a role player. It synthesizes an essentially bifurcated, self-serving theory of motive. We play for advantage, but we play for pleasure too . . . Purposeful striving is invigorated by frequent dips back into the pleasurable resources of pure play . . . The rhetorical view thus stands fundamentally opposed to the West's bad conscience about language, revels in what Roland Barthes . . . has called "the Eros of Language." *Homo rhetoricus* cannot, to sum up, be *serious*. He is not pledged to a single set of values and the

cosmic orchestration they adumbrate. He is
not, like the serious man, alienated from his
own language. And if he relinquishes the
luxury of a central self, a soul, he gains the
tolerance, and usually the sense of humour, that
comes from knowing he — and others — not only
may *think* differently, but *may be* differently.[12]

In line with such an ideal, that which a well dressed man with a
beard might well affirm is, of course, his own distinctive elegance, his sense of
style, taste and choice. Since it implies a fundamental lack of seriousness, as
Lanham points out, and above all of self-seriousness, this outlook tends to
undercut itself in the end. A rhetorical idealist may be capable of affirming a
diversity of things, above all affirmation itself, but by the same token he will be
incapable of solid commitment, occupying instead an incessantly shifting ground,
one which remains, in Derrida's terms, "undecided — between the groundless and
the grounding of the ground" (*VEP* 40). Not surprisingly, the gaiety appropriate
to "The Well Dressed Man with a Beard" verges on satire, on "the satire of the
abyss," the smug self-satisfaction that we might associate with the figure of the
poem's title being, in the final account, self-satirical. "The comic effect,"
Derrida writes, "It is never missing if the abyss never is enough, if it has to
remain — undecided. . . ." What the poem affirms, out of a radical impoverishment, is not the possibility of a satisfaction in which "One thing remaining,
infallible, would be / Enough." It is, rather, the instability of any state of
satisfaction, any fulfilment, the insatiable appetite for more:

> Ah! douce campagna of that thing!
> Ah! douce campagna, honey in the heart,
> Green in the body, out of a petty phrase,
> Out of a thing believed, a thing affirmed:
> The form on the pillow humming while one sleeps,
> The aureole above the humming house . . .
>
> It can never be satisfied, the mind, never.
> (*CP* 247)

2. The Festival of Truth: Scapegoat and Supplement in
"Credences of Summer"

Attaining presence, dying, two equally enchanted expressions.
Maurice Blanchot[13]

Metaphor: The Scapegoat

If any poem of Stevens represents total satisfaction, it is, as Frank
Kermode has noted, "Credences of Summer": "The subject is total satisfaction,
the moment of total summer."[14] This may seem an overly strenuous judgement,
but in this it is only conforming with the poem's explicit thesis. "Credences"
might well be described as a midsummer day-dream come true. At least, the
manifest ambition of the poem is the fulfilment of such a dream, which suggests
a claim to truth made on a firm ground of belief. The "credences" of the title,
however, do not forcibly point to an unquestionable given, for the truth at stake
is not necessarily a self-evident or apodictic one. In any question of credences,
there is always the possibility of deception and error. The poem's complexity
stems, in part, from a fundamental ambivalence, which is born from the inherent
difficulty in representing an uncomplicated immediate presence. There is a
conflict here between two revelations: a description in its proper place and, to
borrow the title from one of Stevens' most apocalyptic works, a "description
without place." This involves the difference between "the indifference of the
eye / Indifferent to what it sees" (*CP* 475), spoken of in canto XV of "An

Ordinary Evening in New Haven," and "a sight indifferent to the eye," "The difference that we make in what we see" (*CP* 343-44) of "Description without Place." This difference of difference itself entails as well the *différance* at play in the supplement, as an irrepressible process of figuration eventually preempts and eclipses the drive towards final identity, which is the poem's express subject.

Other critics, who have perceived an unresolved ambivalence at work in the poem's thesis of a final satisfaction, have recognized the deficiency of Kermode's assessment.[15] For example, Helen Vendler writes:

> *Credences of Summer*, as its title betrays, is the creed of the believer rather than the certain projection of the prophet or the divided commentary of the skeptic, but its intention cannot command all the strings. Its initial impetus of praise and involvement, resolutely kept in the original moment, is maintained through the first three cantos, but from then on the oneness with the here and now diminishes, until by the end of the poem Stevens is at an inhuman distance from his starting point.[16]

Considering the divided critical response to which "Credences" gives rise, the tendency to see it as either a failure or a success of presence, Bloom quite rightly observes that "there is something equivocal about the poem that stimulates sharp disagreement among the critics" (*The Poems* 243). He locates the source of this equivocation in the supreme moment of natural apotheosis celebrated by the poem, that height of summer in which "the celebration is thwarted by the eloquence of mere nature, which resists being reimagined" (243-44). In this view, nature has priority, poetry finding itself condemned to come after, to be inescapably secondary, since it can only hope to *re-present* a self-sufficient plenitude. What Bloom calls "belatedness," a romantic topic to which his revisionary ratios have given new life in psychoanalytic disguise, would be explained, for Derrida, by the supplementary logic of *différance*. Both Bloom and Derrida relate this concept to Freud's *Nachträglichkeit*, the psychoanalytic term for the cunningly evasive deferral and substitution that mark the figurative process of the unconscious in face of repression. With these concerns in mind, we might ask if in "Credences" something potentially divided in the very economy of desire underlies the apocalyptic quest for a proper state untouched by derivative, contingent, merely secondary determinations. How is one to express in language a state of presence beyond language, when the means of expression must naturally interfere with and, to use a Stevensian word, evade the final identity of any assured signification?

But there is a fatality at work here as well. As a poem troubled by its own ambitious thesis, and one which falls so short of its projected satisfaction in an immediate reality, "Credences" anticipates in its failure the ghostlier demarcations and keener sounds of the wintry vision in "The Auroras of Autumn." As Vendler suggests, if "Credences" is Stevens' "Allegro," it is written in the shadow of his "Penseroso," "a day piece matched with a night piece (a night piece nonetheless auroral), his innocent Eden confronted by his true Paradise, where he finds the serpent" (231). But perhaps to call the poem a failure misses the point. That it does not live up to its own claims may be more instructive than its possible success. Once we have gone beyond the benign surface of praise and celebration, we begin to suspect that the drive to attain presence is always already possessed by death. The figurative must then be seen in a new light, for not only does it interrupt and prevent presence − it intervenes and preserves it (and us from it). The "motive for metaphor" here becomes the vital energy of its mobility or movement.[17] The poem's ostensible impulse is in need of a supplementary direction which, reversing the apocalyptic drive, would keep us from ever halting in a definitive identity. If presence and truth are to survive — which means that they can never take place *as such* — they must learn to live in the differing desire for an object that is never to be absolutely approximate, but to remain both near and far, home and away.

* * *

> Now in midsummer come and all fools slaughtered
> And spring's infuriations over and a long way
> To the first autumnal inhalations, young broods
> Are in the grass, the roses are heavy with a weight
> Of fragrance and the mind lays by its trouble.
>
> Now the mind lays by its trouble and considers.
> The fidgets of remembrance come to this.
> This is the last day of a certain year
> Beyond which there is nothing left of time.
> It comes to this and the imagination's life.
>
> There is nothing more inscribed nor thought nor felt
> And this must comfort the heart's core against
> Its false disasters — these fathers standing round,
> These mothers touching, speaking, being near,
> These lovers waiting in the soft dry grass.
>
> (*CP* 372)

The violence of the poem's apocalyptic drive is explicit from the opening line: "Now in midsummer come and all fools slaughtered." Indeed, the celebration of the entire initial canto is a profoundly uncertain one. For one thing, the very situating of the estival moment ("And spring's infuriations over and a long way / To the first autumnal inhalations") makes this crowning middle of life also a reminder of an inevitable end to life. Its subliminal message is that, however far off the auroras are, they are already on their way. Canto IX later exposes the necessity of this auroral declension, which nevertheless dawns on us from the first canto, where the presence of summer is — fatally for it — located exactly between the infuriations of burgeoning life and the sobering inhalations of approaching death. But this negativity is all the more dramatically voiced in the brutal connotations of the opening line, which point to a violent exclusion. The mode of expression employed throughout the poem is pervasively negative, as Vendler has rightly pointed out:

> All of Stevens' praise of summer is put in negative terms . . . . It is with all our memories of negative phrasing used pejoratively that we hear Stevens say "There is nothing more inscribed nor felt," and we feel the truth of deprivation in his paradoxes to come, when he will speak of "The barrenness of the fertile thing that can attain no more," and of "a feeling capable of nothing more." (236-37)

These negatives suggest a presence conceived only in terms of term itself ("This is the last day of a certain year / Beyond which there is nothing left of time"), both as the finality of a becoming and as an end to all extraneous incidentals, to all that is merely aleatory and extrinsic. Heard in this insistence that "There is nothing more inscribed nor thought nor felt" is the cautioning "nothing more than the carnations there" of "The Poems of Our Climate," that *nothing more* that "one desires so much more than" (*CP* 193). The prospect of there being "nothing left of time" should give us as many misgivings as reassurances concerning the fulfilment at hand. It would be reasonable to ask, with some uncertainty: what is this presence on its own, what is this truth, beyond the negations and exclusions that seem to determine its advent?

The estival is, in "Credences," with the addition of an initial letter, a festival, a time for feasting and celebration. But it also involves, as the opening line clearly states, a metaphoric slaughtering. Not only is the slaughtering metaphoric, but the sacrificial victim or scapegoat here is, as the rest of the poem makes explicit, metaphor itself, figurative language. That this slaughtering of fools should prove antithetical and ambivalent is not surprising; such may be the nature of all festivals. It is certainly the case for the word itself in

Stevens, which in this poem appears in canto IV: "The utmost must be good and is / And is our fortune and honey hived in the trees / And mingling of colors at a festival" (*CP* 374). Bloom has analyzed the powerful antithesis at work in Stevens' use of this "primal word":

> "Festival" is itself an antithetical primal word in Stevens' poetry, a word that evokes a defensive turning-against-the-self or a curious kind of masochistic awareness in so massively confident a psyche. Though we use "festival" to mean "feast" or "celebration," deriving our usage from a Latin word for joyousness, its Indo-European root *dhes* has a general religious significance that allies "festival" to such antithetical words as "final," "fanatic," "theism," and "enthusiasm." Something of an uncanny, rather negative quasi-religious flavouring is felt each time Stevens uses "festival" in a poem. (*The Poem* 246)

To extend Bloom's very apt remarks, we might propose the thesis that in "Credences" two alternate understandings of festival are at stake. To a large extent, the two correspond to Bakhtin's distinction between the "official feast" and the "carnivalistic." The former asserts all that is "stable, unchanging, perennial," and reflects "the triumph of a truth already established, the predominant truth . . . put forward as eternal and indisputable," "monolithically serious" and to which "the element of laughter [is] alien." Opposed to this official truth is the feast of fools that celebrates "temporary liberation from the prevailing truth and from the established order," "the true feast of time, the feast of becoming, change and renewal," which is "hostile to all that [is] immortalized and completed," "to all pretense at immutability," "demanding ever changing, playful, undefined forms," and which is "filled with this pathos of change and renewal, with the sense of the gay relativity of prevailing truths and authorities."[18]   The tension between these two outlooks is what we find in "Credences." It provides at least an analogy for the logic behind the poem's development, as the initial official truth of the first few stanzas is eventually *uncrowned*, to use Bakhtin's term, and replaced, in the closing cantos, by a knowledge and celebration of the gay relativity of all things.

What the truth slaughters, naturally enough, is foolishness, folly, the error of fools. This gives us, then, a festival of fools in which the fools are all slaughtered. But if metaphor, which is the foolishness of language, the errancy or vagrancy of words, serves as the scapegoat in the poem, in this case the victim returns in the end to the fold as an indispensable saving supplement. For what begins with the sacrificial slaughter of metaphor turns out, as the poem progresses, to verge on the tragedy of truth. Carried away by a zeal that threatens its own survival, the truth may go too far, so that what is initially excluded and purged in its boundless impulse must now be recovered in order to preserve it — from itself. "The truth kills," Nietzsche remarks, "— it even kills itself (insofar as it recognizes that its foundation is error)."[19] The truth, that is, being truthful, recognizes the truth about itself: that it is only a particular fiction that has been powerful enough to triumph over competing fictions, denouncing them as error. Thus the original "official" festival in "Credences" has to turn to that which it would have done away with: metaphor, the folly of words, that gay knowledge which is the domain of comedy and which counter-balances the poem's hubristic drive. A midsummer night's dream is summoned — cited in fact by the last canto's allusion to Shakespeare's play — to ward off the incandescent purifications of a midsummer day-dream come true. At work in this antithesis and the catastrophic movement it gives rise to is what we might call, after the *pharmakon* of Derrida's "Plato's Pharmacy," a *pharmaceutical* relationship between metaphor and truth. Metaphor, alternately poisonous and medicinal in its effect, plays at first the role of *pharmakos* or scapegoat, yet serves at last to save the truth, to protect it from itself, from the potential disaster of an unmediated (self-)possession.[20]

* * *

From its opening line on, then, "Credences" is a poem troubled by its own thesis, disturbed and unsettled by the very creed it professes. The "young broods / . . . in the grass" of the first stanza in canto I, for all their presumed youthful nonchalance and carelessness, nevertheless "brood" over the scene by virtue of the word itself. Indeed, the introductory stanza is burdened by the mere presence of a series of words which, regardless of the particular use to which they are put in the context, are suggestive of a certain oppressiveness: "broods," "heavy," "weight," "trouble." In this the opening canto radically contrasts with the closing one and its lighter, more "mottled mood." The mind's laying by its trouble still does not allow us to forget the weight of the roses, whether it is a fragrance they are burdened down with or not. This laying by may mean only the trade off of one kind of trouble for an even more imposing sort, the excessive determination of "things as they are." As when Saint John says to the Back-Ache that "We shall be heavy with the knowledge of that day" (*CP* 437), we may begin to suspect the potential burden of presence. The idea of laying by one's troubles, as though only to pick them up again shortly, further suggests that we are perhaps afforded simply a brief respite, and not necessarily from the insufferable fools slaughtered in the first line. It may just as likely be from that other burden just mentioned: the unknown knowledge attendant upon a final accord with reality. There is a sense of suspense, even anxiety, hanging on the repetition in "the mind lays by its trouble. / Now the mind lays by its trouble and considers," while the very attitude of consideration seems to indicate that what impends is by no means certain.

The closing lines of the second stanza, where we learn that what "The fidgets of remembrance come to" is in fact the end of something, only adds to this uncertainty, the question as to whether the moment is foreboding or promising, menacing or desired:

> This is the last day of a certain year
> Beyond which there is nothing left of time.
> It comes to this and the imagination's life.
> (CP 372)

The very expression "comes to this" is one we are apt to associate with misfortune, with a certain dread, at least with an event more happily avoided than undergone. It is natural enough that this poem of presence should feature an eschatological concern with last things, beyond which there is nothing left to consider. What is staked, however, is "this and the imagination's life," a phrase whose meaning is disturbingly open to interpretation. It could point to the fulfilment of the imagination's life in a final accord with a present reality, or to its end, its negation or death in face of an immediate presence that has made the imagination's mediacy superfluous. There is, however, a more inclusive possibility, and one more consistent with Stevens' characteristic championing of interdependencies. To say "It comes to this and the imagination's life" may mean that what the poem takes for the real is not simply "the very thing and nothing else," as in canto II, but a supplementary interrelationship between reality and the imagination. If "Credences" marks, as Stevens has confirmed in letters, a turning away from "the imaginative period of 'Notes'" to the reality represented by this apex of summer ("When that poem was written my feeling for the necessity of a final accord with reality was strongest"),[21] this is not to identify reality with a simple exclusion of the imagination. "Credences" begins at one end of an extreme antithesis and, as it moves from a negative, exclusive impulse focused on the thing itself to conclude in canto X by celebrating the imagination, it depicts a complex and necessary interdependency. "The very thing and nothing else" is shown — even if the demonstration is only subliminal — to threaten not only the life of the imagination, but the real itself with asphyxiation, when the latter is left to inhale nothing but the stale air of its own stark propriety: "Here, the sun, / Sleepless, inhales his proper air, and rests" (*CP* 373). Reality, in order to survive its own deprivation, must look beyond the things itself to something else, to everything else in fact. In need of a breathing-space of *différance,* it must transcend itself in the imagination, without which its own restrictive identity would suffocate it.

This necessity is evident in the very first canto where presence can be interpreted as both a desired and vital plentitude and a potentially fatal disaster against which we must defend ourselves. It is as though, against a menacing finality, we were offered at first little more than the limited comfort of a philosophic resignation. As Bloom notes, concerning the final stanza of the canto, the proclaimed satisfaction is peculiarly negative and vicarious: "Whether the heart's disasters were ended is put in question by the 'must' of 'must comfort,' yet Stevens seems ready enough to accept a second-best in the fulfilment of others" (*The Poems* 245). The "total satisfaction" of which Kermode speaks is off to a rather lame start. Bloom may even be assuming too much in calling it "a second-best in the fulfilment of others." The ambiguous syntax suggests, among possible readings, a total engulfment in catastrophe. If we decide that the clause "There is nothing more inscribed nor thought nor felt" is the antecedent of "this" in "this must comfort," then what comforts the heart's core "against / Its false disasters" is, ironically, disaster itself, the end of something beyond which nothing is left, the destruction of all future possibility. At the same time this interpretation would make "false disasters" refer to "these fathers standing round . . .," as the placing of the dash seems to indicate. The possibility of such a reading makes it uncertain whether the proximity of this human presence, these fathers, mothers, and lovers, is the comfort or the disaster in question. Do these presences serve to attenuate and ward off the heart's disasters, or are they to be identified with a catastrophe which has become redundant and all consuming? Is presence itself the catastrophe? The syntactical uncertainty could, of course, be dismissed as giving a perverse and unacceptable reading of the stanza. But there is, indeed, significant support for such an interpretation in the rest of the poem and in the antithetical way it poses the immediacy of summer's reality. Is it not precisely the overly insistent desire for presence, for the absolutely approximate, for an immediate intimacy with reality, that defines the danger in "Credences"? Nor is such a catastrophic reversal — or, to use Bakhtin's word, uncrowning — strange to Stevens' work as a whole, the most dramatic example being the famous canto VIII of "It Must Give Pleasure" in "Notes," where the last stanza degrades and destroys the elaborately developed affirmation that has preceded:

> These external regions, what do we fill them with
> Except reflections, the escapades of death,
> Cinderella fulfilling herself beneath the roof?
> (CP 405)

There is perhaps in the closing lines of the first canto a reference as well to the lines from Yeats's "Sailing to Byzantium":

> That is no country for old men. The young
> In one another's arms, birds in the trees
> — Those dying generations — at their song,
> The salmon-falls, the mackerel-crowded seas,
> Fish, flesh, or fowl, commend all summer long
> Whatever is begotten, born, and dies.

This Yeatsian echo contributes to the uncanny sense that "the soft dry grass" where fondly and idyllically linger the "dying generations" of Stevens' poem, those parental and amorous presences, "these fathers standing round, / These mothers touching . . ./ These lovers waiting," is that glade already infiltrated by the menacing diabolic serpent of "The Auroras of Autumn": "the flecked animal, / The moving grass, the Indian in his glade" (*CP* 412). As that which is begotten and born is already caught up in the trammels of degeneration and death, so the communicative presence and human warmth of these parents and lovers may already be beginning to "Look like frost" as boreal night approaches, their intimate domestic space already beginning to dissolve and crumble. The festival of presence in "Credences" looks ahead even in its opening flourishes to the stinging question of "Auroras": "What festival? This loud, disordered mooch?" (*CP* 415). It is perhaps already — at least potentially — a festival "made up of this: / That there are no lines to speak? There is no play. / Or, the persons act one merely by being there." The word "disaster" itself in the phrase "false disasters," with its etymology of an astral undoing (*dis-astro*), if we also consider that other key word in the stanza, "consider" ("to move with the stars"), may punningly point to the inevitable uncrownings of all fortune, to a tragic human destiny ruled from a distance by the stars, by extra-human forces of time and change.

But another festival is possible, one that combats the first, one that is "hostile to all that [is] immortalized and completed," that celebrates instead "the true feast of time, the feast of becoming, change, and renewal."[22] This alternative understanding involves the recognition that it is impossible to hold onto presence, which is that knowledge of the gay relativity of all things towards which "Credences" can be seen as subtly moving from the start. If, as in the imperative which opens the next canto, the "anatomy of summer" is to be postponed, it could be that it is deferred as a truth repressed: that it is already its autopsy which is taking place. Is an autopsy not, literally, "a seeing with one's own eyes"? Such a seeing is certainly significant in a poem that categorically demands: "Let's see the very thing and nothing else."

*　*　*

> Postpone the anatomy of summer, as
> The physical pine, the metaphysical pine.
> Let's see the very thing and nothing else.
> Let's see it with the hottest fire of sight.
> Burn everything not part of it to ash.
>
> Trace the gold sun about the whitened sky
> Without evasion by a single metaphor.
> Look at it in its essential barrenness
> And say this, this is the centre that I seek.
> Fix it in an eternal foliage
>
> And fill the foliage with arrested peace,
> Joy of such permanence, right ignorance
> Of change still possible. Exile desire
> For what is not. This is the barrenness
> Of the fertile thing that can attain no more
> (*CP* 373)

A series of violent imperatives govern the syntax of canto II: "Postpone," "Let's see," "Let's see," "Burn," "Burn," "Trace," "Look," "And say," "Fix," "And fill," "Exile." The series culminates in an antithetical combination of terms: the barrenness of extreme fertility ("This is the barrenness / Of the fertile thing that can attain no more"). The command to "to see the very thing and nothing else" sets off a crescendo of violent images intensifying into those of branding and incision: "Burn everything not part of it to ash. / Trace the gold sun about the whitened sky. . . ." Sight, "the hottest fire of sight," finally amounts to a fiery engraving. Vision becomes an incandescent writing of the eye, ruthlessly purging anything extraneous to the thing itself. Speech too aims at fixing the naked object at the point of its "essential barrenness" so as to declare at last without qualification: "this is the centre that I seek." Thus possessed, the object's plenitude cannot be distinguished from a radical exclusion.

Entirely predicated on a militant sense of propriety, its fulness is paradoxically determined by a primarily negative desire: "Exile desire for what is not." The repeated assertions ("This is the centre," "This is the barrenness") and the accumulating imperatives suggest that "the very thing and nothing else" is only disclosed by an act of will, and is therefore less an advent than in imposition.

Indeed, the use of the imperative in canto II resembles a magical decree. Its fierce insistence is simultaneously a recognition that the desire for a proper vision of reality *is* now fulfilled and the wilful demand that such a desire *be* now fulfilled. The present indicative of "to be," which conveys presence, is — in this canto in any case — conditioned by the optative mood; a "would that it were" thus translates into an "it is," desire into reality, but only by a rhetorical sleight-of-hand.23 This gap between decree and presentation calls to mind the critical distinction in canto VI, "It Must Give Pleasure" of "Notes" between an imposed order and a discovered reality: "But to impose is not to discover" (*CP* 403). Throughout "Credences," except perhaps in the last cantos, the main note is strongly assertive, betraying an imperious insistence so top-heavy that it tends to work against itself. The very urgency threatens presence with a dangerous precociousness, as though its ripeness were forced, taken by force. In canto II the opening command to "Postpone the anatomy of summer, as / The physical pine, the metaphysical pine" looks ahead, in the very gesture of deferral, to the corpse of summer, to that tomorrow when, used up and spent, this warm-blooded reality will be the colder subject of a sober analysis. A ghostliness haunts the passage and anticipates the "complex of emotions" falling apart in canto IX. We are already part of an auroral imagination that, "As grim as it is benevolent," "in the midst of summer stops / To imagine winter" (*CP* 417). In pretending to transcend the cloven fiction dividing the "proper" pine between two worlds, the physical and metaphysical, the poet's "unmediated vision" (to invoke the early Hartman) turns out to be the opposite of an inclusive one. Uniting as it does an extreme plenitude and an equally extreme impoverishment, a complete satisfaction and a fiery purgation, "Credences" is haunted by a pre-posthumousness that defines the very victory of presence and truth the poem attains: a Pyrrhic one, and pyrographic, or pyromaniacal as well. The implication is that the summer pine *an sich*, far from seen at last prospering in the fullness of its growth, has in fact been set aflame and burned to the ground in the forest fire of a fanatically apocalyptic eye.

The order to "Trace the gold sun about the whitened sky / Without evasion by a single metaphor" attests to the ultimate desire of all "white mythology": that a proper meaning be grounded in a presence beyond language, that the thing itself be spoken in a "Pure rhetoric of a language without words," as it is put in canto VI.[24] This correspondence between being and language — a language beyond or without language, since it is "without words" — is itself, of course, metaphorically posed, evaded "by a single metaphor," the figure of "the gold sun" traced "about the whitened sky." The dream of a proper name for the sun is the subject of Derrida's essay, which concerns the *helio-trope* (the troping of and the turning of, and towards the sun) as a figure for the movement away from an origin that grounds literal meaning, a movement which is, at the same time, metaphor's parabolic route to an end that finally restores a proper state of being and meaning. The sun's trajectory is, then, a metaphor of metaphor. In this case, metaphor represents, for the metaphysical epoch, a detour whose wandering has its *telos* in the advent of "proper" meaning. This makes the goal of metaphor its own self-destruction.

> Philosophical discourse — as such — des-
> cribes a metaphor which is displaced and

> reabsorbed between two suns. This *end* of metaphor is not interpreted as a death or dislocation, but as an interiorizing anamnesis (*Erinnerung*), a recollection of meaning, a *relève* of living metaphoricity into a living state of properness. This is the irrepressible philosophical desire to summarize-interiorize-dialecticize-master-*relever* the metaphorical division between the origin and itself, the Oriental difference. (*MP* 269)

But the way in which Stevens' poem develops its thesis, instead of convincing us of the arrival of presence and the proper, seems to expose instead the inevitability, the inescapable nature of metaphor. What cannot be evaded are metaphor's evasions. Not only is the advent of the proper itself *figured* in the *helio-trope* of white mythology — a recourse to metaphor even in the affirmation of its overcoming — but the poem's entire logic finally demonstrates the undesirability of such an effort to bring *différance* to a close. If tracing the sun's proper name allows the sun of canto III "sleepless" to inhale "his proper air" and to rest, it can do so only by a potentially fatal amputation. It expunges that which escapes a final identity, that which threatens, through metaphor, trope, and figure, to evade us "as in a senseless element" (*CP* 396), "in the intricate evasions of as" (*CP* 486). This very evasiveness, however, saves us in the end, saves us from the end, that point "Beyond which there is nothing left of time." Metaphor preserves presence and the proper name from a potentially dangerous self-possession. Both a curse and a blessing, its evasions not only defer certain truth, but in so doing they save us from an excessive stringency and by the same token save and preserve the truth as well — from itself.

"We have been a little insane about the truth," Stevens writes in "The Noble Rider and the Sound of. Words," "We have had an obsession. In its ultimate extension, the truth about which we have been insane will lead us to look beyond the truth to something in which the imagination will be the dominant complement" (*NA* 33). In the passage that immediately follows in the same essay, Stevens speaks of that noble element in art which evades all definition, all identity: "Nothing could be more evasive and inaccessible. Nothing distorts itself and seeks disguise more quickly. There is a shame of disclosing it and in its definite presentations a horror of it" (*NA* 34). The essay's closing lines suggest quite clearly that the relationship between metaphor and literal meaning or truth, that "truth about which we have been insane," is one not of antithesis, of an opposition we might hope to transcend, but finally of preservation, in which the differential struggle between two violences, the rhythm of their *différance*, is both conflictual and profoundly vital.

> It is not an artifice that the mind had added to human nature. The mind has added nothing to human nature. It is a violence from within that protects us from a violence without. It is the imagination pressing back against the pressure of reality. It seems, in the last analysis, to have something to do with our self-preservation; and that, no doubt, is why the expression of it, the sound of its words, helps us to live our lives. (*NA* 36)

For all its contradictoriness, then, it is perhaps no accident that canto III turns out to be, ironically enough, one of the most explicitly metaphoric sections of the poem. It is as though "Credences" can only contradict itself at this point, and so it does so as blatantly as possible. "It," the impersonal pronoun which, however indefinitely, stands for "the centre that I seek," the thing itself of the preceding canto, is identified in a sequence of almost allegorical figures, one piled on top of another.

> It is the natural tower of all the world,
> The point of survey, green's green apogee,
> But a tower more precious than the view beyond,
> A point of survey squatting like a throne,
> Axis of everything, green's apogee

> And happiest folk-land, mostly marriage-hymns.
> It is the mountain on which the tower stands,
> It is the final mountain. Here the sun,
> Sleepless, inhales his proper air, and rests.
> This is the refuge that the end creates.
>
> It is the old man standing on the tower,
> Who reads no book. His ruddy ancientness
> Absorbs the ruddy summer and is appeased,
> By an understanding that fulfils his age,
> By a feeling capable of nothing more. (*CP* 373-74)

The images unfold here rather predictably, the metaphors suspiciously resembling ones we might find among the allegorical devices of a Tarot pack: tower, throne, marriage, mountain, hermit. The idea of an ascent at the end of which the sun is discovered resting in its proper place at last, beyond all degree of figurative distortion, is itself a *topos* that has been well used, and used up. Plato, of course, figures such an ascent to represent the quest after a vision in which the philosopher will finally "be able to see the Sun, and not mere reflections of him in the water, but he will see him in his own proper place, and not in another."[25] Stevens' sun, however, does not particularly strike us as in his proper place and inhaling his proper air at last, but gives the impression of being buried and suffocated beneath a stylized series of tropes. If "This is the refuge that the end creates," it is a refuge in perpetual retreat from the truth — at least from any truth but a figurative one — and not the place, that proper place, from which metaphor withdraws and makes place for the proper.[26] Especially in the light of canto II with its demand for a presence presented "Without evasion by a single metaphor," it is impossible to ignore this chain of allegorical figures which so explicitly undermine the imperatives of the poem. We note again as well the negative character of the satisfaction celebrated in "Credences": that this "old man standing on the tower" should be appeased "By a feeling capable of nothing more." Such a feeling is phrased in a strikingly negative manner, so that what is emphasized is the incapacity of the feeling, the fact that all feeling has been spent and exhausted, that beyond this point "there is nothing left of time," as it is phrased in the opening canto. As Bloom comments: "To have a mind of midsummer is to write no more poetry, because one has been absorbed as part of 'a feeling capable of nothing more'" (*The Poems* 245). The dilemma, however, may not be that no more poetry is written but that what is written is bound to be uninspiring, nothing but the sun inhaling its own hot, stale air, as it were. It would be the poetry one encounters in "The Man on the Dump," where the freshest poetry "has been fresh a long time" (*CP* 202). The images in canto III of "Credences" might almost be said to make up a dump of images, as one well worn figure is used up after another, each with relatively little more resonance than "aptest eve," "Invisible priest," or "stanza my stone" (*CP* 203). What is important is the refreshment of our vision of the world, not its maintenance, and this refreshment always implies a deviation from any presently held truth or reality. Since it is precisely the truth that is at stake in this poem of ultimate satisfactions, it is impossible not to hear, in all its skeptical force, the question that closes that other poem: "Where was it one first heard of the truth? The the."

* * *

A proper naming of the sun[27] is the well known inaugural theme of "Notes," where an ironic reversal makes explicit the logic only implicit in the opening cantos of "Credences." The first two cantos of "It Must be Abstract" portray two distinct desires in relation to language. The first involves purging the idea of the sun of all its accumulated figurative coverings so that it be "Washed in the remotest cleanliness of a heaven / That has expelled us and our images" (*CP* 381). This is the dream again of a "white mythology," the desire for purity that is such a part of Stevens' poetry, the wish, in the terms of "Sailing After Lunch,"

> To expunge all people and be a pupil
> Of the gorgeous wheel and so to give
> That slight transcendence to the dirty sail. (*CP* 121).

But in "Notes," the second canto abruptly reverses this purifying drive and turns around and asserts the opposing necessity, that for the truth's own sake the first idea must become "The hermit in a poet's metaphors, /Who comes and goes and comes and goes all day" (*CP* 381). This second moment reveals by re-veiling, re-covers the truth in metaphor and apotropaically wards off the inherent menace of its "ravishments," which are a result of the original *immodest* — "There is a shame of disclosing it and in its definite presentation a horror of it," as Stevens puts it in "The Noble Rider" — cleansing made in view of gaining an immediate vision. This immediacy is now depicted as fatal.[28]

In Stevens, metaphor and truth are not in opposition. The logic of their relation is supplementary, steered by that economy which, in the discussion of a similar logic at work in Rousseau's conception of desire, Derrida says "exposes and protects us at the same time according to the play of forces and of the differences of forces," so that if "the supplement is dangerous in that it threatens us with death," it is equally the case that "pure presence itself, if such a thing were possible, would be only another name for death" (*G* 155).

> It is the celestial ennui of apartments
> That sends us back to the first idea, the quick
> Of this invention; and yet so poisonous
>
> Are the ravishments of truth, so fatal to
> The truth itself, the first idea becomes
> The hermit in a poet's metaphors,
>
> Who comes and goes and comes and goes all day.
> (*CP* 381)

"The celestial ennui of apartments" does not only suggest "a socially induced dissatisfaction" in "the distaste at being surrounded by apartment-dwellers" (*The Poems* 179), as Bloom has rather literally explicated the image. It may be a more imaginative play on the idea of a poetic naming of the sun, a "celestial" naming whose space is the poem itself, partitioned into stanzas. *Stanza* in Italian means "room," which would make of the poem a kind of apartment or apartment-building, made up of rooms, as it were, as in Donne's famous pun in "The Canonization" of building "in sonnets pretty rooms," or as in Stevens' own "Extracts from the Academy of Fine Ideas," where the completed and permanent "stanzas of final peace" which "Lie in the heart's residuum" are promised to replace the merely provisional "camp" (*CP* 258) in which we now dwell. In "Notes," they are "celestial" rooms because it is in the poem that we invent names for the sun, names "for something that never could be named," like the catachrestic "gold flourisher." But a proliferation of metaphors may become an unruly clutter, expanding to such an extent as to take over whole cities in a high-rise urban sprawl, as in "Someone Puts a Pineapple Together," where one is nostalgic for a time

> When a pineapple on the table was enough,
>
> Without the forfeit scholar coming in,
> Without his enlargings and pale arrondissements,
> Without the furious roar in his capital. (*NA* 85)

The excess of metaphor has come into being originally to supply, as in "Notes," the dearth of a proper name (for the sun), or, as in "Pineapple," the loss of a plenitude of pineapple or of an authoritative pineapple *an sich*. But now the poet is threatened by the hegemony of the supplement, by "The metaphor that murders metaphor" (*NA* 85). He must reverse the bias and in cleaning out the clutter of his rooms restore the space of poetry's vital *différ-*

ance. In "Notes," the motive for exiling metaphor is not finally the desire for the first idea in its pure form, for truth, at least not if we mean by truth something attainable *as such*, on its own terms. To purge the sun of its tropes aims first at saving metaphor from the danger of its own surfeit. But that very purification bears with it a new and added danger that metaphor, only apparently exiled, now returns to ward off, as the first idea becomes an eternal "hermit in a poet's metaphors."

Indeed, if green in the golden age of pure pineapple "had, those days, its own implacable sting," it is well to remember that a sting — and an "implacable" one at that — may have quite fatal consequences. This explains in part why "a habit of the truth has formed" in the first place, and why, when the scholar speaks of the "one," he must speak instead "always of many things." It is for the scholar's self-protection, to clothe and "protect him in a privacy" from a perilously unitary truth or presence:

> Green had, those days, its own implacable sting.
> But now a habit of the truth had formed
> To protect him in a privacy, in which
>
> The scholar, captious, told him what he could
> Of there, where the truth was not the respect of one,
> But always of many things. He had not to be told
>
> Of the incredible subjects of poetry.
> He was willing they should remain incredible,
> Because the incredible, also, has its truth,
>
> Its tuft of emerald that is real, for all
> Its invitation to false metaphor. (*NA* 85)

Metaphor, then, is alternately scapegoat and saviour, fatal poison and medicinal antidote. If it preserves us from a poisonous truth, it can do so only at the risk of corrupting us with its own "invitation to false metaphor." Just as the alternate risk is at play in the subtle tempering of metaphor, where the cure by truth may end up killing off the patient. The risk is irreducible on both sides. The cure does not lie in making whole, in a complete healing, but rather in what might be called a counter-wounding.[29] The one power must combat the other. Thus the healthy and vital purgation that sets off "Notes" is abruptly answered by the spectre of a debilitating ennui of the first idea, the antithesis of that other celestial one that drives us to purify the first idea in the first place: "May there be an ennui of the first idea? / What else, prodigious scholar, should there be?" (*CP* 381) Purged of all that is extrinsic, the truth may become venomous in its very immediacy, unless it withdraw again in metaphor. For metaphor is the habitat, the permanent but ever changing residence of a "hermit" truth, which is without a proper place *per se*, nothing but, in the perpetuity of its sojourn in the wilderness, a borrowed home or retreat.

*   *   *

This digression through "Notes" and "Pineapple" has been necessary to set the stage for the recognition in "Credences" of the necessary supplementarity of metaphor and truth. Although it is not the lesson of the moment, truth, as in the metaphor that murders metaphor, is itself supplementary; that is, it remedies a metaphoricity dangerously left to itself. Indeed, this is how we can make sense of the powerful drive for presence that opens the poem, so exuberant that it would slaughter all the fools in its way.

The recognition of this logic of the supplement, however, is — at least until the later cantos — only the negative lesson of "Credences." Canto IV just as insistently continues the effort to overcome the secondary, evasive aspect of language and realise what canto IX of "An Ordinary Evening" calls "The poem of pure reality, untouched / By trope or deviation" (*CP* 471). In this "land too ripe for enigmas, too serene," "the distant fails the clairvoyant eye" and we attain at last, in the absolute proximity of word and thing, the "Pure rhetoric of a language without words":

> One of the limits of reality
> Presents itself in Oley when the hay,
> Baked through long days, is piled in mows. It is
> A land too ripe for enigmas, too serene.
> There the distant fails the clairvoyant eye
>
> And the secondary sense of the ear
> Swarm, not with secondary sounds, but choirs,
> Not evocations but last choirs, last sounds
> With nothing else compounded, carried full,
> Pure rhetoric of a language without words.
>
> Things stop in that direction and since they stop
> The direction stops and we accept what is
> As good. The utmost must be good and is
> And is our fortune and honey hived in the trees
> And mingling of colors at a festival. (*CP* 374)

The limit of reality which "Presents itself" has, presumably, transcended the rhetorical and merely evocative function of language. It is conveyed in a language beyond language, since it is "without words." The secondary and extrinsic ("secondary sounds," evocations") disappear in face of nothing but "last choirs, last sounds / With nothing else compounded." This is the real that in the last part of "Notes" is prophesied: "that in time / . . . will from its crude compoundings come" (*CP* 404). As in the preceding cantos, the eschatological mode of the revelation, with its emphasis on last things ("last choirs, last sounds"), stresses the negativity of the limit involved, which is the end of something, with nothing else beyond. Indeed, the plenitude of language here, "carried full, / Pure rhetoric of a language without words," is achieved at the cost of the very thing most essential to language: words themselves (here we can take words to mean signs, the signifying level of any language, verbal or not). This language of presence means the disappearance of language, a divestment of all difference and mediacy beyond which language, however, is properly inconceivable. The swarming "secondary senses of the ear" may verge upon a hearing whose unitary object is absolutely present and immediate to it(self), but in that case we are dealing with a language "without words" or signs and to call it a "Pure rhetoric" is a bit like calling death pure life. A language that has dissolved all difference is no longer language.

Both Bloom and Vendler have noted the antithetical irony of canto IV: ". . . we can see the canto as Stevens' beautiful but wholly momentary acceptance of, or resignation to, his defeat by nature, by the 'pure rhetoric of a language without words'" (*The Poems* 247); "Stevens' aim is to disappoint us subtly as he pairs each word of potential, like 'full' or 'capable,' with a negation of potential" (Vendler 242). This canto, however, may hold in reserve those very features presumably purged in the name of presence. First of all, we may have misgivings about the plenitude at hand, central to which is the idea of a stoppage: "Things stop in that direction and since they stop / The direction stops and we accept what is / As good." Although this cessation of movement is affirmed as the acceptance of "what is / As good," the affirmation could easily be confused with a resignation and even with the subliminal denial of a negative truth. The specious logic of these lines makes them sound more like fatalism, as though merely asserting the positive were enough to make it so, as though "The utmost must be good and is," simply because "we accept what is / As good." This logic recalls a passage from Emerson in "Fate," which Bloom, though not in the context of a reading of "Credences," cites in "Emerson and Whitman: The American Sublime," : "The day of days, the great day of the feast of life, is that in which the inward eye opens to the Unity in things, to the omnipresence of law: — sees that what is must be and ought to be, or is the best."[30] Emerson's identification of festival with the omnipresence of law appears to state one thing while suggesting another; as the positive revelation of a fatality, the celebration involves more an assent to the inescapable than a welcoming of plentitude.   Fortunately, however, in this canto of "Credences," no period follows hard upon such an acceptance of finality.   The sentence itself goes on, conjunctively: "And is our fortune and honey hived in the trees / And mingling of colors at a festival."

At this point in the poem, festivity may be moving in another direction than that of a celebration of the "day of days" announced in the fatal slaughter of the first canto.   "Stevens subsides," Bloom observes, "yet finds his defense in the single counterthrust of 'festival' which restores the sense of enigma and allows for the poem's middle movement . . ." (*The Poems* 247).   The change, however, may be explained less by a restoration of enigma than by a turn, also Emersonian in character, to carnival and to what Bakhtin calls the gay relativity of all things, to that fearless knowledge that laughs at the official, eternal, serious truth imposed by dogma and custom, such as the belief in an unswerving course of events, the belief, for example, in something like fate or an eternal order, imposed by an omnipresent law.   Indeed, canto IV's mention of "fortune" suggests instead the temporal and changing nature of the moment, which is reversible and part of a process of becoming, not a fixed state of being, while the "mingling of colors" looks ahead to the joyous mood of the closing canto, with its characters "mottled, in the moodiest costumes /   Of blue and yellow," "half pales of red, / Half pales of green" (*CP* 377-78).

It is no accident, then, that the poem should begin to question itself at this point and even reverse its thesis.   In canto V we find the only interrogatives of the poem: "Or do the other days enrich the one? / And is the queen humble as she seems to be, / The charitable majesty of her whole kin?"

The question, as to whether one day enriches the year or the days enrich the day, makes an important difference between arrested maturity and prospective potential, between recollection and hope. It affirms the triumph of an as yet unrealized future which is "Stripped of remembrance" and "without souvenir" over a backward-looking retrospection and nostalgia. Presence here is not present — it is an outlook, propelled and expectant. Stevens' representative man, who like Emerson's poet "stands among partial men for the complete man,"[31] is the vital deputy of a growing humanity, essentially forward-looking, "a filial form," not a culmination so much as a new beginning: "The youth, the vital son, the heroic power." The day contains and enriches the years only because it renews time and transforms it into an open end, a commencement. The sense of a vital potential and incipient energy eclipses the idea of reality as a final achievement. This reversal allows the poem to surpass the stoppage it has conceived for itself in taking plenitude as a limit, an end, in both sense of end: goal and finality-as-death.

> One day enriches a year. One woman makes
> The rest look down. One man becomes a race,
> Lofty like him, like him perpetual.
> Or do the other days enrich the one?
> And is the queen humble as she seems to be,
>
> The charitable majesty of her whole kin?
> The bristling soldier, weather-foxed, who looms
> In the sunshine is a filial form and one
> Of the land's children, easily born, its flesh,
> Not fustian. The more than casual blue
>
> Contains the year and other years and hymns
> And people, without souvenir. The day
> Enriches the year, not as embellishment.
> Stripped of remembrance, it displays its strength —
> The youth, the vital son, the heroic power.
> (*CP* 374-75)

But as though simply to ignore the danger, canto VI stubbornly returns to the poem's initial thesis and again *presents* us with a final presence or truth beyond all evasion, beyond all figure, proclaimed from within and not without the veil of language. The truth in question is said to be an audible and visible one ("the visible rock, the audible") which is immediately apprehensible as at once a physical and a metaphysical reality. This is that world of "Description without Place" that has shrunk — the shrunkenness of such a world should be a caution in itself — "to an immediate whole" and is "complete / Without secret arrangements of it in the mind" (*CP* 341). Although the denial itself would seem to belie it, since it puts metaphor to such good use, it is not, we are told "A hermit's truth nor symbol in hermitage." Rather, it is the *parousia* of a truth affirmed upon "this present ground," a living presence fixed like an unbreakable rock in the permanence of "Things certain sustaining us in certainty."

> The rock cannot be broken. It is the truth.
> It rises from land and sea and covers them.
> It is a mountain half way green and then,
> The other immeasurable half, such rock
> As placid air becomes. But it is not
>
> A hermit's truth nor symbol in hermitage.
> It is the visible rock, the audible,
> The brilliant mercy of a sure repose,
> On this present ground, the vividest repose,
> Things certain sustaining us in certainty.
>
> It is the rock of summer, the extreme,
> A mountain luminous half way in bloom
> And then half way in the extremest light
> Of sapphires flashing from the central sky,
> As if twelve princes sat before a king.
> (*CP* 375)

The truth Stevens so elaborately praises here is a perfect example of that idealized eternal order of which Bakhtin speaks, one inimical to life's festive relativity of becoming and change. Elsewhere Stevens himself perceives the potential danger of such an absolute, as in "Of Bright & Blue Birds & The

Gala Sun" where he conceives in its stead the laughter of "A gaiety of being, not merely knowing," thus affirming a truthless belief over the belief in truth, the triumph over Being of being-as-becoming. Happily, the case for presence made with such conviction and assurance at this point in "Credences" is far from completely consistent and free of contradiction. The most obvious contradiction is that however immediate, certain, and integral the truth of this canto may claim to be, the world which conveys it is nevertheless composed of supplementary halves ("half way green and then, / The other immeasurable half"). It is a world both fully alive and fully allegorical, green and yet still cast in "secret arrangements," a world whose self-presence is still sealed by figures. Not only is the metaphoric denied in a metaphor, but it is, significantly, the same "hermetic" image of the truth that we find in "Notes," where to counteract the poisonous "ravishments of truth" the first idea must become "the hermit in a poet's metaphors" (*CP* 381). This cross reference alone should make us think twice before swallowing the truth of this canto whole and without antidote. The entire canto is, moreover, perhaps the most figurative one in "Credences," if it is possible to measure such things quantitatively. Most notably, in the closing stanza, the emblematic imagery of spiritual victory recalls Revelation, a book whose finally revealed truth is paradoxically translated in a hermetically sealed language; if any book is composed of symbols "in hermitage" it is that book, which "Credences" here seems to imitate, if somewhat allusively. In spite of the claim, then, that this presence or truth is beyond all verbal evasiveness, it is precisely such an evasiveness that dominates in this complex extended metaphor and closing simile of a rock of summer, which is a mountain of light, half in bloom, half in celestial splendour, compared to twelve princes sitting before a king. What better example of what is expressly repudiated as "A hermit's truth" than such apocalyptic imagery?   In canto IX of "An Ordinary Evening in New Haven," A similar paradoxical reversal occurs in the quest for "The poem of pure reality, untouched / By trope or deviation"   when, in an abrupt turnabout, "A view of New Haven, say, through the certain eye, / The eye made clear of uncertainty" is said to include both "Nothing beyond reality" and

Within it,

> Everything, the spirit's alchemicana
> Included, the spirit that goes roundabout
> And through included, not merely the visible,
>
> The solid, but the movable, the moment,
> The coming on of feasts and the habits of saints,
> The pattern of the heavens and high, night air.
> (*CP* 471-72)

Canto VI resists the affirmation of "An Ordinary Evening," where this curious conjunction of the transparent and the parabolic, of certain truth and festive relativity, of an immovable reality and temporal vicissitude points to a blatant contradiction that creatively challenges the way we conceive of truth and presence.   In resisting the affirmation, the canto does not persuade us of the opposite.   Indeed, another cross reference provides a further hidden warning against the perils of unqualified presence.

The extreme assurance proclaimed in canto VI of "Things certain sustaining us in certainty" can be compared to the very beginning of "Notes" and the less stringent affirmation of that "uncertain light of single, certain truth, / Equal in living changingness to the light / In which I meet you" (*CP* 380).   The difference here is critical.   A truth that embraces change and uncertainty, that is rooted in time and remains open-ended and versatile, contrasts significantly with the dangerously absolute and double certainty affirmed in "Credences."   It is as though in these opening lines "Notes" were able to recognize and ward off the lapidary menace of a transfixing decisiveness and immutability, and to make a relative and much less ambitious claim to what is sure. To be held in the "uncertain light" of truth, no matter how single or certain that truth is perceived as being, is to be at a healthy remove from the possible fatal petrifications of any absolute assurance. It is to be granted a vital breathing-space. Nor is it any accident that these petrifications take the added form of a fixed hierarchical ordering of being, as reflected especially in the final image of twelve princes sitting before a king. In the final account, that "the rock cannot be broken" is hardly a totally positive pledge. Indeed, the assertion of "Things certain sustaining us in certainty" seems motivated by nothing other than the extreme desire for certainty, for a principle of permanence, an eternal order of truth. The object of certainty is, in a tautological way, simply the certain. This redundancy implies not only a truth that kills itself, as Nietzsche would have it, but one whose excessive insistence makes for an even more perilous overkill. No wonder that at this particular juncture we should welcome in place of the absolute proximity of presence a certain intermittence of desire, and thus the spaciousness afforded by a certain *différance*.

The next four cantos mark a definite change in the poem's direction. A growing insistence on the supplementary role of the imagination now counters the almost obsessive concern with presence that has dominated so far:

> Far in the woods they sang their unreal songs,
> Secure. It was difficult to sing in face
> Of the object. The singers had to avert themselves
> Or else avert the object. Deep in the woods
> They sang of summer in the common fields.
>
> They sang desiring an object that was near,
> In face of which desire no longer moved,
> Nor made of itself that which it could not find . . .
> Three times the concentred self takes hold, three times
> The thrice concentred self, having possessed
>
> The object, grips it in savage scrutiny,
> Once to make captive, once to subjugate

Or yield to subjugation, once to proclaim
The meaning of the capture, this hard prize,
Fully made, fully apparent, fully found.
(CP 376)

Absolute proximity to the object means the imagination's death. This is certainly a possible interpretation of the ambiguous proclamation, in the poem's opening canto, that "It comes to this and the imagination's life," which could mean that that life is either fulfilled or negated. Canto VII certainly suggests that the imagining mind thrives not when overly near to the desired object, as in the earlier canto IV where "the distant fails the clairvoyant eye," but when at a liberating distance, "far in the woods" and "secure," singing "of summer in the common fields." We sing, naturally enough, of that which we do not fully possess.

But the canto goes even further. Leaving behind the poem's primary thesis of presence, it juxtaposes the new terms of a productive interdependency. The imagination's desire for an object that is near is ambivalent, since it implies at the same time an "aversion" for an absolutely approximate object: "The singers had to avert themselves, / Or else avert the object." It must alternate — as the ellipsis in the middle of the canto seems to suggest — with a creative act consisting of a positive subjugation of the object, which is deliberately gripped, made captive, overmastered, and proclaimed. This event takes place in an appropriate present tense, since it involves an object made fully present to the self. This violent mastery points, however, not to an accommodation but to almost a violation of presence. This hard won "prize," "Fully made, fully apparent, fully found," has been made present and brought close because it has been forcibly seized, the object an its truth proclaimed — asserted, not necessarily discovered. The object's meaning is now ultimately something created. Presence and truth here have no priority, no preeminence, when the object in question is "Fully made" and therefore determined by an arbitrary decision, an artistic choice. Signification is something won by a resolve, which imposes rather than represents meaning. There is something essentially Nietzschean about such an event. As a product of the self's will to power as art, meaning is not an essence fixed and arranged for good. It can never be a settled thing but remains reversible and always open to diverse and changing interpretations. The interpreter's power, the action of that "thrice concentred self," is decisive, because it includes in its scope the simultaneous capacities of making, discovering, and inventing. Thus, whatever truth is so determined can never be a definitive or final one, unlike that belief in certain truth of the preceding canto VI; it can never be "the respect of one," as Stevens says in "Pineapple," but "always of many things" (NA 85).

Canto VIII reinforces this shift from an initial thesis of truth and presence to an affirmation of the imaginative and the creative. The final aim of the preceding canto "to proclaim / The meaning of the capture" prefigures the apocalyptic trumpet which now announces, however, not a fully present object but the advent of "the more visible, the more / Than sharp, illustrious scene." This scene is at the same time "the successor of the invisible." The certain audible and visible presence of canto VI is here replaced by the more and less than present: the possible. Thus what claims to be a limit beyond which nothing more is possible ("right ignorance / Of change still possible," "the barrenness / Of the fertile thing that can attain no more," "a feeling capable of nothing more" [CP 373-74]) proves to be in need of supplementation, in need of something more than what is, of something other than either the visible or invisible. But this something is not the thing itself. It is, on the contrary, the tremendous force of change represented by "Man's mind grown venerable in the unreal." Our way again lit by the star that "shines" in canto XXII of "An Ordinary Evening," which "From the sleepy bosom of the real, re-creates, / Searches a possible for its possibleness" (*CP* 481), we now find ourselves at a long remove from the poem's beginning where "There is nothing more inscribed nor thought nor felt." The imagination poses reality not as a term but as a beginning, for "that's the difference," and the *différance*, to look to that other canto of "An Ordinary Evening": the difference between "the end and the way / To the end," for "Alpha continues to begin / Omega is refreshed at every end" (*CP* 469). In canto VIII of "Credences," the repeated ideas of succession, substitution, usurpation, and replacement strongly suggest this force of irresistible supplementarity.

> The trumpet of morning blows in the clouds and through
> The sky. It is the visible announced,
> It is the more than visible, the more
> Than sharp, illustrious scene. The trumpet cries
> This is the successor of the invisible.
>
> This is its substitute in stratagems
> Of the spirit. This, in sight and memory,
> Must take its place, as what is possible
> Replaces what is not. The resounding cry
> Is like ten thousand rumblers tumbling down
>
> To share the day. The trumpet supposes that
> A mind exists, aware of division, aware
> Of its cry as clarion, its diction's way
> As that of a personage in a multitude:
> Man's mind grown venerable in the unreal. (*CP* 376)

Imagination here supplements the negative limit of a fully present object, as in the reversal of "Notes" when desire, in "an ennui of the first idea," concludes that "what it has is what is not," confirming not the end but the "ancient cycle" of desire:

> It knows that what it has is what is not
> And throws it away like a thing of another time,
> As morning throws off stale moonlight and shabby sleep.
> (*CP* 382)

Canto VIII thus introduces a strategic shift in "Credences," a new ploy of the strategic itself or "stratagems of the spirit," which imply by their very nature contextual differences and differential balances. The plenitude of "Credences" eventually turns out to be that which *is not*. In this new context, in order to avoid a deathly arrest in satisfaction, it must look to that which it first banished as a danger but which now "in sight and memory, / Must take its place, as what is possible / Replaces what is not." Ironically, this leaven of the possible is announced as a triumphal procession of revelation when it actually signifies the very thing that takes the place of "the centre that I seek," "the refuge that the end creates," replaces, that is, the more properly apocalyptic "very thing and nothing else." The announced transcendence is in fact a reawakened desire and imagination that "throw off" a stringent presence "like a thing of another time, / As morning throws off stale moonlight and shabby sleep."

What is not possible is identifiable precisely with that which *is*, in and for itself, a state of being realized beyond all evasion. But since this is a state of exhausted potential, incapable of further growth or becoming, it negates itself in the very fulfillment. A purely negative limit now, it is "a thing of another time," to be thrown off and purged as "what is not." As in "Notes," "It knows that what it has is what is not, / And throws it away like a thing of another time." The element of the unreal in the imagination, of course, *is not* in another sense; it is a pure undifferentiated potential that evolves from "the sleepy bosom of the real" (*CP* 481). It takes place, then, as that which as a reality does not take place, since, like "The weather and the giant of the weather" of canto VI of "It Must Be Abstract" in "Notes," it is "Not to be realized because not to / Be seen, not to be loved nor hated because / Not to be realized" (*CP* 385). As both "successor of the invisible" and "the more than visible," this ghostlier demarcation and keener sound meets the conditions of the peculiar inclusive disjunction proposed in that same canto:

> It must be visible or invisible,
> Invisible or visible or both:
> A seeing and unseeing in the eye.
> (*CP* 385)

In contrast to the values prescribed by a belief in presence — exclusivity, identity, unity, proximity, and centrality — the trumpet's cry which announces this other ascendancy and which is compared to "ten thousand tumblers stumbling down / to share the day" suggests a much more carnival-like event and looks ahead to the mottled mood and figures of the closing canto. We are free now to *suppose* "that / a mind exists, aware of division"; we are to entertain, that is, suppositions about the speculative nature of reality, or of the mind of humanity itself as the prime speculator, this "mind grown venerable in the unreal." That "its diction's way" is "that of a personage in a multitude" accords with Richard Lanham's depiction of *Homo rhetoricus* as someone who, having no stake in "a single set of values and the cosmic orchestration they adumbrate" and having abandoned "the luxury of a central self," gains by the same token "the tolerance . . . that comes from knowing he — and others — not only may *think* differently but *may be* differently."[31] The values affirmed by the orator stand for everything the quester after presence seeks to reduce and eradicate: complexity, difference, multiplicity, distance, and perspective.

Canto IX significantly reinforces this implicit affirmation of a rhetorical point of view by depicting the inevitability of change and of the degeneration promised to any attempt to fix reality. The temptation to eternalize what can only be a momentary, temporally limited, and contextual truth here meets the maker of that truth: time itself, that uncrowns and destroys just as it gives birth and renews. The poem is thus brought to one of its two ends:

> Fly low, cock bright, and stop on a bean pole. Let
> Your brown breast redden, while you wait for warmth.
> With one eye watch the willow, motionless.
> The gardener's cat is dead, the gardener gone
> And last year's garden grows salacious weeds.
>
> A complex of emotions falls apart,
> In an abandoned spot. Soft, civil bird,
> The decay that you regard: of the arranged
> And of the spirit of the arranged, *douceurs*,
> Tristesses, the fund of life and death, suave bush
>
> And polished beast, this complex falls apart.
> And on your bean pole, it may be, you detect
> Another complex of other emotions, not
> So soft, so civil, and you make a sound,
> Which is not part of the listener's own sense.
> (*CP* 377)

The canto's closing allusion to "The Snow Man" suggests that if in that early poem the listener achieved a fulness in vacancy and nothingness, in "Credences" the plenitude is shown to sacrifice and expend itself precisely because it is complete. This spending of force is already latent in canto II's "barrenness / Of the fertile thing that can attain no more" (*CP* 373). The snow man listens without thinking "Of any misery in the sound of the wind" that "is blowing in the same bare place" for him and, "nothing himself," beholds "Nothing that is not there and the nothing that is" (*CP* 10). In "Credences," in contrast, the "cock bright" makes a sound "Which is not part of the listener's own sense," thus dispelling the dream of any identity between the beholding subject and a natural presence. Taking its place is the pathetic fallacy of a barbarous force, "Another complex of other emotions, not / So soft, so civil," which differs from the empty neutrality of the earlier poem and looks ahead to the crisis of "The Auroras" where the poet is confronted by that diabolic imagination "which in the midst of summer stops / To imagine winter" (*CP* 417).

This is the poisonous aspect of living in time, in a world that becomes and changes, that lives, dies, and renews itself by casting off the dead body of the past ("The gardener's cat is dead") and giving birth to the new. It destroys the dogmatic belief in an eternal truth, in the security of an immortal presence beyond all change. This truth is deconstructed not only because it has decayed but because it is shown to be in its essence "of the arranged / And of the spirit of the arranged." It is deconstructed because it is shown to be *constructed*. It is exposed as a perishable ordering of experience that is of the moment and therefore part of nature — because it is part of us — party, that is, to the law of becoming and therefore to both life's *"douceurs"* and its *"Tristesses*, the fund of life and death." The poem's thesis of ultimate satisfaction is, to use Bloom's phrase, a lie against time. Since the limit of reality in "Credences," of this "land too ripe for enigmas," is a negative limit as well, it inevitably tends beyond itself. In being temporally placed, this summer presence is merely temporary. But its constructed nature also means that it is an order imposed, not discovered — an arrangement, a formal limitation only, an inflexible construct which cannot be maintained against the flow and reverses of time.

The echoes of Yeats's apocalyptic "Second Coming" serve further to suggest catastrophe. In Stevens' complex which "falls apart" we cannot help but hear the famous "Things fall apart; the centre cannot hold," while the notorious prophetic *"rough* beast, its hour come round at last" is perhaps parodied by Stevens' *"polished* beast" [emphases added], the "cock bright" whose "suave bush" is now a cruder, *rougher* "bean-pole," and who is ordered: "Let / Your brown breast redden, while you wait for warmth." An old reality has been discarded and, as in the final poem of The Collected Poems "Not Ideas about the Thing but the Thing itself," a "new knowledge of reality" is about to make its advent, a force whose effect, however, may be so impoverishing as to defeat utterly the quest for "A civil nakedness in which to be" (*CP* 310), that goal of the orator in "Repetitions of a Young Captain." The reality announced as "not so soft, so civil" may well be beyond the civilizing power of words to order and transform, and thus remain a barbaric one, the poet's attempted eloquence falling short as "of barbarous tongue" (*CP* 415), as do the father's failed fetchings in "The Auroras." This is the risk of all change. The "civil" bird's distressful alien cry testifies to the extreme nature of that risk, and to its sinister implications: that an inhuman violence from without is about to invade a defenceless within. It is no accident, then, that Stevens should end the poem with a counter-violence, with "the imagination pressing back against the pressure of reality," with a powerful influence both meditative and rhetorical.

Metaphor: The Inhuman Meditation

> The personae of summer play the characters
> Of an inhuman author, who meditates
> With the gold bugs, in blue meadows, late at night.
> He does not hear his characters talk. He sees
> Them mottled in the moodiest costumes,
>
> Of blue and yellow, sky and sun, belted
> And knotted, sashed and seamed, half pales of red,
> Half pales of green, appropriate habit for
> The huge decorum, the manner of the time,
> Part of the mottled mood of summer's whole,
>
> In which the characters speak because they want
> To speak, the fat, the roseate characters,
> Free, for a moment, from malice and sudden cry,
> Complete in a completed scene, speaking
> Their parts as in a youthful happiness.
> (*CP* 377-78)

The significance of the "inhuman author" in the closing canto of "Credences" has been variously judged and accounted for. The major cause of the discrepancy is perhaps the unavoidable negative connotations of the adjective "inhuman." Helen Vendler reads the word more or less as a synonym for inhumanity, depicting the author as a pernicious Prospero figure, a "puppet master" whose impersonal virtuosity dominates the creatures of his imagination: "This final canto in 'Credences' begins very coldly indeed, with the poet as a deliberate and distant manipulator of marionettes" (243). Bloom attacks this reading in his own synopsis of the poem, but at the cost of a certain critical mistrust. He strikes, indeed, a somewhat humanistic note, and if he provides a corrective to Vendler's denigration of the canto — she concludes by accusing Stevens of risking "sentimentality in the ending" (244) — he still falls short of providing a convincing analysis of the word "inhuman." Bloom himself, indeed, might be justly accused of sentimentality:

> It is appropriate that the poem's most problematic canto should be its last, as Stevens strives to close on a note not wholly estranged from celebration. By seeing himself as "an inhuman author," Stevens means something like "not yet wholly human," that is, not yet knowing himself wholly beyond illusion. He does not mean that he has come to an inhuman distance from his own fictions. (*The Poems* 251-52)

These very different readings are revealing in the way they emphasize two possible poles in the interpretation of this word "inhuman." The one insists on the impersonal estrangement; the other, resignedly but optimistically, looks to the provisional necessity of that estrangement, to be overcome eventually in the appropriation of a fully human identity. What Stevens actually means, however, by this inhuman author may fall somewhere, not between , but outside of the compass of these two poles.

Stevens word "inhuman" evokes the speculative process of what is called, in the closing lines of "Of Ideal Time and Choice," "the inhuman making choice of a human self" (*NA* 89). This process does not mean that such a choosing ends in the fully human, which would then inhabit, beyond all further illusion, the "centre of resemblance" or "of ideal time" envisioned in the same poem. This inhuman power may, on the contrary, make "choice of a human self" only perpetually to estrange the self from any proper identity. The only way, indeed, of conceiving of a finalizable identity would be to imagine that there is a being, a consciousness, a self, a presence, outside of language, outside of, that is, a system of differences, a system affected, through what Derrida calls *différance*, by an irreducible deferral of presence. Stevens, of course, allows us to imagine this all the time. He is always pointing to a beyond of language, what appears to be a beyond at any rate, a place called reality or truth, both terms that he highly favours and obsessively employs. Throughout his poetry, this is reflected in his remarkable obsession with the "proper," whether it be proper being, proper sound, proper speech, terms that all designate in one way or another an apparently attainable, finally unalienable realm where being and language are one, where all difference collapses from the weight of sheer identity. The idea of a fully attained human identity is another case of such an imagined reality or truth *beyond language*; or if *in language*, an impossible one, the "Pure rhetoric," as it is put in that earlier canto of "Credences," "of a language without words." The goal of Stevens' poetry seems *at times* to be the establishment of such truths, or such a truth, since presumably all such truths must be, in the end, one. At times: the qualification is crucial, since Stevens always seems to take his reader to one extreme, in this case (let us call it) the appropriation of reality, only to confront its impossibility and turn us paradoxically in the other direction. One of the best examples of this sort of turn-about, overturning, or *catastrophe*, as it were, of apparently opposed terms is that which plays itself out between the "human" and the "inhuman."

Terms such as human and inhuman are supposed to *work* according to certain predictable rules, rules that Stevens' poetry so often disrupts. Derrida's name for such a set of rules is "the law of the proper," by which he means the discursive economy that governs Western metaphysics and which organizes the deployment of concepts like presence, self-presence, truth, identity, essence, being, etc. This economy, according to him, is inextricably bound up with the concept of man, of the human as an end, *telos*, finality, as the pending goal or destiny of history. In "The Ends of Man," Derrida points out that this concept of man, of the human, of which the most notable latest version is perhaps Heidegger's understanding of man as *Dasein*, as the guardian of being, is now in a serious state of crisis. Derrida's further and crucial point is that inherent in the metaphysical concept of the human has always been its finality and therefore its death, since

> In the thinking and the language of Being, the *end* of man has been prescribed since always, and this prescription has never done anything but modulate the equivocality of the *end*, in the play of *telos* and death. In the reading of this play, one may take the following sequence in all its senses: the end of man is the thinking of Being, man is the end of the thinking of Being, the end of man is the end of the thinking of Being. (*MP* 134)

And then, the two sentences which follow in the passage, which should be given in French, to capture the play on the word "propre": "L'homme est depuis toujours sa propre fin, c's est-a-dire la fin de son propre." Man has always been his own — proper — end, that is, the end of his properness.

Stevens, then, may be worrying the human in equally original ways, and specifically when it comes to the question of properness, of what is proper to the human. Throughout his poetry, Stevens reveals an obsession with thresholds, and in particular the threshold, the boundary between the properly human or human proper and its other, that which expropriates or depropriates the human, the inhuman as he often calls it. Ultimately, this obsession points to the impossibility of conceiving the properly human and the proper itself except as something always already divided by the difference from itself, by this difference from itself that is the inhuman. These lines from the closing section of "The Sail of Ulysses" present the paradox in one of its most striking forms:

> The englistered woman is now seen
> In an isolation, separate
> from the human in humanity,
> A part of the inhuman more,
> The still inhuman more, and yet
> An inhuman of our features, known
> And unknown, inhuman for a little while,
> Inhuman for a little, lesser time. (*OP* 105)

In Stevens, woman is often a figure of figuration. As the object of desire, she is an image of the truth: that which is veiled, and which only appears as an alien shining or seeming, a glittering, glistening, or glistering. This image of woman as an image of the truth, as a truth necessarily alienated in a figurative or fictional clothing or covering, this image – a constant in Stevens' work from at least "To the One of Fictive Music" and on – always brings into play, as a consequence of figuration, this "inhuman more, / The still inhuman more" which is at the same time a projection of the human: "And yet an inhuman of our features." There is a chiasmatic threshold effect here, an intersection, an irreducible exchange. "Separate / From the human in humanity," this woman is part of the "inhuman more" in humanity, and this crossing is captured in the very phrase "the human in humanity," which when read aloud is absolutely ambiguous, since it can be heard as an oxymoronic *human inhumanity*. The inhuman and human are never strictly separated in Stevens. Rather, they invade and cross into one another in that space "in which opposites are opposed" through "the movement and the play that links them among themselves, reverses them or makes one sidecross over into the other," that space which Derrida speaks of in "Plato's Pharmacy" as "the movement, the locus, and the play . . . the differance of difference"(*D* 127). This threshold or frontier space is a space of figuration that extends the human into the inhuman, or gives the inhuman a human face. The threshold is also a temporal one, for it involves a prolongation that never issues in a finality or fully attained identity, not at least without bringing into play its *other*. The inhuman is never fully absorbed by the human; the human is never absolutely alienated in the inhuman. The adverbs in the lines are telling, since they suggest by themselves the perpetuity of such a space: "The still inhuman more, and *yet* . . . inhuman for a little while, / Inhuman for a little, lesser time."

This passage, and other passages like it in Stevens, is the source of Bloom's interpretation of the "inhuman author" as "not yet wholly human, not yet knowing himself wholly beyond illusion." The only thing wrong with Bloom's reading is the strong statement of a *telos* that Stevens himself only brings into play so as to problematize and complicate. Stevens' "englistered woman" is separate from the human, "and yet / And inhuman of our features." She is "known / And unknown," still this — and yet something else, something *other*. She inhabits a threshold space that never becomes one thing without being another at the same time. The insistence on "a little while," "a little, lesser time," emphasizes the not-yetness, the ever deferred definition of any final identity. No imaginable end is indicated at this culminating point in the poem. Rather, any such indication is undercut by the dilatory, differing, differential prolongations that seem always to inhere in the midst of Stevens' endlessly complicated approaches, proximities, nearnesses, his tantalizing closing-ins and close-comings. Heidegger has a word for this sort of teasing imminence, for this advent of presence that is never quite an arrival of presence: "saving nearness," *Sparende Nähe*, a word he uses, in his reading of Hölderlin's great poem of homecoming, "Heimkunft/And die Verwandteten," to describe the distancing at work in the proximity to home, to the source, to the most proper.[32]   All of Stevens' homecomings involve precisely such a saving or reserving movement, this protection of an irreducible, unclosable space or recessive difference from the origin, or from the end, the end being, as *telos*, always a resumption, repossession, or reappropriation, with interest, of the origin. Or if there is an end, it is nothing proper, but an *otherness* that, like Derrida's "end of man" is both *telos* and death. Thus, at the end of the volume *The Palm at the End of the Mind*, we find a poem entitled "Of Mere Being," a poem whose title would seem to suggest some final state of being, that proper *end* of the mind suggested by the title of the volume that contains it, some final identity or presence "Beyond the last thought."   What this presence turns out to be is a Yeatsian bird of inhuman origin, who sings "without human meaning, / Without human feeling, a foreign song."   What is such an end, as pure foreignness, pure otherness, but death, final identity as death.

In canto X of "Credences," the inhuman is associated with the singular activity of meditation, a word with a weight all its own in Stevens' poetry.   Its significance is most fully outlined in "The World as Meditation," where it is described as the *inhuman* activity of which Stevens' Penelope sees her musings as part. In the epigraph by Georges Enesco, "l'exercice essentiel du compositeur" is said to be "un rêve permanent, qui ne s'arrête ni nuit ni jour," an endless speculation, a voyage in the blue like the homecoming of Ulysses who, although he keeps "coming constantly so near" (*CP* 521), confirms again and again, in his constant approach, his abysmal distance.   In spite of this irreducible *différance*, the practical effect of this "inhuman meditation" which so absorbs Penelope but which is "larger than her own" is a vital and healing one, an influence that makes whole: "The trees are mended. / That winter is washed away. This wholeness, however, does not correspond to some final identity, whereby name and thing, self and desired object would be made one. It announces, rather, a catachrestic naming of the rising sun, a world invented — and a world discovered, in this sense of invention — not resolved. The world meditated in the poem is a world made new by metaphor. "It was Ulysses and it was not," Penelope recognizes, which is perhaps the only way of recognizing a man — or sun — of many turns, who is only willing to reveal himself by troping himself. His uncanny presence *in absentia*, his way of simultaneously being and not being there, is Stevens' way of saying that Ulysses is a metaphor for the sun, or that every sun is a metaphor and every homecoming a *nostos* which must remain a nostalgia for a presence always already withdrawn in metaphor.

Although Penelope, in Stevens' poem, is said to want "no fetchings," "nothing he could not bring her by coming alone," it is as an ambiguous "Two in a deep-founded sheltering" (it being uncertain whether they are sheltered from others or from each other) that she imagines the momentous encounter between herself and Ulysses. Their coming together as one may still be conditioned by a drawing back. As something only possible in metaphor, their face to face is more of a figure to figure, between the self "she has composed" and a Ulysses who is and is not himself, who, like "that brave man" of an earlier poem, if it can be said that he walks "without meditation" (*CP* 138), does not — thanks to this very anthropomorphism — ever walk alone, at least not without the shadow of a trope.

Metaphor, then, is the vehicle of this speculative, inhuman meditation, essential to the poetic imagination. Penelope weaves and unweaves the
sun's name, as an exercise in composition, in rhetoric, which is also a composing
of the self, a figured self with which to meet her metaphoric Ulysses (the
implied metaphor being that the sun is Ulysses — or is Ulysses the sun? —
approaching from the East). The two, Penelope and Ulysses, like "love's
characters come face to face" in canto IV of the third part of "Notes," remind
us that we come together only by being apart, and by playing a part, revealed to
one another at last only in metaphor, in the retreat, withdrawal, or remarking —
Derrida's "retrait" — of a differential and abysmal naming, "in a deep-founded
sheltering" that has always already divided and dispersed (self-)presence.

* * *

Thus what may at first appear in Stevens as a nostalgic gesturing
towards some final identity that one might reach by transcending the realm of
signs and figures is really always something else; it is, indeed, a gesturing
towards something *other*. For if it is not death, then it can only be an
otherness that indefinitely carries the human beyond itself. It can only be a
transformation of the human by the inhuman, and a transformation that is
primarily oratorical and rhetorical, at least in Stevens' peculiar sense of these
terms. One of Stevens' favorite words is elegance, a word derived from the
Latin *eligere*, which means to "choose or select." It is a word that often
accompanies his depiction of human striving as a figurative project, and its Latin
derivation is a clue to understanding the idea, for example, of "the inhuman
making choice of a human self," which we find in "Of Ideal Time and Choice":
"Of how much choosing is the final choice made up, / And who shall speak it"
(*NA* 88). Stevens ultimately makes no distinction, at least no "proper" distinc-

tion, between the oratorical and the imaginative, between the rhetorical and the creative. His poetry deconstructs the notion that the one should relate to the other as the primary to the secondary, the spirit to the letter, the extrinsic to the essential. The "ultimate elegance" is also "the imagined land," as Mrs. Alfred Uruguay discovers halfway on her journey to the real. The elegant is not necessarily just supplementary but integral. The imagination is always an elegant imagination, and this goes so far that revelation, even of ultimate realities, must itself finally be understood as a verbal or figurative effect:

> . . . it might have been thought that I was rhetorical, when I was speaking in the simplest way about things of such importance that nothing is more so. A poet's words are of things that do not exist without words. Thus, the image of the charioteer and of the winged horses, which has been held to be precious ["precious" here may carry the further sense of excessive elegance] for all of the time that matters, was created by words of things that never existed without words. . . . Poetry is a revelation in words by means of the words.
> (*NA* 32-33)

> The images in Ecclesiastes . . . are not the language of reality, they are the symbolic language of metamorphosis, or resemblance, of poetry; but they relate to reality and they intensify our sense of it and they give us the pleasure of "lentor and solemnity" in respect to the most commonplace objects. . . . A group of images in harmony with each other would constitute a poem within, or above, a poem. The suggestion sounds euphuistic. If the desire for resemblance is the desire to enjoy reality, it may be no less true that the desire to enjoy reality, an acute enough desire today, is the desire for elegance. Euphuism had its origin in the desire for elegance and it was euphuism that was a reason in the sun for metaphor.
> (*NA* 77-78)

Stevens could hardly state more plainly that for him the desire for elegance not only does not contradict the desire for reality but is in fact an expression of just that desire. The two desires enhance, intersect, and finally fuse with each other. Even such a transcendent thing as nobility, which is what this high-flown "image of the charioteer and of the winged horses" exemplifies, Stevens understands as primarily the effect of a rhetorical decision, of a verbal construct, a composition or figuration.

Thus Stevens forces us to rethink the rhetorical and makes us recognize the possible meditative value of a devotion to eloquence, even at its most euphuistic. The right images, however ornate and artificial, "relate to reality and they intensify our sense of it." This is what metaphor does in "Pineapple" where, in an "outlandish" periphrasis, we are commanded to "Divest reality of its propriety" and "Admit the shaft / Of that third planet to the table" (*NA* 86). And then: the world, made new in metaphor, is extended, our human reality made to reach into another alien reality through "the chance / concourse of planetary originals" (*NA* 84). This intensification or extension does not exclude the properly human. This addition to reality is still, "as it seems, of human residence." Nothing, indeed, is more human than the power of metaphor. That is what a human is: a maker of metaphors. But what if the human itself should turn ut to be a metaphor, a construction, that metaphor itself, as a force that estranges us and carries us beyond ourselves, has the power to deconstruct? For metaphor is both the point of departure and the endpoint in an endless meditation, a meditation marked by an unrestricted supplementarity. "What our eyes behold may well be the text of life," Stevens writes in "Three Academic Pieces," "but one's meditations on the text and the disclosures of these meditations are no less a part of the structure of reality" (*NA* 76). Or, in the words of "An Ordinary Evening":

> The eye's plain version is a thing apart,
> The vulgate of experience. Of this,

> A few words, an and yet, and yet, and yet
>
> As part of the never-ending meditation,
> Part of the question that is a giant himself. . .
>
> (*CP* 465)

In this regard, then, the meditative author in canto X of "Credences," as precious as he is contemplative, as elegant as he is pensive, is neither Vendler's "poet as deliberate and distant manipulator of marionettes," nor Bloom's "not yet wholly human" genius, "not yet knowing himself wholly beyond illusion." What makes this author inhuman also makes him human: metaphor. The very thing human beings use to construct their realities may end up deconstructing the idea of the human itself, at least inasmuch as the human presupposes a centred subject in control of language and capable of arresting the dissemination of meaning, that increase in "The profusion of metaphor" (*NA* 83). "The proliferation of resemblances extends an object" (*NA* 78), but this enlargement or expansion of reality may also threaten to carry us away. If "The gaiety of language is our seigneur," that particular lord and master may in fact finally unmaster the human pretender.[33] Pointing to neither the impersonalism condemned by Vendler nor the idealism defended by Bloom, the adjective "inhuman" that describes Stevens' author suggests rather a Bakhtinian carnivalizing force, within language itself, the influence of a knowledge of the gay relativity of all things — at least of all words.

This sense of gay relativity is precisely what we find in the figures that close the poem. Like "the appropriate creatures" in "Description," "jubilant, / The forms that are attractive in this air" (*CP* 344), canto X's "personae of summer" are creatures of an imagination whose talent for the euphuistic is acutely developed. It does not follow, however, that such an imagination is manipulative, even if there is this connotation in the idea of the *rhetor* as he who pulls the strings of language, directing and designing his words rigorously to elicit the desired responses from his audience. Far from being so commanded, as if the Hoffmannesque victims of an inhuman puppet master, as Vendler would have it, these *dramatis personae* are significantly distinct from the compulsive singers of unreal songs in canto VII, who are constrained by an inhibiting presence. They possess, rather, a freedom, though not necessarily without control, of play, speaking only "because they want / To speak." Released in a universe of metaphor and theatre, they do not suffer the ambivalence of an simultaneous desire and aversion for "an object that was near," to near, "in face of which desire no longer moved" (*CP* 376). They enjoy a sort of relaxed *sprezzatura*, at their ease in "The huge decorum, the manner of the time," practitioners of a mannerism like the one affirmed in "Description." There an age is said to be "a manner collected from a queen":

> Its identity is merely a thing that seems,
>
> In the seeming of an original in the eye,
> In the major manner of a queen, the green
>
> The red, the blue, the argent queen. If not,
> What subtlety would apparition have?
>
> In flat appearance we should be and be,
> Except for delicate clinkings not explained.
> (*CP* 340)

Thus "Credences," a poem with such a stake in presence, with an almost terroristic insistence on seeing "the very thing and nothing else," counterbalances this midsummer-daydream-come-true with its own closing midsummer night's dream, where apprehension belongs to "The lunatic, the lover, and the poet" whom Theseus in Shakespeare's play asserts are "of imagination all compact" (V.i.7-8). To this list we might just add, for Stevens' sake, the *rhetor* or orator as well, who can claim an equal power. The imagination, in this canto, is rhetorical, just as it is almost everywhere else in Stevens; its signature is its elegance. It is not just the imagination but, more pertinently, a rhetorically motivated "appropriate habit for / The huge decorum" (*CP* 378) that completely eclipses the poem's ostensible concern with an immediate "proper" reality. Decorum is a rhetorical concern, and a decision about what is appropriate or "proper" in a given context is a very different thing from the quest for a non-mediated presence or truth, where the "proper" is the unique, the indivisible and undifferentiated, conceived as existing outside of any system of differences. Propriety, in the rhetorical sense, is on the other hand an entirely relative matter and involves a recognition of *differences*. It quite explicitly involves a decision about the difference among any number of possible things. This means that it has no faith in the absolute identity of anything nor is it interested in any such assurance. Both Nietzsche's gay science and Bakhtin's gay relativity of all things come to mind here. They both involve what Richard Lanham calls the rhetorical view of life, which "begins with the centrality of language." This *other* "proper," this rhetorical ideal, happily opposes any Platonic idea of a state where "The Sun, / Sleepless, inhales his proper air, and rests" (*CP* 373) at last in a world without *différance*, with neither the need nor the desire for any further figurative mediation. Happily — because what is finally suffocating and unlivable, undesirable and menacing, is not the irresistible drift of difference and sense away from a stringent unique object, but indivisible presence itself.

And so we are saved by the night of canto X, by this feast of colour and garish apparel, a festival in which such tricks as strong imagination has have, indeed, the power to turn everything, reality most of all, upside down, to turn day into night, for example, or night into day, as on this occasion a meditation by dark becomes a vision made luminary by the variegated colours of the day, "Of blue and yellow, sky and sun," "half pales of red, / Half pales of green." Evoked is a world where motley is worn, where change, variety, and heterogeneity define this "unmottled mood of summer's whole" and its inhabitants, "mottled in the moodiest costumes." These characters are significantly described as "fat" and "roseate." Their colour describes their vitality and optimism, as they look head to what is possible as opposed to what is not. Their obesity, besides being the natural mark of the truly festive, like Falstaff, and generally appropriate to the fulsomeness of the canto's "huge decorum" and "completed scene," may also suggest the shape of their language which, as they are free to "speak because they want to speak," may tend to be expansive, enlarging, dilatory, what Stevens conceivably would deem euphuism, the great example given in "Three Academic Pieces" as the "reason in the sun for metaphor," that "desire for resemblance" which is also "the desire to enjoy reality," it being no less true "that the desire to enjoy reality, an acute enough desire today, is the desire for elegance" (*NA* 78). Thus the two adjectives "fat" and "roseate" describe both a rhetorical and a temporal *dilation*, an expatiation and an expectancy. The canto's theatrical "scene" is completed and whole only in being differentiated, partitioned and divided, composed of multiple parts. The characters are "*Part* of the mottled mood" and, in speaking "their *parts*" (my emphasis), recall by their idiosyncratic playfulness and freely improvised speech Peter Quince and his mechanicals, whose "palpable-gross" — large, fat — play is said by Theseus to have "well beguil'd/ The heavy gait of night" (V.i.376-77). Shakespeare's clowns also rehearse their parts "in the palace wood, a mile without town, by moonlight" (I.ii.106-07), like Stevens' clownish counterparts whose inhuman author "meditates / With the gold bugs, in blue meadows, late at night."

"Credences," then, which starts out as a poem of certain truth and presence, ends up by depicting a total of separate parts — both parts and apart — in which difference and *différance* are vital factors. We are reminded again of "An Ordinary Evening" which opens with "a thing apart" from which "a few words" grow to build an ongoing *composition* ("Of what is this house composed . . .") as "part of the never-ending meditation, / Part of the question that is a giant himself." The same opening canto closes with the grotesque vision of the poem as an androgynous giant body, its parts or members regathered at last, like one of Aristophanes' titanic men before their division and fall into sexual difference, in that goofy explanation of erotic desire in *The Symposium*:

> A larger poem for a larger audience,
> As if the crude collops came together as one,
> A mythological form, a festival sphere,
> A great bosom, beard and being, alive with age.
> (*CP* 465-66)

Canto X of "Credences" celebrates a similar "festival sphere," a "completed scene" that is not one thing but many, complete not as something arrested and finished but — "alive with age" — as a still to be defined, growing living form, open-ended and forward-looking, ever-renewed and turned to the future.

* * *

So the poem ends with a meditation that is at the same time a feast, a festival, a conjunction as "Platonic" ultimately — witness *The Symposium* — as the sun of that earlier canto which, taking in its own proper air at last, threatens to breath its last, being oppressed by a too strict propriety. Feasts of thought and philosophical dialogue, meditations that are gay and Saturnalian, that welcome the clown and reveller instead of banishing them, are of course one of Bakhtin's great subjects: the vital carnivalization of life in the world of thought. Socrates is the great example here, but a more recent philosophical exponent of festive meditation, who may not come so easily to mind perhaps, is Heidegger, who equally conceives of thinking or meditation in its most authentic form as a literal festival, a feast of thought. He introduces his lectures on Nietzsche with a meditation on the latter's sense of philosophy as "feast and frenzy," which his own interpretation may in fact rob of much of its carnivalizing force. But Heidegger does take the idea of feast and festival seriously — perhaps a little too seriously, when its very heart is laughter — and concludes:

> Feasts require long and painstaking preparation. This semester we want to prepare ourselves for the feast, even if we do not make it as far as the celebration, even if we only catch a glimpse of the preliminary festivities at the feast of thinking — experiencing what meditative thought is and what it means to be at home in genuine questioning.[34]

The *Besinnung* of the "inhuman author" in canto X is in the same way a festival. To pursue Heidegger's sense, it is a pre-festival (this may be true of all festivals, by their very nature preparatory, since they renew time and look ever to the future), the threshold or pre-liminary of a celebration we are never to know, since it is always only in preparation of itself. We are never to know the absolute homecoming, the advent of the proper as *Er-eignis*, the very event, the coming into its own place of the proper. If language is the house of Being, as Heidegger expresses it, it is for him and for Stevens as well, even if they pose this *différance* in significantly different ways, a residence in which we remain in a condition of perpetual petition, never passing out of the vestibule, the threshold, into the proper living room of presence. But as in Heidegger's reading of Hölderlin's "Heimkunft," where "The discovery comes about as the already reserved and remains in fact as that which is sought after,"[35] to be festively at home engages us in a different economy of the proper and way of knowing an immediate living presence than the one we initially find in "Credences."

To meditate, in Stevens' sense, means we are always at home in a home away from home, for meditation is a process of metaphoric extension which exceeds any "proper" human reality. The revelatory function of meditation involves an effect of estrangement that only diminishes along with the disclosure. The one depends on the other. Reality is not only revealed but in fact produced by an effect of difference:

> It is as if a man who lived indoors should go outdoors on a day of sympathetic weather. His realization of the weather would exceed that of a man who lives outdoors. It might, in fact, be intense enough to convert the real world about him into an imagined world. In short, a sense of reality keen enough to be in excess of the normal sense of reality creates a reality of its own. (*NA* 79)

Stevens' Penelope meets her elusive, ever-approaching, never-arriving spouse with the help of "a planet's encouragement" and her own "barbarous strength," two expressions which can be read as metaphors of metaphor. They can also, significantly, be read the opposite way. The "barbarous strength within her" may allude to the estrangement or *foreignness* of metaphor or its opposite, the inhuman otherness of an unmediated, unnameable reality or nature. As in one of Stevens' very early poems, "Nuances of a Theme by Williams," the "strange courage" inspired by the sun or evening star is that of a world that has not yet fallen into a linguistic dimension. For to name is already to introduce a deviation, to alter, to make other, through the foreignness of metaphor, as we find, for example, in the "antipodal, far-fetched" provenance of the creature in "A Discovery of Thought" (*OP* 96); or in the exotic antipodes of those "hale-hearted landsmen" in "The Auroras," "For whom the outlandish was another day / Of the week, queerer than Sunday" (*CP* 419), as queer as those "unherded herds of barbarous tongue" (*CP* 415) that the father in the same poem fetches from afar for his masque but fails to translate.

Originary naming in Stevens always involves this catachrestic abuse, this profound rupture with the proper. So too can we read Stevens' planetary metaphor, where this *outlandishness* becomes extraterrestrial. The "planet's encouragement" can refer to the influence of the earth or sun, to a reality beyond language, to that which is other than the names we give to it ("shine alone, shine nakedly"; "Be not an intelligence, / Like a widow's bird / Or an old horse," as Stevens puts it in "Nuances"). But the metaphor can also refer to the error and wandering of language and naming, originary naming as always improper, catachrestic, metaphoric. For the metaphor of the planet here can be taken two ways. First, as an expression of white mythology, it would mean that Penelope takes courage from an ever-returning sun, which daily revives the expectancy of a proper name, that word to identify and contain that which is other, a presence beyond language. But it also suggests the unsettling contrary: the planetary as a verbal dimension which heightens our sense of the real precisely to the extent that it de-propriates reality, and threatens to make the visible not just a little difficult to see — but even unrecognizable. In "Three Academic Pieces," Stevens uses indeed an "E.T." figure to illustrate what he means by metaphor which works at the "level of resemblance of the imagination" and surpasses the level of resemblance in nature:

> If, to our surprise, we should meet a monsieur
> who told us that he was from another world,
> and if he had in fact all the indicia of divinity,
> the luminous body, the nimbus, the heraldic

> stigmata, we should recognize him as above the
> level of nature but not as above the level of
> imagination.   (*NA* 74)

This planetary metaphor of metaphor is also one of the threads running through "Pineapple," where "The ephemeras of the tangent swarm, the chance / Concourse of planetary originals" (*NA* 84) and the battle-cry of metaphor is: "Divest reality / Of its propriety.   Admit the shaft / Of that third planet to the table and then . . ." (86).   The third planet in the solar system is, of course, the earth, but here it appears to be a metaphoric name for metaphor and its power of estrangement, of de-propriation.   For twelve metaphoric visions of pineapple then follow, as strange as anything we might expect from an extraterrestrial traveller — and many of them as grotesque.   "Planet" originally means "wandering star," which suggests not only the influence of an alien perspective but also the connected idea of metaphor as a deviation or wandering from "proper" meaning.

The inhuman force behind meditation, then, is metaphor, verbal deviation, "the accent of deviation in the living thing," the distortion that quickens any trope or "far-fetched creature worthy of birth" (*OP* 96).   This deviation produces disclosure, revelation, discovery, not as (self-)presence but as that which has always already broken with it, sending us on our way, away from any proper human reality and *en route* to another.   This is how we can explain the *inhuman* character of the meditating author in "Credences" and why, in that final canto, in place of celebrated presence the gay relativity of metaphor and play gain the day, or at least the night.   With this new ascendancy comes a new danger.   No longer from a stringent and asphyxiating presence, the danger now comes from evasion.

What saves us from the delusion of presence, from an overly stringent law of the proper, that freedom in which the characters "speak because they want to speak," might also be seen as an evasion, an escapism that shrinks from the unpleasant truth of "malice and sudden cry." The idyll is only for a moment because it would be a lie that cannot last against the destructive force of what is real.

But there is another evasion as well, and another danger. Not just the abuse of play and illusion as means of escapism, but the possibility of a grave injury to sense, the wound of an irreparable semantic loss. Metaphor may escape meaning and resist the intelligence completely, and not just "almost successfully" (*OP* 171), as poetry must always do. Divesting "reality of its propriety," enhancing our perception of human reality by an effect of alienation, can be a treacherous operation. The new meaning may be inaccessible, so far in excess of any human touchstone that it is out of reach. The poet's freedom of speech may turn into the license to speak unintelligibly, as we go "from the poet's gibberish to / The gibberish of the vulgate and back again" (*CP* 396). This anxiety, the fear that the poet become a mere jabberer, is the subject of canto IX in "It Must Change" of "Notes":

> There's a meditation there, in which there seems
>
> To be an evasion, a thing not apprehended or
> Not apprehended well. Does the poet
> Evade us, as in a senseless element?
>
> Evade, this hot, dependent orator,
> The spokesman at our bluntest barriers,
> Exponent by a form of speech, the speaker
>
> Of a speech only a little of the tongue?
> (*CP* 397)

The risk cannot be eradicated, except at the cost of poetry itself. An irreducible "senseless element" is the source of both unintelligibility and the transfiguration of reality that is the work of successful metaphor and the function of the poem. It is not a case of trying to rid oneself of the danger, of schooling poetic language to extirpate all threat of loss. It is, on the contrary, more rightly a matter of knowing when to go too far. The deviation, the irrepressible excess is vital to poetry. In canto X of "Credences," the author is termed "inhuman" not because he is a tyrant dominating the creatures of his imagination, nor because, as in Bloom's reading, the inhuman is the route to a fully human identity. It has more to do with what our philosophical tradition understands as the potential menace of metaphor, what Derrida deconstructs as "white mythology":

> Each time that polysemia is irreducible, when no unity of meaning is even promised to it, one is outside language. And consequently, outside humanity. What is proper to man (*le propre de l'homme*) is doubtless the capacity to make metaphors, but in order to mean some thing, and only one. In this sense, the philosopher, who ever has but one thing to say, is the man of man (*c'est l'homme de l'homme*). Whoever does not subject equivocalness to this law is already a bit less than a man: a sophist, who in sum says nothing, nothing that can be reduced to a meaning. (*MP* 248)

Stevens' inhuman author is not, in this philosophical sense, a "man's man." But what is inhuman about him does not put him "outside of humanity," beyond the boundaries of the properly human. As "spokesman at our bluntest barriers," he is "of human residence" and yet beyond. He is at the passageway of a translation between the two: the human and the inhuman, the intelligible and the unintelligible, the proper and the improper. By the medium of metaphor, "he meditates a whole," contrives a "balance to contrive a whole" (*CP* 420). Metaphor is human and inhuman at once, making us human only as the vehicle of our own unmaking and constant transformation. "To speak humanly from the height or from the depth / Of human things, that is acutest speech," says "Chocorua to Its Neighbor" (*CP* 300). But "acutest speech," like the sharpest or "acutest end / of speech" which is "to pierce the heart's residuum" (*CP* 259) in "Extracts," if it heals our humanity by wounding, is at the same time only possible because of unrestricted metaphor. In the depths of the human it has already introduced an inhuman other, has always already divided and dispersed the centre, presence, the human truth.

3. The Satire of the Abyss

> . . . in pure
> Affirmation that doesn't affirm anything
> John Ashbery, "Self-Portrait in a Convex Mirror"[36]

> To be satisfied is to have one's needs or desires fulfilled, and even to have accomplished the will's revenge against time and so against time's mocking statement "It was." But etymologically it means to make something suffice, to make enough, and the root *sa* appears ominously also in the words "sad," "sated," and "satire." To be satisfied is to be sated and to be sad, to be self-satirized, and we can recall Freud's melancholy reflection that for the human psyche there can be no satisfaction in satisfaction anyway.
> (Harold Bloom (*The Poems* 213)

The Wisdom of the Supplement

Canto V of "It Must Give Pleasure" in "Notes" introduces the extended parable of the Canon Aspirin, a figure who, as his name suggests, romantically "aspires" to cure us of the Back-Ache of Saint John's fallen world, which divides us from presence or *parousia*.[37] The canonic status of Aspirin derives from, among other things, the very canon he proclaims, that "canon central in itself, / The thesis of the plentifullest John" (*CP* 345) spoken of in "Description without Place." This thesis or book is, to be playful, the ultimate spiritual aspirin. In a sense, this could be said of Revelation as well, where the book of prophetic knowledge is not simply read, it is eaten, as though it were the definitive reader's digest — to be literally digested. "So I went to the angel and told him to give me the little scroll; and he said to me, 'Take it and eat; it will be bitter to your stomach, but sweet as honey in your mouth!'" (Rev. 10.9-10) The bitter-sweet knowledge in the Canon's case, however, results from a wisdom that is essentially antidotal or "pharmaceutical," in that he counteracts and remedies the deficiencies of prior half-successes in his pursuit of an ultimate satisfaction.

Satisfaction, in the end, proves not to be a project of the ultimate. The Canon can admire and sympathize with the motives of propriety in his sister's "sensible ecstasy," which consists in a radical impoverishment. Still, he cannot agree with its fundamental perversity, for the results are purely negative and reductive. His is a sensibility inseparable from his senses, from his aesthetic good sense. He is not after the thing itself, but the "taste" of it, the "taste at the root of the tongue," as it is expressed in "Holiday in Reality," of "the unreal of what is real" (*CP* 313). Whence his penchant for "Mersault . . . lobster Bombay . . . Mango Chutney," not to mention an oratorical tendency of equal extravagance, declamatory, profusive and, one surmises — since it is a fugue he outlines — somewhat "flighty."

> The Canon Aspirin, having said these things,
> Reflected, humming an outline of a fugue
> Of praise, a conjugation done by choirs.
> (*CP* 402)

Unlike his ascetic sister, the Canon is a strong romantic who yet, for all his apocalyptic compulsiveness, shares with Professor Eucalyptus a "eucalyptic" vision of things. He can find only a provisory satisfaction in his sister's bleak *askesis*, which leads her to paint "The way a painter of pauvred color paints," to paint her daughters "appropriate to their poverty," holding them "closelier to her by rejecting dreams" and fighting "off the barest phrase." This simplifying reduction is one side of Stevens' muse. In "To the One of Fictive Music," the initial aim is an impossible absolute proximity to the object. But that aim must be qualified: "Yet not too like, yet not so like to be / To near, too clear, saving a little to endow / Our feigning with a strange unlike" (CP 88). Or, as in "An Ordinary Evening," "The vulgate of experience" must always be supplemented by "A few words, an and yet, and yet, and yet " (*CP* 465).

The lesson of the Canon's widowed sister, however, is an unremittingly negative one. The loss she mourns is a belief in fiction, which she has lost to the real. In this she resembles Mrs. Alfred Uruguay, presumably a widow as well, of identical circumstance, who proves herself an equally exemplary and perverse visionary in her struggle and martyrdom for the real. Her illustrious counterpart and foil is "The Well Dressed Man," who shares with Aspirin an affirmed sense of taste and elegance. What makes him and the Canon close cousins is, among other things, their tell-tale association with a peculiar humming sound,[38] whose source may be, among others, Melville's Captain Ahab, "lowly humming to himself, producing a sound so strangely muffled and inarticulate that it seemed the mechanical humming of the wheels of his vitality in him."[39] The well dressed man affirms "The form on the pillow humming while one sleeps, / The aureole above the humming house," while Aspirin reflects, "humming an outline of a fugue / Of praise." This noise expresses the mind's essential dissatisfaction and the ultimate evasiveness of any finally satisfying reality, as in canto IX of "It must Be Abstract," where major man is described as that elusive "object of / The hum of thoughts evaded in the mind" (*CP* 388). It is the mark of the irrepressible in Stevens, the noise of the running and unarrestable machinery of desire.

Witness to his sister's extreme ascetic propriety, the Canon thus finds himself in the place of Uruguay's donkey, "Wishing faithfully for a falsifying bell." To demand a bare minimum of enough remains much too little, utterly deficient. It can never satisfy because it represents an evasion of evasion itself, of the necessity of an evasion of the real in the fictive, which is perhaps not quite the same thing as an evasion of the fictive in flight from the real. In the end, it appears to be need, dearth, or lack which is the object of such a perverse quest for propriety, the repression, not the culmination, of desire, a state in which, as for "Mrs Alfred Uruguay," "To be . . . could never be more / Than to be, she could never differently be" (*CP* 249). In canto II of "It Must be Abstract," a similar tedium, "an ennui of the first idea," makes us fly back into the arms of metaphor from whose "celestial ennui of apartments" we had originally sought refuge in an extreme propriety. Desire discovers in a monotonous being without difference "that what it has is what is not," and so it "throws it away like a thing of another time, / As morning throws off stale moonlight and shabby sleep" (*CP* 382). The latter simile ("As morning throws off . . .") is curious in the context, for it is employed elsewhere in a completely antithetical sense.

In "Notes," it is the toxic influence of an unchanging identity, a reductive clarity, order, and propriety that must finally be purged if we are to survive, that is, if our desire, which is vital, is. The same image of moonlight and shabby, "muddled," or muddy sleep, in another context, represents the excess of unreality which the puristic Uruguay wipes "away like mud" ("She wiped away moonlight like mud") and which the Canon's puritanical sister fights off, demanding "in the excitements of sleep / Only the unmuddled self of sleep" — and not "The form on the pillow humming while one sleeps, / The aureole above the humming house." The simile's double duty is a particularly significant indication of the need for a differential relationship between reality and imagination, or between "proper" (literal) meaning and the impropriety of metaphor, in accordance with that pharmaceutical logic which Derrida, in a discussion of Plato's *Phaedrus*, explains in the following manner:

> Philosophy thus opposes to its other this transmutation of the drug into a remedy, of the poison into a counterpoison. Such an operation would not be possible if the *pharmako-logos* did not already harbor within itself that complicity of contrary values, and if the *pharmakon* in general were not, prior to any distinction-making, that which, presenting itself as a poison, may turn out to be a cure, may retrospectively reveal itself in the truth of its curative power. (*D* 125)

Steven's simile of moonlight and sleep may refer to the pernicious influence of an over-insistence on either the imagination or reality, an alternation possible only because of this effect of the *pharmakon*, "the movement, the locus, and the play: (the production of) difference . . . the differance of difference" (125).

In *The Philosophy of Literary Form*, Kenneth Burke speaks of the magical use of language in similar terms. Even more fascinating is how Burke's language evokes the Cannon Aspirin's crisis in canto VI: "He had to choose. But it was not a choice / Between excluding things. It was not a choice / Between, but of" (*CP* 403).

> The choice here is not a choice between magic and no magic, but a choice between magics that

> vary in their degree of approximation to the truth. . . . The ideal magic is that in which our assertions (or verbal decrees) as to the nature of the situation come closest to a correct gauging of that situation as it actually is. Any *approximate* chart is a "decree." Only a *completely accurate* chart would dissolve magic, by making the structure of names identical with the structure named. This latter is the kind of chart that Spinoza, in his doctrine of the "adequate idea," selected as the goal of philosophy, uniting free will and determinism, since the "So be it" is identical with the "It must be so" and the "It is so." A completely adequate chart would, of course, be possible only to an infinite, omniscient mind.[40]

The magical element in language is, according to Burke, irreducible; there is no proper language "as such", no discourse that can absolutely approximate reality. The lack of recognition that this is so, that verbal decrees are essentially arbitrary and limited by their relativity turns out to be the major stumbling-block for Aspirin in his quest for a final satisfaction. Indeed, this is the source of his eventual downfall, when he follows his positive decision in canto VII to "include the things / That in each other are included" by imposing orders in canto VIII ("He imposes orders as he thinks of them . . ."). He makes use of the verbal decrees of which Burke speaks, but he takes his decrees as absolute ends in themselves. They signify an imposed, not a disclosed or revealed, reality. The lyrical voice thus takes over in canto VIII, and opts for an imitation of the utterly "proper" language that Burke observes "would, of course, be possible only to an infinite, omniscient mind." However hubristic such a satisfaction may be, however ultimately doomed and self-satirical the effect — the significance of which we will discuss below — Stevens' lyrical "I" chooses, in what Vendler aptly calls "the risk of the personal voice" (Vendler 197), a language in which "So be it" ("Be silent . . . and hear / The luminous melody of proper sound"), "It must be so" ("It must / Be possible. It must be that in time

. . ."), and "It is so" ("There is a month, a year, there is a time . . .") merge into a single affirmation: "I have not but I am and as I am, I am" (*CP* 405). The apparent end of this achievement is the attainment, in a personal voice, of presence as self-presence.

But the apocalyptic hysteria in canto VIII is first preceded by the initial and provisory wisdom of Aspirin who is otherwise limited from the beginning by a purely formal feature: he is merely the hero of his parable, unable to say "I," that locus of self-presence, without being quoted. As befits his name, which shares with Professor Eucalyptus of New Haven a pharmaceutical connotation, the Canon depicts a medicinal wisdom, a wisdom reflected in Stevens' predilection for the proverbial or adagial. Gnomic sayings often have a corrective or remedial import, which is precisely the nature of the Canon's response to his sister's dangerous repressions. He acts by way of remedying her excessive zeal for propriety. He corrects her austerity with a more inclusive balance, "Contriving balance to contrive a whole" (*CP* 420), as it goes in "Auroras." Testing out the limit "Beyond which thought could not progress as thought," he dramatically answers the competing limit "Beyond which fact could not progress as fact." The logic of his action is differential and supplementary, leading to an impasse he overcomes, but only provisionally, in an apparently viable decision: *inclusion*, then, not exclusion, is the answer. Beyond a severe and unsupplied reality, beyond a purely solipsistic contemplation, the Canon posits an all-embracing imagination. The Canon is wise because he rejects the possibility of an unmediated absolute for the better belief in a necessary interdependency.

"To be at the end of fact," Stevens writes in his *Adagia*, "is not to be at the beginning of the imagination but it is to be at the end of both" (*CP*

175). The preceding adage that "Eventually an imaginary world is entirely without interest" describes the state of affairs that has lead Aspirin's sister to go into mourning for the fictive in the first place and to embrace an austere art of reality. Not only, then, do these two aphorisms suggest the necessary supplementarity of imagination and reality, but their very juxtaposition performs what they prescribe — they actually supplement each other. The one limited, partial perspective corrects the other. In this wisdom the Canon's explorations culminate. Recognizing the limits of the merely factual, he takes a pensive flight to the abysmal limits of thought. But this effort will prove just another isolated extreme, a dangerously solipsistic one, in which a scholar's erudition conceives a golden source "audible in the mountain of / His ear, the very material of the mind," so that the "aspiring" Aspirin becomes the "ascending wings he saw / And moved on them." The highly romantic effect of the passage is derivative, parodic. In its imitation of Milton (a truly romantic vice if ever there was one), it draws attention to its own speciousness, as Aspirin shoots forth to his sublime peak in an outburst of transcendence: "Forth then with huge pathetic force / Straight to the utmost crown of night he flew" (*CP* 403). In accordance with the question Stevens asks in "A Collect of Philosophy," "Does not philosophy carry us to a point at which there is nothing left except the imagination?" (*OP* 200), the Canon comes upon the impasse of the mind that seeks to satisfy itself in things of the mind alone, beyond any interest in either fact or imagination: "The nothingness was a nakedness, a point / Beyond which thought could not progress as thought."

Having proven the abysmal nature of extremes, he reaches a turning-point or crisis. Decision here, paradoxically, is a decision not to choose but to suspend choice, at least as a choice between diverse terms. What Aspirin's trial had demonstrated is that to choose *between*, to choose one thing over another, is not simply to sacrifice one sphere to another. The act of choosing between finally leaves one unable to progress at all, since without their interdependency, neither fact, thought, nor the imagination can progress on their own beyond a certain negative limit. The Canon's testing of the limits teaches him to remain *suspended* among diverse things. This is the crux of a passage in "The Noble Rider and the Sound of Words" which follows hard upon an affirmation of Milton as a figure of capable imagination (in this case, Milton is an inspiring prototype and not, as in the Canon's parody in canto VI, an anxiously imitated precursor). The equally positive mention, in the same breath, of Don Quixote, whom we associate more ironically with the fantastic and madly unreal side of the imagination, is evidence of Stevens' own refusal to choose among poetry's diverse manifestations:

> Don Quixote will make it imperative for [the poet in his creative formation] to make a choice, to come to a decision regarding the imagination and reality; and he will find that it is not a choice of one over the other and not a decision that divides them, but something subtler, a recognition that there, too, as between these poles, the universal interdependence exists, and hence his choice and his decision must be that they are equal and inseparable. (*NA* 24)

Thus, it must be a choice *of* — of diversity — and not *between* diverse terms. For the world is most satisfying when it is experienced as an interdependency of different poles, "complicate" and "amassing," like that "object the sum of its complications" in "Pineapple," "As of sections collecting towards the greenest cone" (*NA* 87), or like the "venerable complication" of the "being of sound" in "The Creations of Sound," from whom "we collect," as "An accretion from ourselves" (*CP* 311).

> He had to choose. But it was not a choice
> Between excluding things. It was not a choice
>
> Between, but of. He chose to include the things
> That in each other are included, the whole,
> The complicate, the amassing harmony.
>
> (*CP* 403)

To affirm the truth of inclusiveness over the exclusiveness of truth is to recognize, as it is put in "The Road Home," that "Words are not forms of a single word," for "In the sum of the parts, there are only the parts" (*CP* 204). As we have seen, at a similar turning point in canto IX of "An Ordinary Evening," the drastic search for "The poem of pure reality" is abruptly reversed by an additional paradoxical specification. I will take the liberty of quoting the passage again:

> We seek
> Nothing beyond reality. Within it,
>
> Everything, the spirit's alchemicana
> Included, the spirit that goes roundabout
> And through included, not merely the visible,
>
> The solid, but the movable, the moment,
> The coming on of feasts and the habits of saints,
> The pattern of the heavens and high, night air.
>
> (*CP* 471-72)

However, that the imagination's parabolic inclusiveness depends on more than the mere recognition of its necessity seems to be the moral of the Canon's subsequent failed orderings in canto VII. Oddly, Aspirin contravenes the very lesson he has just come to learn. The decision to make the choice *of*, instead of *between*, may remain a purely theoretical and not yet a practical wisdom. Even more — almost by an irony inherent in that very wisdom — the very nature of a supplementary logic may be such that the wisdom remain provisional, never approaching any proper state of realization *as such*. At the risk of too nice an observation, we might say that the wisdom of the supplement is itself in need of supplementation. We have only the notes towards a supreme fiction, not the fiction *an sich*. The best we have are "things chalked / On the sidewalk so that the pensive man may see," and see metaphorically, always only according to a figurative model of reality. The attempt practically and properly to apply such a theoretical wisdom may inevitably entail the fatal misprision of the Canon's arbitrary orderings in canto VII:

> He imposes orders as he thinks of them,
> As the fox and snake do. It is a brave affair.
> Next he builds capitols and in their corridors,
>
> Whiter than wax, sonorous, fame as it is,
> He establishes statues of reasonable men,
> Who surpassed the most literate owl, the most
>   erudite.
>
> Of elephants.   (*CP* 403)

The Canon's error is his inability yet to reason with anything more than bare reason. He does not supply reason with a "later reason" and mistakenly translates the imagination into a fixed imaginary order. Such an ordering reminds us that the Canon's title means, among other things, "authority" or "law," as in "the body of rules, principles, or standards," for example, "accepted as axiomatic and universally binding in a field of study or art" (*RHD*, "canon" (1), def. 3). The word "canon" derives from the word for "rule" or "measuring rod," which suggests Aspirin's own procedure as he mounts a kind of scholastic order in canto VII. The problem is that all measure is conventional, and therefore arbitrary. Thus, the Canon's very authority precludes a freely given revelation. He only gains in order what he loses in imaginative vision. Equally pertinent here is the idea of a canonic ordering of texts in literature, whose epitome, for our own century at least, would be "Canon" Eliot's effort to create and ensure the ground of a "modernist" classical tradition for the individual talent. But we might also think of Stevens' more flexible sense of canon, the collected works of romance and romantic writing that he is reordering, revising, rewriting, that is to say, supplementing throughout his poetry. Stevens' answer to Eliot's "Tradition and the Individual Talent" is his reasoning with a later reason. Aspirin, of course, is still reasoning only with a contemporary or past reason. His willing of a fixed order which enlists the intellect's cunning and power of recollection can never become more than an imaginary construct and an empty repetition. The mind that builds empire and colonizes is itself always only commanded and colonized by the orders of the past. But a supplementary logic demands more than an imitation, "more than an imitation for the ear" (*CP* 311).

The Canon's building of "capitols and in their corridors . . . statues of reasonable men" resembles the work of "the forfeit scholar" in "Pineapple." This scholar's "coming in" to supply the loss of the pineapple's green sting of truth also represents the incursion of a "dangerous supplement." The scholar, like nature, abhors a vacuum but, in saving us from the drastic loss of pure pineapple, he brings with him, in "an age / When pineapple on the table" is no longer "enough," the invasion of an order tainted by a vicious secondariness. The supplement, in this case, supplies, then, a loss of original meaning whose debilitation it repeats and extends, violently usurping the place of which it is "forfeit," to which it has no claim or right.

> There had been an age
> When a pineapple on the table was enough,
>
> Without the forfeit scholar coming in,
> Without his enlargings and pale arrondissements,
> Without the furious roar in his capital.
>   (*NA* 85)

Canon Aspirin's failure in canto VII also prefigures the debacle of the father figure in canto V of "The Auroras." The latter seeks to fetch by fiat a festive harmony out of thin air, only to find himself defeated and diminished, a connoisseur of chaos cowering before an inarticulate "loud, disordered mooch" (*CP* 415). Although we are not shown the collapse of Aspirin's order, we assume it. The elliptical turn to the lyrical voice of the canto's second half leaves us to imagine he will find himself in the place of "The scholar of one candle" who "sees / an Arctic effulgence flaring on the frame / Of everything he is," and "feels afraid":

> The theatre is filled with flying birds,
> Wild wedges, as of a volcano's smoke, palm-eyed
> And vanishing, a web in a corridor
>
> Or massive portico. A capitol,
> It may be, is emerging or has just
> Collapsed.   (*CP* 416)

The shortcomings of Aspirin's capitols and corridors arrayed with "statues of reasonable men" anticipate the expressed hope in the closing lines of the penultimate canto of "Notes" that "They will get it straight one day at the Sorbonne." The Sorbonne is, of course, that central place of rational learning, that capitol of cultural capitols filled, quite literally, with the "statues of reasonable men." But what is needed is not reason but more than reason, "a later reason," "the more than rational distortion, / The fiction that results from feeling" (*CP* 406) spoken of in that same canto IX, which is precisely the fictional excess Aspirin's imperious orderings seem bent upon checking and finally excluding. "That I should name you flatly, waste no words, / Check your evasions, hold you to yourself," as the poet accosts his expansive, dilatory, enlarging "Fat girl, terrestrial, my summer, my night" (*CP* 406), are words we have little trouble imagining in the mouth of Aspirin as well.[41] He may recognize the necessity of a "complicate" and "amassing harmony," but the realization he effectively bungles. His betrayal of the very truth he decides upon in canto VI — "to include the things / That in each other are included" —

is not entirely surprising if we keep in mind the pitfalls of evasion which Stevens lays out in "The Noble Rider and the Sound of Words." One stipulation in that essay is, ironically, that Stevens himself almost completely evade a definition of the word "nobility." Unfortunately, the Canon is not as captiously, punctiliously talented at evasion as is his author. For Stevens, to say that "The squirming facts exceed the squamous mind" (CP 215) would go without saying if the whole point were not to say it as well as one can, repeatedly, and in so many different ways. Aspirin slips up precisely because he is not quite slippery enough himself to recognize that the one thing which cannot be evaded is evasion, that the real, protean and multiform, will always evade us in the fictional:

> Nothing [Stevens is referring to what he calls by the provisory name of "nobility"] could be more evasive and inaccessible. Nothing distorts itself and seeks disguise more quickly. There is a shame of disclosing it and in its definite presentations a horror of it. But there it is. . . . The manner of it is, in fact, its difficulty, which each man must feel each day differently, for himself. I am not thinking of the solemn, the portentous or demoded. On the other hand, I am evading a definition. If it is defined, it will be fixed and it must not be fixed. . . . To fix it is to put an end to it. Let me show it to you unfixed. (NA 34)

Apocalyptic Hysteria: The Catachrestic Moment

"Eucalyptus" as against apokalypsis, or the sudden, extraordinary uncovering of things" is how Eleanor Cook, in a remarkable gloss on the name "Professor Eucalyptus" in "An Ordinary Evening in New Haven," has charac- terized Stevens' uncanny sense of revelation as re-veil-ation: "'Eucalyptus' means well-covered, as the flower of the eucalyptus tree is, until its time for uncovering arrives in the ordinary course of things."[42] At the same time,

Stevens repeatedly attempts apocalypse — if we can put it that way — and constantly impresses us with the urgency of the need for an uncovering of things as they are. If the only satisfaction lies in the quest for a satisfaction that is perpetually lacking, Stevens' poetry does not by the same token ever forego the dream of presence, of a plenitude without difference or *différance*. The dream remains as irresistible as the evidence of its impossibility. In Derrida's words, used in another context to describe the puzzling effect of Rousseauian desire (what he calls its "destiny of non-satisfaction"), "Differance produces what it forbids, makes possible the very thing that it makes impossible" (*G* 143). For Stevens as for Rousseau, it makes indeed an obsession of presence — one as compelling as the very forces that inevitably resist its pull.

Nowhere is this propulsion more pressing, more promising than at this critical juncture of "Notes" where the Canon's imposed order is dramatically refused in the name of discovery. But even here the disclosure still teasingly withholds the truth, even as it proffers it. The fascination of this closing crescendo of canto VII can be explained, indeed, by the peculiar tension at play between a purported apocalyptic unveiling of the real, which is so emphatically announced, and the "hysterical" use of syntax upon which that epiphany depends, between a "proper" revelation and the discovery here predicated on the *suspension* of any "law of the proper," to use Derrida's term for the economic rule governing all truth-oriented discourse:

> But to impose is not
> To discover. To discover an order as of
> A season, to discover summer and know it,
>
> To discover winter and know it well, to find,
> Not to impose, not to have reasoned at all,
> Out of nothing to have come on major weather,
>
> It is possible, possible, possible. It must
> Be possible, It must be that in time

> The real will from its crude compoundings come,
>
> Seeming, at first, a beast disgorged, unlike,
> Warmed by a desperate milk. To find the real . . .
>   (*CP* 403-04)

The event of disclosure at this point in "Notes" is curiously speculative. This proper event, or event of the proper, this Heideggerian *Er-eignis* turns out to be essentially conjectural, which accounts for the compulsive tone that seems to invade the canto. We sense the effort to give birth to something that is already a ghost of itself, the event of the proper as a simulation of the proper: not paradise regained, but paradise refeigned. Belief here hardly suggests belief in the truth of disclosure. Like Coleridge's willing suspension of disbelief, or like the belief in metaphor in "The Pure Good of Theory" which sticks "to the nicer knowledge of / Belief, that what it believes in is not true" (*CP* 332), it is a belief in the fiction of something, the recognition that the real is revealed only when "secreted" in a figurative covering ("Secrete us in reality," the orator is commanded at the end of "Repetitions of a Young Captain" [*CP* 310]). Not surprisingly, the contradiction of such a belief "in a fiction, which you know to be a fiction, there being nothing else" (*OP* 163) induces a visible note of hysteria, which takes the form of an impossible effort to translate the speculative into the actual, the present — and into a presence as well.

Stevens' use of tenses is especially crucial. It reflects what Helen Vendler calls, also accounting for similar shifts in "Owl's Clover" and "Description without Place," the "manipulation of tenses to yield apocalypse, as conjecture . . . becomes hypothesis . . . and hypothesis is hypostatized to a visionary present tense" (Vendler 220). This "manipulation" makes the reader a bemused but skeptical observer trying to follow a sleight-of-hand that has already slipped the nut under another shell.   First of all, we are in the subjunctive, the realm of mere possibility: "It is possible, possible, possible."   The urgency conveyed by the repetition seems to indicate that an hysterical need for the eventual is encroaching on an object which is still completely speculative.   It is a true invocation, as though by mere insistence on the event's possibility we may be assured that "the real will from its crude compoundings come."   This driven lyrical voice has left far behind the cautionary doubt of Saint John's Back-Ache who, if he admits the possibility of an absolute, unmediated presence, does so only grudgingly: "It may be, may be.   It is possible" (*CP* 437).   With the repeating of "possible" we shift surreptitiously from the indicative "is" of "is possible" to the imperative in the auxiliary "must":   "It must be possible." Expressed is a certain propriety, not of that which necessarily is, but of that which *should* in fact be.   But the "must" here is even more sneaky, since it still affirms only the possibility, not the event itself.   There is something syllogistic (in the pejorative sense) about Stevens' furtive shifts of verb tenses and moods here; it is reminiscent of the speciousness in the equally stealthy change from "must" to "is" in the lines from canto IV of "Credences":   "The utmost *must* be good and *is*" (*CP* 374, emphasis added).   Just as the critical distinction between the initial subjunctive mood and the imperative is lost forever in the shuffle (in the move from the speculative to an unconditional, categorical necessity, as "may" becomes "must"), so too in the next step the significant difference between the actual event and the mere demand for it is skirted and eluded in the shift from the imperative "must" to the future "will" of the subordinate clause in the lines: "It must be that in time / The real will from its crude compoundings comes. . . ."   What began as only conjecture or possibility, hypothetical and speculative, has now become a future actuality, an assured, foreknown event. The merely speculative is treated here as a proper (authentic) event, which, in an almost Heideggerian fashion, is also an event of the proper. But the speciousness of the logic only succeeds in undercutting the very ground of such an affirmation. Moreover, the deceptive, syllogistic, elliptical turn of the argument is intended to be only partially concealed. The suspect nature of the invocation not only is, but is expressly shown to be an indispensable aspect of this apocalyptic event, which is affirmed as both proper and entirely speculative at once. This advent of the real may, in fact, ask that we think of it as purely conjectural, hypothetical, but without — paradoxically — unilaterally or unequivocally rejecting its "reality." Otherwise this event cannot take place, cannot take place as that by which, to invoke Mallarmé's "RIEN N'AURA EU LIEU QUE LE LIEU"[43] from *Le Coup de dés*, nothing will have taken place but place, which means that nothing takes place, nothing but an effect of pure speculation.

Vendler quite rightly describes this elliptical shifting as a "manipulation of tenses to yield apocalypse." But it does not follow that Stevens is simply manipulating the reader. The reader may in fact be invited to catch the cheating going on, to recognize that with this apocalypse we have ironically never left the speculative even for a moment. For if Vendler's extraordinary sensitivity (hard to find equalled in any other critic) to the quirks of this poet's use of words allows her to nab Stevens every time he slips another card from the bottom of the deck, an all-important question still remains to be asked: what if "the sleight-of-hand man" is doing everything in his power to get caught, yet without ever seeming to want to get caught? In that case, is he actually cheating, and what could be the ulterior motive behind such a red-handed clumsiness, which is perhaps all too clever by half? Stevens discusses, in a letter, a similar invocation of apocalypse in "Owl's Clover" (the passage beginning "Time's fortune near . . ." [*OP* 61]), and outlines, presumably to his own disadvantage, the same overtly specious and hysterical argument for an eventual final disclosure of reality.   Just as in "Notes," the event exposes itself as groundless speculation, with signs as well of the same obsessive insistence: "Time's fortune near = now that the disinherited are to come into an unexpected inheritance: Time's categorical inheritance, the fortune concealed in it *must* be so, it *cannot* be otherwise (It will, it will be changed and things that will be realized.)"[44]

Apocalypse is finally the fiction of apocalypse.   This may seem a rather nice distinction, but we are concerned here, after all, with the "nicer knowledge of / Belief" (*CP* 332), with "apocalypse," not apocalypse; that is, with the supreme fiction *as* fiction, with the remarking or quoting of a signifier that, in this case, has the peculiar irony of signifying the end of the signifying process, the fading away of all signifiers in face of a compelling, transcendental signified.   By remarking or quoting, I mean that the passage alludes to, cites or summons "apocalypse" by the metonymic use of the "beast" that is such a notable companion of revelation in the Biblical and literary sources.   Stevens' "beast disgorged" is, by the detour of Yeats's "Second Coming," a summoning of the apocalyptic beasts in Daniel and Revelation:

> It must be that in time
> The real will from its crude compoundings come,
>
> Seeming, at first, a beast disgorged, unlike,
> Warmed by a desperate milk.

The image of these "crude compoundings," which as the real emerges dissolve and vanish, recalls that perfected "proper" scene in "The Poems of Our Climate," which, clean and white, has "Stripped one of all one's torments, concealed / The evilly compounded, vital I" (*CP* 193).   As these lines suggest, this stripping is still only another form of concealment.   In "Notes" one is stripped in a similarly ambiguous way —   "of every fiction except one," that of revelation itself, which is still a fiction and therefore suggests that in Stevens' apocalypse the real has not evaded every covering; in fact, it is only disclosed in this very evasion of the real.   As Ozymandias knowingly observes in his put-down of Nanzia Nunzio's offering of her favours in canto VII of "It must Change":   "the spouse, the bride / Is never naked. A fictive covering / Weaves always glistening from the heart and mind" (*CP* 396).   Also of moment here is Pierce's analogy for *unlimited semiosis*, the infinite regression of representations and interpretants;   he uses the kindred image of a "stripping," and equally recognizes that meaning, however progressively diaphanous, is always clothed by interpretation, by a representation or sign:

> The meaning of a representation can be nothing but a representation.   In fact it is nothing but the representation itself conceived as stripped of irrelevant clothing.   But this clothing never can be completely stripped off; it is only changed for something more diaphanous.   So there is an infinite regression here.   Finally, the interpretant is nothing but another representation to which the torch of truth is handed along; and as representation, it has its interpretant again. Lo, another infinite series.[45]

Purity, as shown in "The Poems of Our Climate," is only a fiction that conceals and threatens to obstruct a vital imperfection.   So in "Notes" the real invoked as shedding "its crude compoundings" may suggest a result as fatal as it is compelling.   If the compounding is vital, the fading away of this complexity may well be the opposite.   What saves us from this unmediated disclosure is, ironically, the real itself.   We are not to be stripped of *every* fiction, not to be divested of this final one: "The fiction of an absolute."   This fiction is recognized *as a fiction*. The ultimate revelation is that revelation is itself a figure, that a disclosure of the real is possible only "in the intricate evasions of as" (*CP* 486). We enter reality only secretly, in the nicer knowledge that there is no way *not* to cover one's nakedness. Nor is this to insist that the real is a fiction but, rather, that we only ever know the real *as* fiction, which is a significantly different proposition.

Not surprisingly, in light of the impossibility of any unmediated disclosure of the real, a certain hysteria pervades this passage of "Notes." It is reflected in the very image of "a beast disgorged, unlike, / Warmed by a desperate milk." "Disgorged," this apocalyptic creature of the throat ultimately gives voice to "The luminous melody of proper sound" which, at the end of canto VII, the competing Angel is ordered to take in silence. But it is brought into the world only by the need for itself; the advent of such a beast only calms the very want or desperation that, like its mother, has brought it forth and nursed it into life. This *hysterical* self-generation recalls "the weaving round the wonder of its need" of the form in "The Owl in the Sarcophagus," where the figures attendant upon our extreme experience with death are "visible to the eye that needs, / Needs out of the whole necessity of sight" (*CP* 432), as though they only ever evolved from their own acute necessity. A similarly insatiable desire for a proper speech appears in canto VIII of "An Ordinary Evening": "Our breath is like a desperate element / That we must calm, the origin of a mother tongue / With which to speak to her" (*CP* 470-71). Once again, necessity is the mother of invention, need, in a circular way, the origin of the very speech that satisfies, as though need fulfilled itself in its own self-expression.

The apocalyptic beast in "Notes" is also a close cousin of that "Fire-monster in the Milky Brain" or "beast of light" in "The Pure Good of Theory."

In canto IV of that poem it is equally a case of "a beast disgorged": a guttural monster, a deformed creature born from the throat, a future being of speech or sound whose specular emergence suggests, as in "Notes," a bottomless, abysmal desire. A desperate self-fulfillment marks "the beast of light," as it groans

in half-exploited gutturals

The need of its element, the final need
Of final access to its element —
Of access like the page of a wiggy book,

Touched suddenly by the universal flare
For a moment, a moment in which we read and repeat
The eloquence of light's faculties.   (*CP* 333)

The "need of its element" gives birth here, spontaneously, to that which fulfills it, an apocalyptic speech or script, a book that is primarily a rhetorical achievement, an effect of "The eloquences of light's faculties." The "universal flare" is also homonymically the "flair" of an acute sense of style or manner. Vision, for Stevens, is not a seeing beyond all fiction. It is a verbal fluency. We "read and repeat" a final reality that is only imaginatively and figuratively accessible, which we enter only as a world of words, "like the page of a wiggy book." The "beast of light," like the apocalyptic "beast disgorged" of "Notes," is born, groaning in "half-exploited gutturals," from the throat's drastic hunger for a final eloquence, for a fiction that its own hysteria, "The final need / Of final access to its element," generates to satisfy itself.

The inherent lack of satisfaction in Stevens' demand for the "fiction of an absolute" or "luminous melody of proper sound" recalls Mallarmé's "Don du poème," where the poet presents his starved, half-dead poem to his nursing wife, desperately pleading that she resuscitate it at "le sein / Par qui coule en blancheur sybilline la femme / Pour les lèvres que l'air du vierge azur affame." Rimbaud's famous closing line from "Conte" also comes to mind: "La musique savante manque à notre désir." For Stevens, this insatiability means that a proper speech is always exorbitant. "The supplement itself," as Derrida sums it up, "is quite exorbitant, in every sense of the word" (*G* 163). This idea of the exorbitancy of all signification is also theoretically very similar to Lacan's depiction of the desire for the real, which is always "situated in dependence on demand — which, by being articulated in signifiers, leaves a metonymic remainder that runs under it, an element that is not indeterminate, which is a condition both, absolute and unapprehensible, an element necessarily lacking, unsatisfied, impossible, misconstrued (*méconnu*), an element that is called desire."[48] That word which fulfills apocalypse brings into play at the same time an irreducible extra, like that "wiggy book" in "The Pure Good of Theory," which if it supplies a lack is also purely additional, excessive ("wiggy" suggests that the book is artificial, supplementary, and eccentric as well). It is certainly not an event of the proper in Heidegger's sense of *Er-eignis* but, as eloquence, affirms propriety or decorum in the rhetorical sense. The beast slouching to be born in "Notes" resembles that "antipodal, far-fetched creature worthy of birth" (*OP* 96), which is a metaphor of metaphor in "A Discovery of Thought," a poem whose subject is also a version of apocalypse. Revelation in that poem does not culminate in a transcendence of signification in a final meaning. Rather, it is a moment in which we are born again and live on, "the effort to be born / Surviving being born, the event of life" (*OP* 96). Even if this "first word," which is "of susceptible being arrived, / The immaculate disclosure of the secret no more obscured," seems to suggest at first glance an original word of being which has overcome all figuration before the pure evidence of the real, the event of disclosure in this poem, and by extension in "Notes," announces, on the contrary, the *difference* of this "event of life" as an emergence of "The accent of deviation in the living thing," as a birth of metaphor, not its end.

I have been using the word metaphor, but more specifically what concerns us here is a very particular species of metaphor: catachresis. The hysterical (from *hysterikos* 'of the womb') generation of a new and deviant word typifies a recurrent topic in Stevens' poetry; it is even a sort of *topos*, the commonplace of un-commonplace, the staging of the trope of invention, of a word born out of nothing which itself gives birth to reality. The real is disclosed only as a figurative effect or verbal issue. The need for a new word, in order to name a reality that has no name and no reality until named, impregnates itself (hysterically, if you like) and gives birth to a monster, a grotesque deviation from any natural, normal form or type: a gross verbal impropriety. This deviation corresponds in fact to the very definition of catachresis as "an improper use of words"; etymologically, "contrary-to-usage-ness." In "The Owl," the extreme need for the vital forms that can help us to cope with death gives birth to a trio of bewildering figures, "monsters of elegy" (*CP* 435) like the centaur-like, misaligned and hybrid figure of "peace, godolphin and fellow, estranged, estranged, / Hewn in their middle as the beam of leaves" (*CP* 434), which is an example of two-bodied grotesquery analogous to the verbal misapplication that goes by the name of catachresis. So in "Notes" the real is born in the monstrous shape of an unseemly and dissonant "beast disgorged, unlike." Like Derrida's "future," as he invokes it in the exergue to *Of Grammatology*, which is only to be "anticipated in the form of an absolute danger," Stevens' violently uttered apocalyptic word. radically open to the unknown, is "that which breaks absolutely with constituted normality and can only be proclaimed, *presented*, as a sort of monstrosity" (5).

Catachresis is the supreme example of figurative impropriety. It is itself not even a proper figure, for unlike metaphor it does not substitute for an already existent name, but replaces nothing, naming by transference something for which there is no name. Catachresis is "A name for something that never could be named," which is how Stevens describes the outmoded use of "Phoebus" for the sun in the opening canto of "Notes"; in that same canto, he then turns around and names the sun, catachrestically, of course: "The sun / Must bear no name, gold flourisher. . . ." (*CP* 381). "Gold flourisher" is a perfect example of catachresis, a name that, like the "legs" of a table or chair, fills a lexical gap, supplies the dearth of a name. This need is always most pressing in limit-situations, at the origin or at the end of a history of naming. Stevens is fascinated by these two turning-points or *crises*: the auroral moment of naming and the setting of a verbal sun. The first two cantos of "Notes" contain between them both the uncrowning of old names ("Let Phoebus slumber and die in autumn umber, / Phoebus is dead, ephebe.") and the crowning of the new ("desire at the end of winter"), the rising and setting, the turning of a sun that language cannot finally name except improperly.[49] This catachrestic moment is as close as we get to an origin in Stevens, for here original naming and original reality intersect and are fully interdependent. In the apocalyptic mode, further-more, as in the climax of "Notes" where the discovery of the real is so urgently announced, original and final naming are joined; the origin is supposedly resumed and reappropriated, with the accrued interest that comes with such deferral, in the finally restored proper name, that name for the sun, for the elusive reality that is the obsessive object of quest throughout Stevens' poetry. This moment, however, is always complicated by another, repressed economy of signification whereby, in Derrida's words, "proper meaning derives from derivation" (*M* 333).

Discovery is *inventio*. The return to an origin through the resumptive advent of a final reality is nothing but a new and radical displacement. The arrival of reality is a derivation, a de-rival.[50]

Stevens' apocalypse, then, even at its most urgent, is still *eucalypse*; it uncovers, reveals, only in re-covering. As in Peirce, the regression towards an approachable truth comes up against an instance which is, significantly, both an end and a beginning, a revolution; the critical return to an origin is at the same time a digression, which opens the sign to its future. The revelatory word affirms no *proper* reality, no restored or recovered truth. It affirms instead a deviation, a distortion, a catachrestic, "monstrous" departure from any stringent state of being or literal meaning.

The Satire of the Abyss

Canto VIII of "It Must Give Pleasure" is perhaps the culminating moment of Stevens' quest for an extreme and certain satisfaction in "Notes." If no word will satisfy, if the hunger for a proper speech seems bottomless, insatiable, here there is still the hope that one might yet achieve some form of self-satisfaction, grounded in the propriety of an identification affirmed between voice and self. The model for such an effort is "The Well Dressed Man with a Beard," and "a speech / Of the self that must sustain itself on speech" (*CP* 247). Canto VII's closing apostrophe, "Be silent in your luminous cloud and hear / The luminous melody of proper sound" (*CP* 404), sets the stage for canto VIII's self-conscious *agon* between the poetic self and his angel. John Hollander ingeniously associates "the luminous melody of proper sound" with Wittgenstein's statement that "A tune is a kind of tautology, it is complete in itself; it satisfies itself."[51]   Indeed, this circularity aptly characterizes the flight of the lyric self in canto VIII, as it turns in the abyss of a circle without any centre but its own uncertain self-affirmation:

> Angel,
> Be silent in your luminous cloud and hear
> The luminous melody of proper sound.

VIII

> What am I to believe? If the angel in his cloud,
> Serenely gazing at the violent abyss,
> Plucks on his strings to pluck abysmal glory,
>
> Leaps downward through evening's revelations, and
> On his spredden wings, needs nothing but deep space,
> Forgets the gold centre, the golden destiny,
>
> Grows warm in the motionless motion of his flight,
> Am I that imagine this angel less satisfied?
> Are the wings his, the lapis-haunted air?
>
> Is it he or is it I that experience this?
> Is it I then that keep saying there is an hour
> Filled with expressible bliss, in which I have
>
> No need, am happy, forget need's golden hand,
> An satisfied without solacing majesty,
> And if there is an hour there is a day,
>
> There is a month, a year, there is a time
> In which majesty is a mirror of the self:
> I have not but I am and as I am, I am.
>
> These external regions, what do we fill them with
> Except reflections, the escapades of death,
> Cinderella fulfilling herself beneath the roof?
> (*CP* 404-405)

This extraordinary passage comes as close as Stevens' poetry ever will to a finally sufficing speech, as close as ever to a *saturating* fiction. So pressing is the desire for a final satisfaction that a certain hysteria carries over from canto VII. The canto's sustained rapture is marked by a notable lapse of the strategic or of those "stratagems / Of the spirit" (*CP* 376) on which Stevens usually relies, and remains unguarded, at least at first glance, by any irony, except in the final stanza which abruptly satirizes the lyrical fairy-tale that has preceded it. The shift in canto VII from pure speculation to future actuality ("It is . . . It must be possible . . . that in time / The real will . . . come") finds a counterpart in canto VIII in the building sequence "there is . . . there is . . . there is." We move from mere hypothesis and questioning, which however persuasive as rhetoric still comes across — and perhaps because of the obvious hope to persuade, to convince — as uncertainty, to the culmination in a diminished but curiously satisfying affirmation: "I have not but I am and as I am, I am."[52] This lyrical trajectory, undoubtedly eloquent and powerful in its effect, betrays nonetheless a suspicious compulsion and speciousness. The fulfilment remains in the final analysis purely speculative, and moreover recognizes itself as such: "These external regions, what do we fill them with / Except reflections. . . ."

Bloom's interpretation of the apparent hysteria in the closing stanzas of canto VII, a mood that spills over into canto VIII in the unilateral insistence on self-affirmation, differs significantly from that of Vendler whom Bloom claims "reads the tone as desperation":

> That there is an anxiety of influence at the origin here I do not doubt, and I myself called this a dignified desperation in a commentary written some years ago. But I would dissent now both from Vendler and my earlier self. Repetitive and accumulative the rhetoric certainly is here, but it is too controlled to be hysterical, and Stevens is too shrewd and too sure of himself, at this point, to be desperate. He is overinsistent, because he is arguing against his own reductiveness, but his insistence is upon the possibility of a middle path between reduction and expansion, between Mrs. Uruguay and the rabbit as king of the ghosts.
>
> (*The Poems* 211)

This navigated "middle path between reduction and expansion" consciously steers between extremes. It is, paradoxically, even a deliberate strategy or manoeuver of hysteria, a desperate obsessiveness that is not serious since it recognizes itself as a ploy, a provisional feint or fiction, the better to lead us to a supplementary truth which, in this case, is the very truth of the supplement — which is, of course, no "truth" as such.

From the first line of canto VIII ("What am I to believe?"), the affirmation has already posed itself in the interrogative from which it is not to escape. The aporia here is initially rooted in the poetic self's anxiety that it equal and even surpass the prowess and satisfaction of the angelic power ironically emanating from its own imagination. This anxiety is never really overcome, nor is the questioning ever dropped. The ensuing affirmation never eludes the conditional and interrogative, but remains subordinated to the latter, if only syntactically. By the time we arrive at the lines "I have not but I am . . . ," we still have never left the shadow of initial hypothesis and speculation. What appears to be a definitive self-assertion is still pitched in the inaugural note of questioning and urgency. Given this, it comes as no surprise that it should immediately uncrown itself in the very next words as nothing but "Reflections . . . Cinderella fulfilling herself beneath the roof," as nothing, that is, but a speculative majesty, a specular and specious image of crowning fulfilment, "In which majesty is a mirror of the self." The self may hold up majesty to its gaze for a moment as though it were to look into a mirror, and yet the self in this canto — "I that imagine this angel" — is no more than an imagination, a source of, and a speculator in, images and reflections.

The "violent abyss" evoked in canto VIII. from which the poet would, like his angel, "pluck" "abysmal glory" brings to mind further such abysmal instances in Stevens' poetry.[53] Canto IV of "It Must Be Abstract" speaks of those "Abysmal instruments" which "make sounds like pips / Of the sweeping meanings that we add to them" (*CP* 384). Such instruments evoke, of course, not only the one twanged by the "insatiable actor" or "metaphysician in the dark" in "Of Modern Poetry," but also the "abysmal melody" in "The Owl in the Sarcophagus," which originates in "a likeness of the earth, / That by resemblance twanged him through and through" (*CP* 433). Significantly, canto IV of this first part of "Notes" also concerns a later reason, which is an equal concern of canto II in "The Owl." There "the forms of thought" make our passage into death "as into a time / That of itself stood still, perennial, / Less time than place, less place than thought of place" (*CP* 432-33). Place here is only accessible as a figure, or thought, of place. In canto IV of "It Must be Abstract," the same logic means that all priority reverts to a secondary stage of supplementarity. Such a reversion is endless, because there is no "first idea" which is not itself preceded by a precursor:

> The first idea was not our own. Adam
> In Eden was the father of Descartes
> And Eve made air the mirror of herself,
>
> Of her sons and of her daughters. They found them-
> selves
> In heaven as in a glass; a second earth;
> And in the earth itself they found a green —
>
> The inhabitants of a very varnished green.
> (*CP* 383)

But even this Edenic presence, this earthly paradise which is only a speculative, "varnished" reproduction of earth ("gross effigy and simulacrum" [*CP* 87]), and not the earth itself, is also preceded — not by an unmediated presence, but once again by a supplement of place, a mythic earth.

> But the first idea was not to shape the clouds
> In imitation. The clouds preceded us
>
> There was a muddy centre before we breathed.
> There was a myth before the myth began,
> Venerable and articulate and complete. (*CP* 383)

From a prior myth of the earth we have fallen into mere mimicry, which at the same time supplies the absence of that myth through the capacity of reason and imagination to imitate and replicate. These instruments are a belated development, a later reason, postdating the retreating origin they supplement and which, in a sense, they have themselves forfeited. We live in a derivative place, in the mere images of "a place / That is not our own and, much more, not ourselves" (*CP* 383). The poem has sprung from the need to remedy our dispossession and estrangement on earth with a mimetic energy. But we inhabit therefore only "a place dependent on ourself" (*CP* 401), a place that is only a secondary interpretation, and not a *locus pro prius*.

But because this movement towards an original presence or absolute priority returns us always to an earlier idea, there is no reason that is not a later reason, no idea that is not itself the supplement of a supplement. A "before," a prior, a precedent, always antedates us but by the same token no pure priority is conceivable, only the later of an inevitable *Nachträglichkeit*. What claims priority here is "a myth before the myth began," not only "Venerable" and "complete," but moreover "articulate." But the earth, then, would never be anything more, anything less, than the myth of earth, venerable and complete only in a language always already cultivating its broken soil. Meaning is always already under way, *en route*. We have been dispossessed of an original place, of what, in canto XXII of "An Ordinary Evening," is called "the predicate of bright origin" (*CP* 481), not because we have fallen from an "original earliness" in which the first idea immediately inheres, but because the first idea is always already a later idea, always already implicated in a *semiosis*, in a signifying process:

> Yet the sense
> Of cold and earliness is a daily sense,
>
> Not the predicate of bright origin.
> Creation is not renewed by images
> Of lone wanderers. To re-create, to use
>
> The cold and earliness and bright origin
> Is to search.　　　(*CP* 481)

The necessity for this affirmation of a re-creation becomes all the more obvious in the closing passages of "Notes." The very progress of the poem, indeed, is an adventure of discovery by which we re-read the earlier canto VI of "It Must Be Abstract," for example, from the later "supplementary" perspective of a celebration of the supplement in cantos IX and X of "It Must Give Pleasure." There we find the praise of repetition as "a thing final in itself and, therefore, good" (*CP* 406). Repetition is, of course, the very essence of a later reason: the recognition that we are condemned — or freed, released, depending on how one decides to interpret it — only to repeat a prior meaning. In canto VIII, the self is still to some degree under an anxiety of influence, never sure if he is speaking in his own or in his master's voice, overshadowed by that angelic power to which his imagination desperately aspires. Like the melancholic protagonist of Kierkegaard's *Repetition*, he has not yet understood the reality of repetition, and therefore suffers meaninglessly.[54] To be "he that of repetition is most master" is to realize that one is not the master, and that meaning is, since its production depends on repetition, the necessary condition for a later reason being the power to repeat.

There is no "the," no truth of repetition ("Where was it one first heard of the truth? The the"), which is of course the shocking discovery of Kierkegaard's narrator in *Repetition*, when he has completed his investigation into repetition: that there is no repetition *as such*. For there is nothing proper to repetition. Repeatability is the necessary condition for all quiddity and essence, and therefore it cannot itself be understood or explained in terms of that which it in fact makes possible. In canto IX, Stevens joins in with Kierkegaard to observe that "Repetition is reality, and it is the seriousness of life."[55] Both authors also invoke the problem of the "exception," which repetition resolves, since it transcends the opposition between the exception and the universal. In Stevens' words, "Perhaps, / The man-hero is not the exceptional monster, / But he that of repetition is most master" (*CP* 406). The obsessive poet in Kierkegaard's story is, furthermore, cured and restored to life only when he rejects the power of recollection for the gratuitous doubling of repetition. "Is there not then a repetition? Did I not get everything doubly restored? Did I not get myself again, precisely in such a way that I must doubly feel its significance?"[56] Similarly, Stevens begins with an almost hysterical need for revelation, and only in ridding himself of the desire for a merely recollective identity and power comes to affirm at last "the merely going round, / Until merely going round is a final good" (*CP* 405). Thus, the anxiously imitated angel of canto VIII becomes instead, in canto IX, an equal partner in the dance and festival of a repetition fully celebrated for itself alone:

> Whistle aloud, too weedy wren. I can
> Do all that angels can. I enjoy like them,
> Like men besides, like men in light secluded,
>
> Enjoying angels. . . .
>
> . . . .
>
> And we enjoy like men, the way a leaf
> Above the table spins its constant spin,
> So that we look at it with pleasure, look
>
> At it spinning its eccentric measure. Perhaps,
> The man-hero is not the exceptional monster,
> But he that of repetition is most master.
>
> (*CP* 405-06)

This festive canto celebrating "the pleasures of merely circulating" further brings to mind Heidegger's feast of thinking, of meditation, which derives from thought's circular progress, as he evokes it in "The Origin of the Work of Art":

> Anyone can easily see that we are moving in a circle. Ordinary understanding demands that this circle be avoided because it violates logic.
> . . .
> Thus we are compelled to follow the circle. This is neither a makeshift nor a defect. To enter upon this path is the strength of thought, to continue on it is the feast of thought, assuming that thinking is a craft. Not only is the main step from work to art a circle like the step from art to work, but every separate step that we attempt circles in this circle.[57]

This festive circularity of thought converts the vicious circle into a preservative one, which restores and affirms — opens the path or way, instead of completing and closing it. In "Parergon," Derrida speaks of his own discourse on Heidegger's circular discourse on art and suggests it is

> as if a discourse on the circle should also trace (*décrire*) a circle, and maybe that very one it describes (*décrit*), trace a circular movement at the very moment it describes a circular movement, the *décrire* ["to trace" or "to describe"] displacing itself in its meaning; or rather, as if a discourse on the abyss should know (*connaître*) the abyss, in the sense of experiencing an event, an influence (*au sens où l'on connaît ce qui arrive, ce qui affecte*), the way one knows a failure or a success rather than an object. The circle and the abyss, then, the circle in abyss (*VEP* 29; trans. mine)

This conversion of a vicious into a festive circle is what is at stake in "the risk of the personal voice" of which Vendler speaks in reference to canto VIII. The imitation of a prior angelic majesty discloses a circularity that may be taken in either a negative or positive sense. To affirm the circle, which is the explicit theme of canto IX, is to recognize at the same time that the fulfillment in canto VIII, "In which majesty is a mirror of the self," represents a speculation and not just a plentitude reflecting the self, and therefore must be degraded at the same time. This is the rhythm of *fort-da*, of a child playing, as in the logic of uncertain speculation that Derrida in "To Speculate — on 'Freud'" speculates is at work in *Beyond the Pleasure Principle*, a "now-you-see-it-now-you-don't" performed in the mirror of the self, or like "The Sense of the Sleight-of-hand-Man" in which "One's grand flights, one's Sunday baths, / One's tootings at the weddings of the soul / Occur as they occur" (*CP* 222). They must occur as they occur, and they must go as they have come as well — come and go and come and go all day, like "The hermit in a poet's metaphors" (*CP* 381). To know repetition in Stevens' sense involves a vertigo, an abysmal movement, a turning about and "round and round" by which we come to know repetition not as a concept or idea but, in a paradoxical active submission, as an advent ("au sens," as Derrida writes, "où l'on connaît ce qui arrive") that one assents to and even wills and affirms, a saying "yes" to this, "the merely going round, / Until merely going round is a final good, / The way wine comes at a table in a wood" (*CP* 405).

Satisfaction, then, must finally forget need itself, that lack which sustains a proper economy of desire. But if one foregoes lack, "forget[s] need's golden hand," it is because at stake is not the absence of something properly lacking. Gone without is the very syntax of without. Need is not met and satisfied; it is revoked, suspended, foregone. The rejection of "the gold centre, the golden destiny" means that one now abstains from belief in a "white mythology," in the absolute destiny of a proper naming or identity, contradictorily evoked in the opening canto of "Notes," where the desired centre of all naming, the sun, "Must bear no name, gold flourisher, but be / in the difficulty of what it is to be" (*CP* 381). The controlling desire or need for this centre and destiny now foregone, one is released from "need's golden hand," from the quest after that supreme object for which there is the dearth of a proper name. What takes its place is the free affirmation of simply being, without any purpose or end.

I do not possess the world in such an affirmation, nor most of all my self. I do not possess, or command as by fiat, as if to say "I am that I am," nor even simply and assertively do I declare "I am": but without plentitude, with nothing but the relaxed stricture of an open-ended conjunction, what I affirm is "I am only *as* I am." Stevens' affirmation resembles that of one of his most illustrious successors, John Ashbery, in his "Self-Portrait in a Convex Mirror," where the words of the poem are said to be "only speculation / (From the Latin *speculum*, mirror)," while the glance of the subject of the poet's speculation, Parmigianino, who paints himself in the glass is described as reflecting only "a pure/ Affirmation that doesn't affirm anything."[58] In Stevens' case as well, affirmation doesn't affirm anything, except itself, in that gratuitous moment when being and the saying "yes" to being are one and the same thing. But no ground could possibly make firm such an event, except this very act of *af-firmation*. As Bloom has pointed out, such an abysmal satisfaction is connected, in canto VIII, to a certain satirical effect: "To be satisfied is to be sated and to be sad, to be self-satirized, and we can recall Freud's melancholy reflection that for the human psyche there can be no satisfaction in satisfaction anyway" (*The Poems* 213). In the bottomless aspiration of the self, and in this eventually groundless affirmation, there is an inescapable element of comedy, underscored, as we have seen, in the self-satirization of the canto's closing stanza with its image of "Cinderella fulfilling herself beneath the roof."

What does satisfaction and its satire entail, then, for Stevens? It gives perhaps the most formidable evidence of that "lack of repose" with which we began this extended discussion, and of the essential relativity and profound instability of any single position, ground, or foundation, of any determining vantage point from which the signification of Stevens' work might be dominated. Satisfaction will always come to this ultimate — to use Derrida's inspired term — "satire of the abyss." In such a *general* as opposed to a *restricted* or *proper* economy of desire, the abyss is in no sense a negative or nihilistic factor to be warded off. It guarantees in fact the vitality of a limitless process of poetic signification. In "Parergon," as part of his discussion of Heidegger's "The Origin of the Work of Art," Derrida provides the following suggestive and somewhat dizzying commentary, which may also serve to bring the circle of our own discussion to its completion, or rather to a more appropriate open end:

> The encircling of the circle drew us toward the abyss. But like every *production*, that of the abyss managed to saturate what it hollowed out.
>
> It is enough to say: abyss and satire of the abyss.
>
> What enjoyment has the festival, the "feast of thought" (*Fest des Denkens*) involved in the *Kreisgang*, which has entered into the *pas* ["step" and "not"] of the circle? Opening up and filling in the abyss at the same time: *den Kreisgang vollziehen.*
>
> Interrogate its comic effect. You can never miss it, if the abyss is never enough, if it must stay — undecided — between the groundless and the grounding of the ground. The operation of "mise en abyme" is always busy (activity, occupation, mastery of the subject), somewhere, filling up, filled with abyss, filling up with the abyss
>
> (*VEP* 40; trans. mine)

Notes to Chapter 2

1. The law of the proper or the law of the house is a focal point, throughout Derrida's many writings, for his deconstruction of Western metaphysics. In "The *Retrait* of Metaphor," *Enclitic*, 2, No. 2 (all 1978), 17, Derrida gives the following outline of what he intends by the word "economy": "Now I must speak here economically of economy. I name them algebraically.

a. Economy in order to articulate what I am going to say about the other possible tropical system (*tropique*) of *usure* (usury), the one of interest, of surplus value, of fiduciary calculus or of usury rate . . . although it comes as a heterogeneous and discontinuous supplement, in a tropical divergence (*écart*) irreducible to that of being-worn-out or worn.

b. Economy in order to articulate this possibility about the law-of-the-house and the law of the proper, *oiko-nomia*, which had made me reserve a particular status for the two motifs of light and home ('Borrowed home,' says Du Marsais in citation in his metaphoric definition of metaphor: 'Metaphor is a species of Trope: the word which one uses in metaphor is taken in another sense than the proper meaning, *it is*, so to speak, in a *borrowed home*, says an ancient; this is common and essential to all Tropes.' *Des Tropes*, Ch. 10).

c. Economy in order to steer, if one may say so, towards this value of *Ereignis*, so difficult to translate and whose entire family (*ereignen, eigen, eigens, enteignen*) intermingles with increasing density, in Heidegger's last texts, with the themes of the proper, of propriety, of propriation, of de-propriating on one hand, with that of light, of the clearing, of the eye on the other (Heidegger says to implicate *Er-Aügnis* in *Ereignis*); and finally in current usage, with what happens as event: what is the place, the taking-place, or the metaphoric event, or of the metaphoric? What is happening, today, with metaphor?

d. Economy finally, because the economic consideration appears to me to have an essential relation with these determinations of passage or of fraying (*frayage*) according to the modes of the trans-fer or of the translation (*Übersetzen*) which I believe I must link here to the question of metaphoric transfer (*Übertragung*). By reason of this economy of economy, I proposed to give this discourse the title of *retrait*. Not economies in the plural, but withdrawal (*retrait*).

2. Derrida discusses this key notion of the supplement in *Of Grammatology*. See especially part II, 2, entitled ". . . That Dangerous Supplement . . .," pp. 141-164. In commenting upon Rousseau's text, Derrida attempts to specify precisely the link between writing and supplementarity. Although he is concerned primarily here with the logic of Rousseau's depiction of desire, that logic is not singular but is generally true of a certain representation of writing and desire; it is merely that its representation of Rousseau's writings is exemplary: "What we have tried to show by following the guiding line of the 'dangerous supplement,' is that in what one calls the real life of these existences 'of flesh and bone,' beyond and behind what one believes can be circumscribed as Rousseau's text, there has never been anything but writing; there have never been anything but supplements, substitutive significations which could only come forth in a chain of

differential references, the 'real' supervening, and being added only while taking on meaning from a trace and from an invocation of the supplement, etc. And thus to infinity, for we have read, *in the text*, that the absolute present, Nature, that which words like 'real mother' name, have always already escaped, have never existed; that what opens meaning and language is writing as the disappearance of natural presence." (158-59)

3. Harold Bloom observes in *Wallace Stevens: The Poems of our Climate* (Ithaca: Cornell Univ. Press, 1976), p. 143: "In some sense, 'The Poems of Our Climate' comes to rest in a final implication that 'in the way you speak / You arrange, the thing is posed, / What in nature merely grows.' I quote from 'Add This to Rhetoric,' a kind of footnote to the greater poem, and sharing with that still-life vision the Emersonian insight that everything that is not natural is rhetorical, which means that only the Not-Me, including the body, is free of rhetoric, while the soul itself 'lies in flawed words and stubborn sounds.' The play upon 'lies' here is the poem's finest moment. Delight lies *to us* in flawed words and stubborn sounds, and also delight lies or inheres in such words and sounds.' This work, parenthetically referred to in the text, will be designated as *The Poems*.

4. See Richard A. Lanham, *The Motives of Eloquence* (New Haven: Yale Univ. Press, 1976). Lanham's distinction between philosophical and rhetorical man concerns, generally speaking, the difference between signification and signifying.

5. Compare Steven Shaviro, "'That Which is Always Beginning': Stevens' Poetry of Affirmation," *PMLA* 100 (1985), 220-231. Shaviro outlines the workings of what he calls *disjunctive affirmation* in Stevens' poetry. "The production of differences not susceptible to mediation and of similitudes irreducible to identification" (221) means that binary opposition is only "an effect produced within a larger economy of excess and defect" (225).

6. Jacques Derrida, *La vérité en peinture* (Paris: Flammarion, 1978), p. 40. All further references to this work, henceforth known as *VEP*, appear parenthetically in the text.

7. Martin Heidegger, *Nietzsche, Volume I: The Will to Power*, trans. David Farrell Krell (New York: Harper & Row, 1979), p. 16.

8. Steven Shaviro is again quite instructive here, noting that in Stevens "'Poverty' is not a negative term but the point of an affirmation," whose "unlimited affirmation does not assert anything" just as "its irreconcilable statements do not qualify one another. No decision is possible, not even the decision that would relegate the text to undecidability. For excess and defect are not opposed phases or aspects but a single differential movement" (229).

9. "To Henry Church," 8 Dec. 1942, *Letters of Wallace Stevens*, ed. Holly Stevens (New York: Alfred A. Knopf, 1966), p. 430.

10. Jacques Derrida, "LIVING ON: Border Lines," trans. James Hulbert, in *Deconstruction and Criticism* (New York: The Seabury Press, 1979), p. 132.

11. As Shaviro concludes: "The logic of Steven's poetry is repetitive and accretive, not dialectical or progressive. It moves toward no transcendence and proclaims no truth. It neither conveys metaphysical reassurances nor heralds the triumph of the narcissistic ego. . . . Its project is what Nietzsche describes as the highest aim of art: 'to be *oneself* the eternal joy of becoming, beyond all terror and pity — that joy which include[s] even joy in destroying'" (231).

12. Lanham, pp. 4-5.

13. Maurice Blanchot, *Le pas au-délà* (Paris: Editions Gallimard, 1973), p. 29.

14. Frank Kermode, Wallace Stevens (London: Oliver & Boyd, 1960), p. 106.

15. Besides the two important readings of Vendler and Bloom, there is, among others, the "deconstructive" reading of Joseph Riddel, "The Climate of Our Poems," *The Wallace Stevens Journal* 7 (1983), 59-75.

16. Helen Vendler, *On Extended Wings: Wallace Stevens' Longer Poems* (Cambridge, Mass.: Harvard Univ. Press, 1969), p. 234. All further references appear parenthetically in the text.

17. See Patricia Parker, "The Motive for Metaphor: Stevens and Derrida," *The Wallace Stevens Journal* 7 (1983), 76-88. Parker makes use of Derrida's idea of the "retrait" of metaphor and shows the ambivalence of Stevens' theory of metaphor in an ingenious reading of "The Motive for Metaphor." She points out the potentially negative character of both a final identity which would arrest metaphor and a metaphoric evasiveness in retreat from the stringency of a proper state of being or meaning.

18. Bakhtin, *Rabelais*, pp. 9-11.

19. See note 18 to Chapter One. The original is as follows: "Alles Gute und Schöne hängt an der Täuschung: Wahrheit tödtet — ja tödtet sich selbst (insofern sie erkennt, daß ihr Fundament der Irrthum ist)" (Nietzsche, *Nachgelassene Fragmente*, 231). The idea of a deathly truth suggests the need for an effective antidote, the work of a *pharmakon*, as in the following playful aphorism from *Menschliches, Allzumenschliches:* "*Wahrheit*, — Niemand stirbt jetzt an tödlichen Wahrheiten: es gibt zu viele Gegengifte" (Friedrich Nietzsche, *Werke*, Schlecta, I, 698).

20. See Jacques Derrida, "Plato's Pharmacy," in *Dissemination*. In a discussion of Plato's use of the word and concept of the *pharmakon*, Derrida observes: "Philosophy thus opposes to its other this transmutation of the drug into a remedy, of the poison into a counterpoison. Such an operation would not be possible if the *pharmako-logos* did not already harbor within itself that complicity of contrary values, and if the *pharmakon* in general were not, prior to any distinction-making, that which, presenting itself as a poison, may turn out to be a cure, may retrospectively reveal itself in the truth of its curative power. . . . This 'medicine' is not a simple thing. But neither is it a composite, a sensible or empirical *suntheton* partaking of several simple essence. It is rather the prior medium in which differentiation in general is produced, along with the opposition between the *eidos* and its other; this medium is *analogous* to the one

that will, subsequent to and according to the decision of philosophy, be reserved for transcendental imagination, that 'art hidden in the depths of the soul,' which belongs neither simply to the sensible nor simply to the intelligible, neither simply to passivity nor simply to activity" (125-26) ; "If the *pharmakon* is 'ambivalent,' it is because it constitutes the medium in which opposites are opposed, the movement and the play that links them among themselves, reverses them or makes one side cross over into the other. . . . The *pharmakon* is the movement, the locus, and the play: (the production of) difference. It is the differance of difference" (127). See as well Geoffrey H. Hartman, "Words and Wounds," in Saving the Text, pp. 118-57. Hartman examines Derrida's essay and extends certain of its implications within a literary context: "Literature, I surmise, moves us beyond the fallacious hope that words can heal without also wounding. They are homeopathic, curing like by like in the manner of Spenser's 'myrrh sweet bleeding in the bitter wound'" (122-23). Pertinent here as well is Frye's theory of romance and romantic comedy, as developed in *A Natural Perspective* (New York: Columbia Univ. Press, 1965), for example, or as in *The Myth of Deliverance* (Toronto: Univ. of Toronto Press, 1983). The exclusion of the *pharmakos* is, of course, crucial in this structural theory, and such a figure is examined by Derrida in his essay, with particular reference in a note to Frye's *Anatomy of Criticism* (1957), rpt. Princeton: Princeton Univ. Press, 1973), pp. 41, 45-48, 148-49. But the general framework used by Frye in his analysis of the structure of comedy is also suggestive in terms of our present discussion. The climactic moment in romance is a reversal releasing a vital energy and culminating in festival and celebration, representing a victory over the reality principle whose ultimate conclusion is death. The *pharmakos* and the *pharmakon* are also, significantly enough, central and recurrent concepts in Kenneth Burke's *The Philosophy of Literary Form*, 3rd ed. (Berkeley: Univ. of California Press, 1973). See his analysis of symbolic scapegoating (39-45), for example, or the chapter entitled "The Rhetoric of Hitler's 'Battle'" (191-220) which makes the connection between "scapegoating" or the exclusion of the *pharmakos* and the idea of the *pharmakon*, the symbolic need for a medicinal, purgative cure of a designated poisonous element in society, a cure which is, of course, purely "magical."

21. "To Bernard Heringman," 3 May, 1949, and "To Charles Tomlinson," 19 June, 1951, in *Letters of Wallace Stevens*, p. 636, p. 719.

22. Bakhtin, *Rabelais*, p. 10.

23. In *The Philosophy of Literary Form*, Burke speaks of the "magical decree" "implicit in all language": "If magic says, '*Let there be* such and such,' religion says, '*Please do* such and such.' The decree of magic, the petition of prayer. Freud has discussed the 'optative as indicative' in dreams (where 'would that it were' is stylistically rephrased: 'it is' — as when the dreamer, desiring to be rid of a certain person, dreams that this person is departing)" (4).

24. In "The Climate of Our Poems," Joseph Riddel outlines the deconstruction of "white mythology" in "Credences"; see also his "Juda becomes New Haven," *Diacritics*, 10 (June 1980), p. 29, where he discusses the same issue in "Notes."

25. *The Works of Plato*, trans. B. Jowett (New York: Tudor Publishing Co., n.d.) p. 267. In this particular case, I have chosen to use Jowett's translation, because of his use of the expression "his own proper place."

26. Derrida plays on this idea of the withdrawal ("retrait") of metaphor in "The *Retrait* of Metaphor." See also Patricia Parker, "The Motive for Metaphor: Stevens and Derrida."

27. J. Hillis Miller discusses the inevitable "alogic" of such a naming in "Impossible Metaphor: Stevens's 'The Red Fern' as Example," in *The Lesson of Paul de Man*, ed. P. Brooks, S. Felman, J.H. Miller (New Haven: Yale Univ. Press, 1985), pp. 150-62.

28. In "Wallace Stevens: The Transcendental Strain," in *Poetry and Repression: Revisionism from Blake to Stevens* (New Haven: Yale Univ. Press, 1976), Bloom, following a connection originally made by Frank Kermode, discusses Valéry's *Dance and the Soul*, which speaks of the toxicity of seeing things only as they are: "A cold and perfect clarity is a poison impossible to combat" (qtd. in Bloom 280). What is at stake in Valéry's dialogue is precisely the possibility of living without supplement, but only with the core and essence of things, with what — to the exclusion of the merest addition — is nothing but itself. The poison of identity here, like the ravishments of truth in "Notes," can be compared to the dis-illusioning poison in "The Auroras of Autumn": "This is his poison: that we should disbelieve / Even that" (*CP* 411). Kermode himself makes the connection with the passage from Valéry's dialogue in a discussion of "The Snow Man," the poem that could be said to both institute and epitomize in Stevens this passion for a reduction to the first idea, beyond all metaphor and pathetic fallacy. "The Snow Man" is, of course, a metaphor itself — of the desire to come to the end of metaphor; it is "the recurring metaphor of winter as a pure abstracted reality, a bare icy outline purged clean of all the accretions brought by the human mind to make it possible for us to conceive of reality and live our lives" (*Wallace Stevens* 35).

29. In "Riddles, Charms, and Fictions in Wallace Stevens," Eleanor Cook observes, concerning the important element of nonsense in Stevens' poetry: "In *Notes* I. iii, for all the possible defence in the clause 'we say,' Stevens does not end defensively. He ends with a piercing or wounding, even by nonsense-language, even by the 'hoo' we hear the ocean saying, even in the full knowledge that we say these things ourselves. If we read the poem's last line as in part Stevens' gloss on his own nonsense-lines, then he is putting before us the possibility of words as not only a power to bless and pierce and to which we cling because (not although) it pierces us. In *Notes* III. viii, Stevens asks: 'Am I that imagine this angel less satisfied?' Are we who say the riddle and charm of the Arabian less pierced? Only if we defend ourselves completely against the power of all fictions. And a self that cannot be pierced by words cannot be healed or refreshed by them either" (239-40)

30. qtd. in Bloom, "Emerson and Whitman: the American Sublime," in *Poetry and Repression*, p. 238.

31. Ralph Waldo Emerson, "The Poet," in *Selections*, ed. Stephen E. Whicher (Boston: Houghton Mifflin, 1957), p. 223.

31 Lanham, p. 5.

32. See Martin Heidegger, "Heimkunft/An die Verwandten," in *Erläuterungen zu Hölderlins Dichtung* (rpt. Frankfurt am Main: Vittorio Klostermann, 1981), pp. 9-31. Commenting on lines of Hölderlin's poem, Heidegger writes: "Die Nähe zum Ursprung its eine sparende Nähe. Sie hält das Freudigste zurück. Sie verwahrt und hebt es für die Kommende auf, aber diese Nähe hebt das Freudigste nicht fort, sondern läßt es also das Aufgehobene gerade erscheinen. Im Wesen der Nähe ereignet sich ein verborgenes Sparen. Daß sie das Nähe spart, ist das Geheimnis der Nähe zum Freudigsten. . . . Die dichtende Freude ist das Wissen davon, daß in allem Freudigen, das schon begegnet, das Freudige grüßt, indem es sich spart" (24-25).

33. As Patricia Parker remarks: "Metaphor . . . is always on the 'margins of discourse' (Barbara H. Smith), outside the city walls, and its potential incivility generates concern for its 'mastery' (Aristotle), "moderation' (Quintillian), or 'proper management' (Blair). But the 'Rule of Metaphor' contains, as an ambiguous genitive, that mastery's threatened opposite, the rule of metaphor as a Lord of Misrule. As Derrida suggests, the 'master' of metaphor may himself be 'transported'" ("The Metaphorical Plot" 137).

34. Heidegger, *Nietzsche*, 6.

35. This phrase concerns what is called "Das Eigenste der Heimat" (Heidegger, "Heimkunft," 14), an expression which might be understood as utterly pleonastic; it might be translated as that which is most proper to the home, that is, to that which is proper.

36. John Ashbery, *Self-Portrait in a Convex Mirror* (1975); rpt. Harmondsworth: Penguin Books, 1976), p. 70

37. In "Riddles," Eleanor Cook makes the following observations concerning the Canon Aspirin's name: "At the end of this canto [VIII of 'It Must Give Pleasure'], the Cinderella story reverses the angelic moment, as the Arabian's story reverses the world of 'candid' and *candidus*, the two reversals being very different. It also reverses the Miltonic and Biblical world of the aspiring Canon Aspirin in the three preceding cantos (v-vii). 'Candid' is used only once elsewhere in Stevens' poetry ('candor' never again) in a way that associates it with 'canon' and 'canonical.' When we note that a candidate may also be an Aspirant (*OED*, 'candidate,' 2.a), the candid-Canon-canonical association appears firm. In 1909, age twenty-nine, Stevens notes the Cinderella story in his journal in a one-word entry: 'pumpkin-coach.' The entry follows immediately on these lines:
> What I aspired to be,
> And was not, comforts me —
The lines, unidentified, are from Browning's *Rabbi ben Ezra*, so that Browning's rabbi must take his place as another of the aspirers who make up that compound ghost, Canon Aspirin" (241).

38. See Bloom's discussion of Stevens' penchant for humming in *The Poems*, pp. 165-66.

39. Herman Melville, *Moby Dick*, ed. Alfred Kazin (Cambridge, Mass.: The Riverside Press, 1956), pp. 137-38.

40. Burke, pp. 6-7.

41. In "Metaphoric Staging: Stevens' Beginning Again or the 'End of the Book,'" in *Wallace Stevens: A Celebration*, ed. Frank Doggett and Robert Buttel (Princeton: Princeton Univ. Press, 1980), Joseph Riddel discusses these same lines: "The 'Fat girl' evoked in the last poem of 'It must Give Pleasure' appears, on the contrary, as a figure of 'differance,' and not, like the statue, a figure of identity. She is a 'moving contour, a change not quite completed,' a 'more than natural figure' and 'soft-footed phantom, the irrational / Distortion' (*CP* 406). She is always 'more than' her image, a figure of excess. Neither the 'master' of repetition, the 'man-hero' who is always eccentric, nor the 'Fat girl' is properly a center. The 'Fat girl' is a name for a proliferation of images that will not reduce to one; she is 'familiar yet an aberration' (*CP* 406). She is a metaphor itself" (*CP* 324).

42. Eleanor Cook, "Directions in Reading Wallace Stevens: Up, Down, Across," in *Lyric Poetry: Beyond New Criticism*, ed. Chaviva Hosek and Patricia Parker (Ithaca: Cornell Univ. Press, 1985), p. 299.

43. Mallarmé, pp. 474-75. See also Jacques Derrida, "The Double Session," in *Dissemination*, pp. 173-285, an essay that offers an intensive examination of Mallarmé's poetics, specifically in relation to this uncanny suspension of a proper event, this event that takes place only in not taking place, as the "place where nothing takes place but the place" (257).

44. "To Hi Simons," 29 August 1940, *Letters of Wallace Stevens*, p. 37.

45. qtd. in Umberto Eco, *A Theory of Semiotics* (Bloomington: Indiana Univ. Press, 1976), p. 69.

48. Jacques Lacan, *The Four Fundamental Concepts of Psycho-Analysis*, trans. Alan Sheridan (New York: Norton, 1978), p. 154.

49. Patricia Parker, in her subtle concern for what she calls "Stevens' wariness of apocalypse or centre" (240), effectively paraphrases the paradoxical movement of this passage of "Notes": "Even the reduction to the 'first idea' in 'Notes' ends in an 'imagined thing.' The ephebe is to learn that 'Phoebus is dead,' to 'clean the sun' of all its images. But the sun which must 'bear no name' is simultaneously, and beautifully, called 'gold flourisher,' a kenning which reimports figuration in one of its most elemental forms" (238-39). The most elemental form of naming, and the most inventive (indeed, it is famous for providing names for that which has just been invented) is proverbially catachresis.

50. I am grateful to Peter Nesselroth for some of his very suggestive ideas concerning Derrida's interest in catachresis.

51. John Hollander, "The Sound of the Music of Music and Sound," in *Wallace Stevens: A Celebration*, p. 250.

52. Eleanor Cook successfully sums up this uncertain movement towards a paradoxically convincing affirmation in this passage of "Notes": "We might suppose that a movement from first-person plural to first-person singular, from assertive to interrogative mood, from winging our way from immaculate beginnings to immaculate ends to seeing and being a falling angel, from extended to modified adjectives, from excited participation in power to a multiple stance where power is questioned — that all these limitations would make for a lesser canto. But this is not what happens. Stevens' enchanting first world is presented anew here in strength. His canto both enacts and comments on 'that willing suspension of disbelief for the moment, which constitutes poetic faith.' Coleridge's definition and Stevens' canto are powerful and live for us not in spite of their careful limiting but because of it. Stevens' 'I am' claims no more than he can sustain: 'I have not but I am and as I am, I am.'" ("Riddles" 240).

53. Compare Riddel's reading of the significance of the abyss in Stevens' poetry, in "Metaphoric Staging," pp. 325-27.

54. Sören Kierkegaard, *Repetition*, trans. Walter Lowrie (New York: Harper & Ros, 1964).

55. Kierkegaard, *Repetition*, p. 135.

56. Kierkegaard, *Repetition*, p. 126.

57. Heidegger, *Poetry, Language, Thought*, p. 18.

58. Ashbery, p. 70.

CHAR: THE SOVEREIGN TEXT

Whose venom and whose wisdom will be one.
    Wallace Stevens, "Saint John and the Back-Ache"
                                        (*CP* 437)

Of all writings I love only that which is written with blood.
. . .
It is not an easy thing to understand unfamiliar blood: I hate
the reading idler.
    Friedrich Nietzsche, *Thus Spoke Zarathustra*[1]

The Economy of Joy

Les Inventeurs

Ils sont venus, les forestiers de l'autre versant, les inconnus de
    nous, les rebelles à nos usages.
Ils sont venus nombreux.
Leur troupe est apparue à a la ligne de partage des cèdres
Et du champ de la vieille moisson désormais irrigué et vert.
La longue marche les avait échauffés.
Leur casquette cassait dur leurs yeux et leur pied fourbu se posait
    dans le vague.
Ils nous ont aperçus et se sont arrêtés.
Visiblement ils ne présumaient pas nous trouver là,
Sur des terres faciles et des sillons bien clos,
Tout à fait insouciant d'une audience.
Nous avons levé le front et les avons encouragés.

Le plus disert s'est approché, puis un second tout aussi déraciné
    et lent.
Nous sommes venus, dirent-ils, vous prévenir de l'arrivée prochaine
    de l'ouragan, de votre implacable adversaire.
Pas plus que vous, nous ne le connaissons
Autrement que par des relations et des confidences d'ancêtres.
Mais pourquoi somme-nous heureux incompréhensiblement devant
    vous et soudain pareils à des enfants?
Nous avons dit merci et les avons congédiés.
Mais auparavant ils ont bu, et leurs mains tremblaient, et leurs
    yeux riaient sur les bords.
Hommes d'arbres et de cognée, capables de tenir tête à quelque
    terreur, mais inaptes à conduire l'eau, à aligner des bâtisses,
    à les enduire de couleurs plaisantes.
Ils ignoraient le jardin d'hiver et l'économie de la joie.

Certes, nous aurions pu les convaincre et les conquérir,

Car l'angoisse de l'ouragan est émouvante.
Oui, l'ouragan allait bientôt venir;
Mais cela valait-il la peine que l'on en parlât et qu'on dérangeât
    l'avenir?
Là où nous sommes, il n'y a pas de crainte urgente.

(LM 69-70)

The idea of economy is very helpful in reading René Char. First of all, there is the idea of an economy of verbal expression, such as we find in certain literary forms, like the proverb or adage. The use of these forms is quite pervasive in Char's work, and is especially appropriate to the imparting of a sort of experiential wisdom, an administrative concern with life, almost a science of "household management" to apply to human existence. Char's poetry reflects not a poetic faith, but a poetic ethic, which the poems often convey in succinct aphoristic terms. Implied is an economy governing our energies and desires. "Household management" is, of course, the very etymology of the word "economy," a derivation which Derrida has insisted upon: *oiko-nomia*, meaning "the law (arrangement, management, distribution) of the house."[2]

The thought of a "home economics" brings to mind as well Heidegger's somewhat mystifying but infinitely suggestive explorations of the profound connection between poetry and thinking, and between these and the idea of dwelling, building, and habitation. Poetry, for Heidegger, is above all *poieîn*, a making or creating, even a fabricating or building; it is that which originally brings human beings into dwelling and habitation, submitting them for the first time to a law of the house or economy.[3] Poetic invention is the model for all other forms of human inventiveness and creativity that contribute to man's building of a place in which to dwell. Any reader of Char cannot help but be attentive to such speculations. The image or figure of the house recurs throughout his poetry, and the elucidation of a peculiar mode of dwelling and habitation seems to be one of the central objects of his poetic ethic. He is also concerned about how this activity is at the same time mysteriously rooted in a certain condition of homelessness or state of not-being-at-home, an enigma that is involved in the original sense of the English word "dwelling" (OE, *dwellan*) as a "leading or going astray." Heidegger reflects that "as soon as man *gives thought* to his homelessness, it is a misery no longer. Rightly considered and kept well in mind, it is the sole summons that *calls* mortals into their dwelling."[4]

Char's poem, "Les Inventeurs," depicts precisely this enigma of the profound link between a primordial homelessness and the activity of dwelling, of building an inhabitable space. The poem dramatizes the meeting between two alien groups or cultures: the "ils" and "nous" introduced in the opening line: "Ils sont venus, les forestiers de l'autre versant, les inconnus de nous, les rebelles à nos usages" (*LM* 69). The poem has indeed the flavour of a "contact history," to borrow a term from anthropology. The title invites an initial riddle: who are "the inventors"? The reader answers the question by carefully differentiating the two groups in the poem, a process which naturally follows a logic of binary opposition and brings to mind, appropriately enough, Lévi-Strauss and his model of myth and culture analysis. In following such a model, if only for heuristic purposes, we might come up with something like the following:

They	*We*
nomadic ("La longue marche")	sedentary ("nous... sur des terres faciles et des sillons bien clos...")
homeless, uprooted ("déraciné")	inhabitant
barbaric aliens ("de l'autre versant, les inconnus de nous, les rebelles à nos usages")	indigenous civilization

guests	hosts
herd ("leur troupe")	society
foresting ("Hommes d'arbres et de cognée...")	cultivation and building ("ligne de partage des cèdres / Et du champ de la vieille moisson désormais irrigué et vert")
primitive tools ("inaptes à conduire l'eau, à aligner les bâtisses, à les enduire de couleurs plaisantes")	technology
lack of definition ("leur pied fourbu se posait dans le vague")	definition ("ligne de partage," "des sillons bien clos," "aligner des bâtisses")
surprise ("Visiblement ils ne présumaient pas nous trouver là...")	awareness and foresight
lack of control and of self-possession, overpowering emotion ("Mais pourquoi sommes-nous heureux incompréhensiblement devant vous et soudain pareils à des enfants?", "leurs mains tremblaient, et leurs yeux riaient...")	composure, self-possession, calm, command ("Nous avons levé le front et les avons encouragés," "Nous avons dit merci et les avons congédiés," "Certes, nous aurions pu les convaincre et les conquérir...")
fatigue ("échauffés")	ease ("des terres faciles")
overwhelming sense of risk and danger ("Nous sommes venus... vous prévenir de l'arrivée prochaine de l'ouragan...")	complacency ("Mais cela valait-il la peine que l'on en parlât et qu'on dérangeât l'avenir?" / Là où nous sommes, il n'y a pas de crainte urgente")
child-like timidity and spontaneity in speech ("Nous...les avons encouragés. / Le plus disert s'est approché")	adult-like assured and commanding eloquence ("Nous avons dit merci et les avons congédiés," "Certes, nous aurions pu les convaincre...")
absence of economy, randomness ("capables de tenir tête à quelque terreur, mais inaptes à conduire l'eau," etc., "Ils ignoraient le jardin d'hiver et l'économie de la joie")	economy, inventiveness

From this schematic chart of oppositions we might deduce, then, that the poem offers us a little lesson in prudential economics, that it demonstrates the infinite superiority of foresight and technique over a primitive culture living purely at the mercy of natural forces. This reading, however, would be possible only with the omission of the poem's closing few lines, where the inventors in no way deny the real danger of the mysterious "hurricane" against which the nomadic group warns them:

> Certes, nous aurions pu les convaincre et les conquérir,
> Car l'angoisse de l'ouragan est émouvante.
> Oui, l'ouragan allait bientôt venir;
> Mais cela valait-il la peine que l'on en parlât et qu'on
> dérangeât l'avenir?
> Là où nous sommes, il n'y a pas de crainte urgente.
>
> (*LM* 70)

First of all, the inventors seem sure of their rhetorical power over their vulnerable guests who themselves confess that, before their hosts, they are "heureux incompréhensiblement . . . et soudain pareils à des enfants." The inventors are certain their eloquence could easily "convince and conquer" the anxiety of the foresters, and yet they decline to convert them. The implication of this casualness may be that in using the power to that end they feel they would only be abusing it, since their inventiveness does not consist of a technique of control and domination but of a poetic art, a creative capacity. A poetic sensibility, indeed, governs their peculiar attitude towards the "anguish of the hurricane," which they describe as "émouvante," as a noble and moving or sublime experience.

At the same time they share with their guests a belief in the reality of the hurricane, in its impending arrival and in its overwhelming capacity to wreak destruction. Indeed, for all the signs they give of an easy mastery and control, they share with their nomadic visitors the acknowledgment of a fundamental state of insecurity: the perpetual risk of homelessness. The difference is that, curiously, they assent to this limit to their mastery. They seem, almost serenely, to accept this instability. Their initial complacency must thus be reinterpreted. It is the farthest thing from a smugness or false confidence that would claim to be secure from all loss and disaster. It may be, indeed, on the very basis of a necessary instability and insecurity that the inventors have first learned to dwell.

The nomads and their inventive hosts share, then, an identical sense of the reality of the impending catastrophe. What differs is their response to this condition of insecurity: the one plaintively anxious and foreboding, the other happily unconcerned and serene. The apparent complacency of the inventors, in not taking any measures to protect against the hurricane, is not the self-satisfaction of those who imagine they have gained an absolute control over their environment and thus attained a final guarantee against all risk and danger. What the poem suggests is, rather, another, more general economy, one set into play by the unrestricted inventive capacity to build, make, create, and which includes in its organization the possibility of an uncontainable loss. If this uncanny power of invention, to follow Heidegger, brings us to dwell in the first place, it does not, by the same token, protect us from a fundamental homelessness; on the contrary, poetry causes us to dwell in precisely that insecurity, in precisely that possibility of dispersal.

Poetry's "law of the house" — in the poem's words, "le jardin d'hiver et l'économie de la joie" (*LM* 70) — is, it would appear, what the non-inventive ignore. Adrift and rootless, they are perpetually at the mercy of the hurricane. Reacting to their environment in a direct but random way, they are unable to voice anything but their anxiety concerning the catastrophe that constantly threatens to sweep them away. Those who invent have in no way escaped or transcended that same insecurity. Their law of existence, indeed, includes a certain lawlessness and only works in the first place because it lacks any stricture or absoluteness; it is organized as a merely relative force. Let us suppose, for the sake of the reading I would like to develop here, that what makes the difference, between the visitors and their hosts, is the power of invention, and that what the inventors have discovered is what Derrida describes as the ambivalence of the *pharmakon*, a powerful supplementary technique or art similar to the one that the ingenious Theuth, "the inventor of many arts," discovers with "the use of letters," as related by Socrates in his little fable of writing in Plato's *Phaedrus*: "there was a famous old god, whose name was Theuth . . . and he was the inventor of many arts, such as arithmetic and draughts and dice, but his great discovery was the use of letters. . . . To [Thamus] came Theuth and showed his inventions, desiring that the other Egyptians might be allowed to have benefit of them. . . ."[5]

The inventors in Char's poem are curiously — although perhaps understandably when we consider Thamus's ingratitude in Plato's text — much more reserved than Theuth when it comes to offering their created offspring to passing strangers. They expressly resist the temptation to "convince and conquer," to convert and bring around their opposites to their own peculiar mode of existence: "Certes, nous aurions pu les convaincre et les conquérir. . . ." Their inventions are not presumably for everyone, at least not for the non-inventive, for these "Hommes d'arbres et de cognée, capables de tenir tête à quelque terreur, mais inaptes à conduire l'eau, à aligner des bâtisses, à les enduire de couleurs plaisantes" (*LM* 70). In their laxness to convert others, there is a recognition of differences. There may be a suggestion here as well, reminiscent of Thamus's judgement of Theuth's most dangerous toy, writing, that such a gift is always profoundly ambivalent, that often a vicious curse lies hidden in the blessing, a fatal poison in the medicinal power of a new technique. In *Phaedrus* Theuth praises writing as an enhancement of memory, but Thamus's judgement of it as an ultimately pernicious supplement has the last word, at least in Plato's dialogue.[6] Char, however, is careful not to untie the knot of his poem, which may have something to do with the enigma of the *pharmakon* itself. All we can gather from the concluding lines of "Les Inventeurs" is that somehow, like the effect of a potent medicine that neutralizes the ailment or at least strengthens one's defences against its influence, the technical prowess of the inventors in the poem, their mysterious "economy of joy," has some unfathomable beneficial action on their anxiety about the hurricane. The "anguish of the hurricane" has been transformed into a "moving" experience, perhaps transfigured by an inventive wisdom that neither the visiting wanderers of the poem, nor the poem's equally perplexed readers, seem quite capable of fully understanding.

This transformation suggests the work of a mysterious economy, one that is peculiarly nonprudential and "improper" in its essence — a "mixed economy" that freely joins contraries and ignores the law of contradiction. In Derrida's words, "If the *pharmakon* is 'ambivalent,' it is because it constitutes the medium in which opposites are opposed, the movement and the play that links them among themselves, reverses them or makes one side cross over into the other . . ." (*D* 127). This "ambivalence" is exactly what we find in the paradox of "le jardin d'hiver" and the related idea of an "économie de la joie," as though joy, which by its very nature is an excessive emotion, should lend itself to a frugality of expression. "Without Contraries is no progression," in Blake's words.[7] Invention — or art, or poetry, or the creative act — is that activity which makes opposites and contradictory states of emotion communicate, which mixes them and makes them interpenetrate: in the midst of winter a garden blossoms; in a sparing of emotion the exuberance of joy is brought forth. For Char, poetry's power of making or invention (*poieín*) not only allows us to live in the contradiction of our contingent, temporal existence, but even leads us to affirm that contradiction, without any corresponding need for an eventual reconciliation or resolution.

In "Les Inventeurs" this is the recognition above all else that human beings should learn to dwell in the awareness of their homelessness. The poem's mysterious closing statement is the direct utterance of this creative "plight" which, lived and affirmed, is necessarily enigmatic. Its implications are those of Heidegger's understanding of "the real dwelling plight":

> The real dwelling plight lies in this, that mortals ever search anew for the nature of dwelling, that they *must ever learn to dwell*. What if man's homelessness consisted in this, that man still does not even think of the *real* plight of dwelling as *the* plight? Yet as soon as man *gives thought* to his homelessness, it is a misery no longer. Rightly considered and kept well in mind, it is the sole summons that *calls* mortals into their dwelling.[8]

In order to learn to dwell, we must constantly give thought to the impossibility of ending, by transcending, our primordial *Heimatlosigkeit*. This the inventors in the poem appear to recognize in not denying the real danger of the hurricane. Their serenity testifies to the creative enigma of accepting one's originary not-being-at-home, of one's being originarily astray and adrift. They do not attempt to eternalize their desire in an Apollonian state of repose that pretends to have overcome all vicissitude and dispersal, but, as true inventors, have learned above all to pay Dionysus his due, in the constant knowledge that, as it is put in "La Bibliothéque est en feu," "Celui qui invente. au contraire de celui qui découvre, n'ajoute aux choses, n'apporte aux êtres que des masques, des entre-deux, une bouillie de fer" (*LM* 149).

The Tainted Seat

J'habite une douleur

Ne laisse pas le soin de gouverner ton coeur à
ces tendresses parentes de l'automne auquel elles
empruntent sa placide allure et son affable agonie.
L'oeil est précoce à se plisser. La souffrance
connaît peu de mots. Préfère te coucher sans
fardeaux: tu rêveras du lendemain et ton lit te
sera léger. Tu rêveras que ta maison n'a plus de
vitres. Tu es impatient de t'unir au vent, au vent
qui parcourt une année en une nuit. D'autres
chanteront l'incorporation mélodieuse, les chairs qui
ne personnifient plus que la sorcellerie du sablier.
Tu condamneras la gratitude qui se répète. Plus
tard, on t'identifiera à quelque géant désagrégé,
seigneur de l'impossible.
Pourtant.
Tu n'as fait qu'augmenter le poids de ta nuit.
Tu es retourné à la pêche aux murailles, à la
canicule sans été. Tu es furieux contre ton amour
au centre d'une entente qui s'affole. Songe à la
maison parfaite que tu ne verras jamais monter. A
quand la récolte de l'abîme? Mais tu as crevé les
yeux du lion. Tu crois voir ·passer la beauté au-
dessus des lavandes noires . . .
Qu'est-ce qui t'a hissé, une fois encore, un peu
plus haut, sans te convaincre?
Il n'y a pas de siège pur. (*FM* 178-79)

Char's poem "J'habite une douleur" also affirms the necessity of living

within a certain fundamental homelessness, which for Heidegger is paradoxically

the "Not" summoning human beings into dwelling in the first place. The mode

of habitation suggested by the title is not only an inherently painful one, but

one identified with a condition peculiar to pain and suffering, with an irreducible

threshold state that is not simply lamented, but by the end of the poem even

affirmed, if only indirectly, in the negative proposition: "Il n'y a pas de siège

pur" (*FM* 179). The reader's understanding of this liminal pain and sorrow

progressively alters until a suffering normally thought of as a purely passive

experience reveals itself to be an opportunity for becoming and growth.

In his essay "Language," Heidegger focuses on a line from Trakl's poem "A Winter Evening": "Pain has turned the threshold to stone." For Heidegger the essence of language involves a painful separation that remains at the same time a communicating threshold between separated elements, so that the "Unter-Schied," the difference or dif-ference introduced with language must be understood also as a seam, as both "separation of the between" and "gathering middle."[9] This painful separation is a place of articulation, of difference and *différance*; it sets in play the *pharmakon's* ambivalent movement, the *différance* of difference. Heidegger here anticipates Derrida's association of writing with *différance* in using an explicitly "graphic" simile to represent language's threshold-like separating and gathering. The rending of pain, he says, "as a separating that gathers, is at the same time that drawing which, like the pen-drawing of a plan or sketch, draws and joins together what is held apart in separation."[10] As a means of designating a similar simultaneous "difference and articulation", Derrida, in *Of Grammatology*, employs an image suggested to him by Roger Laporte: that of "la brisure" ("hinge").[11] The image is equally appropriate in conveying what Heidegger means in "Language" by "Unter-Schied." A similar "hinge" is also at work in Char's poem, is locatable indeed in the placement of just a single word: "Pourtant." This adverb, set off so that it divides the poem in two at the very middle, serves to separate but at same time bring together the two larger passages. As Mary Ann Caws comments in her discussion of the poem: "A single word may serve as a threshold. Thus, around the central word: 'pourtant,' neutral in appearance, two verbal masses are set in motion, opposed."[12]

The syntactical *tour de force* represented by the astute use and positioning of the word "Pourtant" is, as Caws observes, the very linchpin or hinge of the poem's tremendous energy, stemming from a successful balancing of contradictory movements. In a parallel way, the poem is also the expression of an implicit directive concerning the most creative employment of human energy, through a specific mode of existence. The poem opens with a command ("Ne laisse pas le soin de gouverner . . .") and ends on an assertion ("Il n'y a pas de siège pur") which itself gives the impression of being a concealed but implied prescription. It seems to say that, since there is no pure fulfillment of desire, one should affirm this lack of repose as the potential for further realization, rather than perceive it merely as a negative limit. The final line may be couched in the negative, but it does not express resignation about a necessarily limited fulfillment; rather, it recapitulates the entire poem, which speaks as a corrective and prescriptive oracle. In showing us the inevitable nature of our deceptions, the poem offers an alternative perspective on the proper ends of our desires. It does not simply mourn this painful experience, this cycle of indefinite lack. It suggests a converse point of view in which, for one thing, our deception would no longer deceive us, if only because we are able to recognize it as an inevitable effect — but not the sole effect — of the full play and employment of our desires and energies. To inhabit the threshold between desire and fulfillment would, then, be the source and goal of a fully engaged human activity, which is the proper mode of a poetic existence — one makes one's home in the very recognition that "there is no untainted seat,"[13] and that therefore, to use Heidegger's words, "mortals ever search anew for the nature of dwelling .. *must ever learn to dwell.*"

One of the distinctive marks of Char's lyrical style is its proverbial, almost oracular form. Such an effect is created by the repeated use of imperative and strongly assertive and declarative sentence-forms: "Ne laisse pas

. . ."; "L'oeil est . . ."; "La souffrance connaît . . ."; "Préfère. . ."; "tu rêveras
. . ."; "Tu rêveras . . ."; "Tu es . . ."; "D'autres chanteront . . ."; "Tu condamneras . . .": "on t'identifiera . . ." The phrasing throughout the poem reflects
a wisdom both directive and prophetic in its import, and specifically the change
of tense from the initial to the closing passage of the poem imparts the sense of
a prophetic "future past." What is future in the first part of the poem becomes,
with no warning but the abrupt shift of the intervening "Pourtant," a past tense,
suggesting that what is initially predicted has in some way already taken place,
that what is foreknown has just as surely come to pass. It is the very discontinuity between the two passages of the poem that ensures such an effect. We
have a long initial series of prophetic assertions, which in the opposing part of
the poem are now contrasted with actions in the past indefinite: "Tu n'as fait .
. ."; "Tu es retourné . . ."; "tu as crevé. . . ." The use of verb tenses thus
produces a temporal threshold, a "not yet" which is at the same time already
accomplished, what is "to be" in the first passage having taken place already and
now part of the past in the second.

The heavy irony of the poem is that we never get beyond the threshold
of desire, that between the desire and the reality a shadow falls, the shadow of
a single word: "Pourtant." But seen in a positive light, this simply means that
fulfillment is not the end but a recreation of desire, a renewed threshold in
which our energy is not expended and exhausted but released again in the form
of a potential for realization. The movement from desire to fulfillment and back
to desire is not necessarily simply disillusioning. The impulse to escape from
suffering in the projection of a future freedom, where the gravity of the past
would have dissolved and satisfaction would be immediate and without obstacle,
is dispelled and shown to be vain and immaterial in the second part of the poem.

But it is only partly a deception, and the impetus of desire is not doomed but necessary if, as is clearly suggested in the penultimate line which asks "Qu'est-ce qui t'a hissé, une fois encore, un peu plus haut, sans te convaincre?" there is to be a counter-gravitational movement upwards out of a stagnant past and into a constantly recreated future.

What desire is never entirely convinced of, otherwise it would give up desiring, is that "there is no untainted seat," a maxim which to a certain understanding would seem to imply its perpetual deception and non-fulfillment, but to another may mean its refreshment, its recreation, its renewed potentiality. The poem ends on a pulling upwards, a restless ascent and not the downward momentum that we associate with a perpetual deception. Enjoining us to consider the possibility of another economy, one which alternates between fulfillment and potential, past and future, sorrow and desire, the poem thus closes on a momentary transcendence, as the poet is violently lifted beyond and upwards once more, but unconvinced, not of the fact that there is no untainted seat, but of any certain repose, of any reality that would clearly hold, of any even momentary fulfillment that is not at the same time a threshold and potential for further realization.

This lack of faith in any pure, "untainted seat" is an essential element in the creative economy of human energy. Char sees the moment of creation as initially a decreative one. What *is* must be envisioned as what *is not*, and thereby negated, since fixed and identified it lacks any further potential. This is the sense of the lines: "Tu condamneras la gratitude qui se répète. Plus tard, on t'identifiera à quelque géant désagrégé, seigneur de l'impossible" (*FM* 178). To repeat gratitude is complacently to accept what is, what has already been accomplished, possessed, and mastered, a state of identified meaning and being. Combatting this monotony is the antidote of difference, the beneficial poison of change injected by the "lord of the impossible," whose dispersal resembles the *sparagmos* of a disintegrated giant form, perhaps a fallen Lucifer, with a body, like that of Dionysus, torn to pieces and scattered. This lord is a master of difference, and of *différance* — and of a wisdom which is the science of the supplement and of the *pharmakon*. The epithet "seigneur de l'impossible" means that this sovereign agent is a lover of contradiction, a master of contraries, with the capacity to affirm and deny the same thing at once, as in the poem's prescription: "Songe à la maison parfaite que tu ne verras jamais monter." He commands the impossible as what is real, since for him what has a proper meaning and being is precisely unreal, lacking in the potential to be anything more than what it is. In a contradictory imperative he enjoins us to hope desperately for that which one can only, in hope, despair of. One is to dream of a perfect house without windowpanes, the very image of an untrammelled freedom, in the complete and certain knowledge that, in the end, as the second part of the poem tells us, "Tu n'as fait qu'augmenter le poids de ta nuit" (*FM* 178). This figure, commanding the impossible, holds together in a single contradictory instance the two opposing moments of the poem: the dream of a perfect future freedom and the deception of an identified past reality. In a unified vision, he inhabits the painful threshold between the two moments, the threshold that both separates and gathers the two, which, even in opposing them, allows for their coexistence. The poet is identified with this figure, for his apprenticeship consists in training his voice, when it speaks, to contradict what is, and in contradicting to shatter the "double-bind" of an identified state of proper meaning and being which binds and inhibits creative energy. The motto of the poet should resemble, in a sense, the curious *mot d'ordre* of the

Lacanian analyst: "Soyez réalistes, demandez l'impossible."[14]   To be truly sovereign the poet must be a lover of contraries, affirming in a single creative word a created object whose inevitable decreation is already foreknown as a necessary moment.   Perhaps another word for the element of this lord of the impossible is simply energy and, to pun on the etymology of that word, energy as that which brings work, the work — in this case the work of art or poetry — into play.

The Strategy of the Margin

Le Serpent

Prince des contresens, exerce mon amour
A tourner son Seigneur que je hais de n'avoir
Que trouble répression ou fastueux espoir.

Revanche à tes couleurs, débonnaire serpent,
Sous le couvert du bois et en toute maison.
Par le lien qui unit la lumière à la peur,
Tu fais semblant de fuir, ô serpent marginal!

(*LM* 108)

The creative energy that includes the decreative as a necessary phase of its economy is symbolized in Char's poetry by the figure of the serpent, whose association with Satan, that adversarial "seigneur de l'impossible" and "géant désagregé," is deeply rooted in the Judaic-Christian tradition.   Char's handling of this figure consists in an almost Blakian infernal reinterpretation, as the symbol for illicit desire is reidentified as the type of a successful total engagement of desire and employment of human energy.   The serpent of the above poem, one of the enigmatic creatures in the suite of emblem-like lyrics entitled "Quatre fascinants" — a *fascinant* being a fascinating, binding spell or charm, in this case that of each creature's riddling identity, which enthralls and captivates the reader — is immediately introduced in an apostrophe, as though by epithet: "Prince des contresens," that is, prince of contradictions or counter-meanings, which may be a synonym for the expression "lord of the impossible"; or we might prefer "Prince of anti-order," as in one translation.[15] All of these versions suggest an affirmation of contradiction which excludes the possibility of reconciliation, a rigorous promotion of counter-values, like Nietzsche's practice of an active *Umwertung* or *revaluation of all values*, for which is needed, as it is proclaimed in *Ecce Homo*, "above all, even contrary capacities" that must be "kept from disturbing, destroying one another . . . the art of separating without setting against one another; to mix nothing, to 'reconcile' nothing; a tremendous variety that is nevertheless the opposite of chaos." For Nietzsche this involves ultimately a "saying Yes to and having confidence in all that has hitherto been forbidden, despised, and damned," a pouring out of "tenderness upon ever so many wicked things," giving back to them "their 'soul,' a good conscience, the lofty right and privilege of existence." In this activity, "Morality is not attacked, it is no longer in the picture."[16] In accordance with Nietzsche's controversial project, Char's serpent represents that sovereign being capable of conducting a revaluation which is "an act of supreme self-examination on the part of humanity," and of pronouncing enigmatically: "I contradict as has never been contradicted before and am nevertheless the opposite of a No-saying spirit."[17]

As with Nietzsche, there is a reversal of values, and a corresponding affirmation of an alternative interpretation of the world, the promotion of a saner, more vital order of existence that the present order disguises and distorts. Following the opening apostrophe to the serpent, the plea which begins "exerce mon amour / A tourner son Seigneur" gives the impression of an active mobility which would escape falling into the trap of merely opposing the proper state of affairs. "To turn," in the context, obviously involves a fugitive turning away, but there is also a reversal or reversibility implied in the turning movement. The best name for this kind of mobility, which evades the fixity of any hierarchical order of oppositions, is ambivalence, and perhaps then the most accurate translation of "Prince des contresens" is "Prince of ambivalence." Merely to oppose is only to confirm what is opposed, but the energy that parodically *reverses* meaning into its opposite is that of potential transformation, and is therefore creative.

The lines that complete the first stanza of "Le Serpent" extend the idea of an ambivalent influence or *pharmakon* — that "medium, in Derrida's words, in which opposites are opposed, the movement and the play that links them among themselves, reverses them or makes one side cross over into the other" — to the associated one of a ritualistic *pharmakos*: "exerce mon amour / A tourner son Seigneur que je hais de n'avoir / Que trouble répression ou fastueux espoir." The traditional expulsion is, appropriately, subtly reversed. The prince of ambivalence or contradictions, that traditional embodiment of evil, is here asked to "turn away" or repulse the recognized Lord, the doctrinal God, since as the false object of our devotion, more an image of tyranny than a source of paternal benevolence, He offers only a "disturbing repression" in the luring hope of an indefinitely deferred fulfillment which is finally mere "ostentation" or "show," not a reality. In an alternative version of the poem, the focus is on a reinterpretation or transvaluation of the serpent, understood no longer as a vicious enemy but, in a reversal of its value, as a persecuted scapegoat and, even more significantly, as the very type of a banished but nevertheless whole energy which has evaded the tyrannical forces of repression and deception:

> Prince des contresens, fais que mon amour
> En exil analogue à ton bannissement

Echappe au vieux Seigneur que je hais d'avoir pu,
Après l'avoir troublé, en clair le décevoir.[18]

In these lines, the expelled serpent represents the exile of *real* desire — the desire, that is, for what is real — from the proper social body or order. But this exile is also a necessary escape, a flight not only *from* an imprisoning and persecuting power but *into* a realm of freed energy and creative employment. The scapegoated serpent is thus affirmed as an indispensable ally. He shows us how to elude the dispensation of the "old Lord" who, in repressing desire, stirs it up again with a hope that only cheats it of its real object, the extravagant and false hope in a transcendent beyond which denies the nature and significance of human reality.

This reversal and transvaluation of the traditional meanings of the serpent is continued in the second half of the poem. The serpent is called "débonnaire serpent," connoting an easy-going, light-hearted, and generous nature, which clearly contradicts his traditional role as a "heavy." The half blessing, half call-to-arms evoked in the cry "Revanche à tes couleurs" reflects a similar twist, since revenge is a conventional feature of the demonic (Milton's Satan, for example) but in this context has a converse meaning: revenge is not the spiteful and destructive reaction of a false nostalgia, is not what Nietzsche would call *ressentiment*, but, rather, a triumphant vindication of hope and desire. In view of this vindication a specific strategy is involved, inasmuch as the serpent cannot raise his "colours" or banner in the open field. Concealment and flight, or at least the appearance of such, are necessary. The serpent haunts the borders of society, of the *polis*. He circumvents the law of the house and of the proper, dwelling just beyond the reach of any strictly organized mode of existence: "Sous le couvert du bois. . . ." Yet he still participates in, although without being confined by, such an order: ". . . et en toute maison." Inhabiting the threshold, living on the margins ("ô serpent marginal!"), never actually entering the living room and proper domain of the social body, this fugitive creature flees only in appearance, is said only to "feign flight" ("tu fais semblant de fuir") by the "bond which unites light to fear" ("Par le lien qui unit la lumière à la peur"). The bond uniting light to fear is at the same time a separating margin, a hinge that both articulates and differentiates, gathers and divides, like the bond and margin that concerns Heidegger in "Language," where he speaks of the "Unter-Schied," the dif-ference of the threshold. The serpent in Char's poem, if not entirely engaged in the proper social order, is not entirely excluded in his role of scapegoat, which is a curiously mixed one. In his ambivalence and marginality, he serves to articulate and differentiate a body proper through the mediation of a potentially infinite displacement. In Heidegger's terms, such a figure is a means by which "man *gives thought* to his homelessness," which is "the sole summons that *calls* mortals into their dwelling." It is a question of whether that summons is carefully attended or dangerously repressed, whether the serpent is perceived as ambivalent or as simply demonic.

In Char's poem, then, what appears to be the serpent's flight is in fact only an appearance, so that it would be superficial to interpret his marginality as nothing more than an enforced exile or a mere evasion. The serpent's behaviour involves, on the contrary, a ruse concealing a point of committed strength and attack, a creative strategy, a style of paradoxical mastery gained in the absence of any desire to possess, control, and have power over the world, or over life, as an object or property at one's command. We might call this style the strategy of the margin,[19] after the closing apostrophe of the poem: "ô serpent marginal!" Although such a committed marginality — and how it specifically concerns poetic creativity — is only touched on in "Le Serpent," a more extensive treatment of the strategy is the subject of an earlier poem by Char, "Suzerain," where the serpent again appears in the role of both *pharmakos* and *pharmakon*, exiled scapegoat and, conversely, curative power.

The Serpent's Wisdom

Suzerain

Nous commençons toujours notre vie sur un crépuscule admirable. Tout ce qui nous aidera, plus tard, à nous dégager de nos déconvenues s'assemble autour de nos premiers pas.

La conduite des hommes de mon enfance avait l'apparence d'un sourire du ciel adressé à la charité terrestre. On y saluait le mal comme une incartade du soir. Le passage d'un méteore attendrissait. Je me rends compte que l'enfant que je fus, prompt à s'éprendre comme à se blesser, a eu beaucoup de chance. J'ai marché sur le miroir d'une rivière pleine d'anneaux de couleuvre et de danses des papillons. J'ai joué dans des vergers dont la robuste vieillesse donnait des fruits. Je me suis tapi dans des roseaux, sous la garde d'êtres forts comme des chênes et sensibles comme des oiseaux.

Ce Monde net est mort sans laisser de charnier. Il n'est plus resté que souches calcinées, surfaces errantes, informe pugilat et l'eau bleue d'un puits minuscule veillée par cet Ami silencieux.

La connaissance eut tôt fait de grandir entre nous. *Ceci n'est plus*, avais-je coutume de dire. *Ceci n'est pas*, corrigeait-il. *Pas et plus* étaient disjoints. Il m'offrait, à la gueule d'un serpent qui souriait, mon impossible que je pénétrais sans souffrir. D'où venait cet Ami? Sans doute, du moins sombre, du moins ouvrier des soleils. Son énergie que je jugeais grande éclatait en fougères patientes, humidité pour mon espoir. Ce dernier, en vérité, n'était qu'une neige de l'existence, l'affinité du renouveau. Un butin s'amoncelait, dessinant le littoral cruel que j'aurais un jour à parcourir. Le coeur de mon Ami m'entrait dans le coeur comme un trident, coeur souverain égaillé dans des conquêtes bientôt réduites en cendres, pour marquer combien la tentation se déprime chez qui s'établit,

se rend.   Nos confidences ne construiraient pas
d'église; le mutisme reconduisait tous nos pouvoirs.
　　Il m'apprit à voler au-dessus de la nuit des
mots, loin de l'hébétude des navires à l'ancre.   Ce
n'est pas le glacier qui nous importe mais ce qui le
fait possible indéfiniment, sa solitaire vraisemblance.
Je nouai avec des haines enthousiastes que j'aidai à
vaincre puis quittai.   (Il suffit de fermer les yeux
pour ne plus être reconnu.)   Je retirai aux choses
l'illusion qu'elles produisent pour se préserver de
nous et leur laissai la part qu'elles nous concèdent.
Je vis qu'il n'y aurait jamais de femme pour moi
dans MA ville.   La frénésie des cascades, symbol-
iquement, acquitterait mon bon vouloir.
　　J'ai remonté ainsi l'âge de la solitude jusqu'à la
demeure suivante de L'HOMME VIOLET. Mais il ne
disposait là que du morose état civil de ses prisons,
de son expérience muette de persécuté, et nous
n'avions, nous, que son signalement d'évadé.

(FM 192-93)

　　The title of the poem "Suzerain" suggests that the theme will be a certain form of rule or governorship.   Whether or not the rule will be of a despotic and tyrannical nature, as the word "suzerain" further implies, remains to be seen.   The word has obviously been chosen partially for its sibilance, which evokes the hiss of the serpent who in the poem exemplifies the sovereignty signified by the title.

　　The poem opens with a general observation, proverbial in its import: "Nous commençons toujours notre vie sur un crépuscule admirable.   Tout ce qui nous aidera, plus tard, à nous dégager de nos déconvenues s'assemble autour de nos premiers pas."   The "disappointments" or "set-backs" mentioned here point to the inevitability in life of serious difficulties, of deception and disillusionment. If our beginnings can never hope to know our ends, the key to our extrication and deliverance is still somehow already prepared for in our first tentative steps. A source of disengagement and freedom from future obstacles is already summoned at the inception of our lives, "s'assemble autour de nos premiers pas." What is this source?   "J'habite une douleur" depicts a restless ascent through deceived and yet ever-renewed hopes, and "Le Serpent" celebrates an influence embodied in the figure of the serpent, who reverses the "disturbing repression" and "ostentatious hope" dispensed by the deceiving "old Lord" of the poem. Both poems show the need to dispel the illusory content of our unreal desires. "Suzerain" takes this process even further and provides a demonstration of real desire, the desire for the real to be found in fully realized desire, which, paradoxically, remains desire. Char uses this paradox to define the poem in one of the aphorisms of "Partage formel," in terms, significantly enough, of a formula for a successful marriage: "Le poème est l'amour réalisé du désir demeuré désir" (*FM* 73).

The opening lines of "Suzerain" speak of a sort of adjuvant, the provision of a suppletory force accompanying our first uncertain infantile steps. What follows is the description of an idyllic, almost Edenic world — the world of childhood — later shown in ruin. This world and of its heroic inhabitants are best characterized by one of the adjectives Char uses in "Le Serpent": "débonnaire." The behaviour of the child's adult models is carefree and gracious, light-hearted and generous, the opposite of what will later, if only temporarily, tempt the maturing child, faced with the destruction of his paradise: nostalgia, remorse, and the desire for revenge. The conduct of these men appears as "un sourire du ciel addressé à la charité terrestre": the heavens smiling on earthly charity or love. The charity and compassion, removed as they are from all pettiness, egoism and malignity, stem from a rare and privileged fortune. These men greet evil as merely an evening's prank, and — like the "inventors" of that other poem, who are uplifted by the sublimity of the hurricane — are moved to great emotion by a meteor's passage. Sensible to beauty and unconscious of evil, which they perceive as nothing but a passing "practical joke," they are indeed, to borrow Blake's phrase, what they behold, the world reflecting to them back their own innocent spirit. They are perhaps not so much ignorant of good and evil as inoculated against it, "in-nocent" in the fullest sense of the word: to be without noxious influence, to be conscious of good but without the mediation of a knowledge of evil. At the same time the paradise they live in is not a world without risk, nor without suffering. But in this privileged, because magically protected world of fortune, suffering is its own remedy. That the poet as a child was "prompt à s'éprendre comme à se blesser" and had "beaucoup de chance" suggests an ambivalence towards experience which does not exclude contraries, which accepts fortune and the contradictions that are part of time. In this world, prank and luck, pain and delight, misfortune and happiness fluctuate, interpenetrate and sidecross perpetually.

Nevertheless, prolonged existence in this "natural" Eden or earthly paradise, "sous la garde d'être forts comme des chênes et sensibles comme des oiseaux," is dangerous, since its security can endure only as the debilitating protection and extension of an innocence and an infancy which are essentially passive in nature. This state resembles what Blake calls Beulah, a paradisal world which must be left behind if one is to grow creatively, so that the eventual fall from innocence described in the succeeding stanza of Char's poem must be understood as ultimately a stroke of good fortune, a type of *felix culpa*. Frye comments on a similar version of the earthly or natural paradise in Blake:

> . . . from our point of view . . . Beulah is a place of perilous equipoise, being as it is the region of the imagination which falls short of the disciplined unity of art. . . . Beulah provides only a temporary escape from the world, not a permanent creation out of it. Wonder that does not stimulate art becomes vacuity: gratifications of appetite that do not build up a creative life become destructive. . . . we can see the perils in the state of imaginative passivity that led to the original Fall. . . .

> Childhood to Blake is a state or phase of imagina-
> tive existence, the phase in which the world of
> imagination is still a brave new world and yet
> reassuring and intelligible. In the protection which
> the child feels from his parents and his evening
> prayer against darkness there is the image of a
> cosmos far more intelligently controlled than ours.
> The spontaneity of life which such protection makes
> possible is the liberty of the expanding imagination
> which has nothing to do but complete its growth. .
> . . However the course of life in this world
> indicates that there is a higher world to attain
> to.[20]

Frye's observations regarding Blake's Beulah may be extended in large part to

Char's poem, the essential point being that the passive paradise of childhood can

endure only at the cost of an expanding creative energy. According to this

logic of a *felix culpa*, the fall from innocence and the concomitant exile into the

world and out of paradise involves an immeasurable enrichment (Milton's "happier

far" in *Paradise Lost*), at least in the long run. Paradise regained is infinitely

more fruitful than paradise retained, the overcoming of alienation better by far

than any inalienable happiness. But first, of course, the paradise must be lost,

this "fall" now signalled by the abrupt discontinuity introduced in the third

stanza: "Ce monde net est mort sans laisser de charnier."

That which was is shown to be now in ruin. As he mourns this neat,

coherent world whose form and definition are now no more than "couches

calcinées, surfaces errantes, informe pugilat," the bitterly disappointed ephebe

happens upon a friend and teacher who, like the angel Michael in his role as the

prophetic educator of Adam at the end of Milton's epic poem, will show the

young poet the way out of despair and into hope, out of the labyrinth of a

fallen world and into the new world of *real* desire. This "Ami silencieux" keeps

a vigil at "un puits miniscule," guards it perhaps, as though he were a covering

cherub, and as though the "source" that he guards were the proverbial well to the bottom of which the "truth" has been thrown and lost forever. This friend, whose aspect is later said to be that of a smiling serpent, is traditionally the archetypal adversary of mankind, tempter and cause of the fall from innocence. But the demonic role of instigating the exile from Paradise and the angelic role of guarding man and woman from the dangerous temptation to return to their lost origin and home are perhaps finally only separate moments of the same function, at least in what Blake would consider a necessarily infernal reinterpretation or reading. These two roles impose the single necessity of a creative movement of *différance*, of the *différance* of difference, in Derrida's terms. This simultaneously demonic and angelic friend — both serpent and seraph — sings neither of innocence nor of experience, but of a union of the two, of the marriage in which the two are one, a marriage of heaven and hell. The rest of the poem will show the presiding wisdom in this marriage, this *hymen*, to be implicitly medicinal, or "pharmaceutical," its strength being drawn from the equally poisonous and antidotal power of a *pharmakon*, the sign for which, we might suggest, is the caduceus: emblem of the medical profession but staff of the angelic herald as well — of the one who brings the divine message, who hermetically transmits the difficult kerygma.[21]

The friend and confessor of the poem, then, is at the same time the satanic accuser and enemy of mankind, at least according to the Christian archetype which Char is obviously evoking, if only to revise radically. For the poet's task, among other things, aims at transforming *"vieux enemis* en *loyaux adversaires,"* as it is put in "Feuillets d'Hypnos" (*FM* 87). The emblematic figure of the serpent in "Suzerain" is exactly such a loyal adversary. His means of conversion are not seductive, nor does he proceed dialectically. His method, in fact, is his ambivalence, the initial lesson of this demonic educator, this Socratic corrupter, being a contradictory one, or rather consisting precisely in a contradiction. Contradiction will turn out to be the beginning and the end of the poet's schooling — not only in its form but in its essential content. Thus, the first word of this contradictor is a blunt disputation of a remark made by the ephebe: *"Ceci n'est plus,* avais-je coutume de dire. *Ceci n'est pas,* corrigeait-il." This important correction involves much more than a mere pedantic splitting of hairs. What the contradiction teaches is the illusion, the unreality, of all nostalgia, of all desire for a revenge on time, on what Nietzsche calls "time and time's 'It was.'"

> Thus the will, the liberator, becomes a malefactor: and upon all that can suffer it takes revenge for its inability to go backwards.
> This, yes, this alone is *revenge* itself: the will's antipathy towards time and time's "It was."[22]

To seek revenge on the "It was" or on the "no longer" is to entangle oneself in the labyrinthine fiction of a lost innocence, the idea of a pathetic fall from innocence being joined to the nostalgic belief in the possible restoration of one's original but forfeited home. The use of a "no longer" presupposes an imaginary continuity between the past and the present, and what the ephebe must come to recognize is the absence of any means by which we might span the bottomless gulf separating the "then" from the "now". By insisting upon the radical disjunction between "not" and "no longer" (*"Pas* et *plus* étaient disjoints"), the friend and adversary contradicts the romantic dream of a restorable presence, of a recoverable plenitude.

What then is the precise antidote to this potentially pernicious nostalgia, this poison lurking in the hope for revenge? The friend provides an alternate wisdom, "m'offrait, à la gueule d'un serpent qui souriait, mon impossible que je pénétrais sans souffrir." That the smiling jaw of a serpent should combat the venomous desire for revenge is a contradiction of all doctrinal wisdom. Char's revision of tradition here is not only Blakian but clearly Nietzschean as well. Transvalued, the serpent, rather than the agent of a reactive *ressentiment*, is a victim of the latter, a scapegoat, burdened with the precise sin of which he is guiltless and which properly belongs to those who subject him to their hypocritical wrath. For what Char's beneficial serpent offers is the cure of revenge: "mon impossible que je pénétrais sans souffrir."

What is this "impossible"? In "J'habite une douleur," the impossible is what is real. But the real as what is impossible is only expressible in poetry and art. Poetry is the realization of a desire that remains at the same time a threshold of desire, as in Char's definition of the poem: "Le poème est l'amour réalisé du désir demeuré désir" (*FM* 73). The incarnation of love in poetry is a marriage ("Le poème est toujours marié à quelqu'un," *FM* 69) wherein, as with any successful union between two people, desire is both completely fulfilled and at the same moment renewed as a potential, fully realized only in the form of recreated desire. It is recreated desire that the apprentice to poetic wisdom is offered by his diabolic teacher and contradictor and which serves as a curative to disentangle him from desire for revenge and the dangerous nostalgia for lost presence.

In a much later poem, "Le Mirage des aiguilles," Char presents us with the negative example of those who ignore the serpent's ambivalent wisdom. The title recalls the final imperative of "J'habite une douleur," "Il n'y a pas de siège pur," which affirms an ever-renewed threshold of desire and warns against the *mirage* of any enduring "untainted seat." They who are satirized in "Le Mirage" take "le rire jaune des ténèbres" (*NP* 17) for lucidity, a reworking of the proverbial expression: "laisser la proie pour son ombre." This proverbial tone suggests an almost Biblical voice of wisdom discoursing on the ways of folly. Leaving the prey for its shadow, in Char's universe, means that one has perilously sacrificed a necessary insecurity to the foolish concerns of propriety and of the proprietary. In this regard, Char's idea of wisdom clearly contradicts, even parodies the often prudential sayings of the Bible, at least of the Old Testament, the wisdom of the New Testament being itself a contradiction of the old dispensation, opposing as it does the folly of its own revolutionary message to the considered and safer judgement of the ancient. By attacking a narrowly prudential way of life, "Le Mirage" prescribes the alternative of a dwelling rooted in the recognition of a fundamental homelessness. Those mocked in the poem refuse to see that existence is not an object to possess and command, to insure and protect from all dispersal and loss by acquiring and guaranteeing a fixed property. Homelessness and death are part of a general economy of human existence that cannot be ignored, and are certainly not to be evaded and repudiated hysterically in the manner of those hopeless proprietors in the poem who "soupesent dans leurs mains les restes de la mort et s'écrient: 'Ce n'est pas pour nous'" (*NP* 17). Death is not for them, they proclaim, because they envision life strictly in terms of security and ownership, as something they command in an absolute way. Their Apollonian hubris condemns them to a fatal entropy of unrelentingly deceived desires. The ambivalent but beneficial "jaw of a smiling serpent," which allows the nostalgic ephebe of "Suzerain" to realize the impossible in poetry and art, is ignored and thus degraded and bereft of all curative and creative power: "Aucun viatique précieux n'embellit la gueule de leurs serpents déroulés (*NP* 17). This missing "precious viaticum," as an embellishment that loses its vital force when "unwound," suggests the powerful influence of an art or poetry capable of binding, distributing, and communicating energy, of a technique ruled by a general economy essential to life. But the proprietors in "Le Mirage" have sacrificed this vital organization in the effort to escape all ambivalence.

A "viaticum" is the provision of certain necessities at the beginning of a journey, like the one evoked in the opening lines of "Suzerain" as a beneficial gathering of adjuvant, suppletory forces "autour de nos premiers pas." This influence can be explained by the effect of a *pharmakon*, an element sadly missing in the proprietary attitude of those condemned, on their own account, to what amounts to a living death in "Le Mirage." Their serpents, the household gods of their creativity, have been "déroulés," unrolled or unwound, so that life is no longer experienced as enigma, as a creative knot capable of ambivalence and expansive energy. Because these proprietors refuse to accept the suffering in life, to admit the pain, loss, and death which is the power of life to wound, they are also sadly unable to be healed — "sans souffrir" — by the impossible gained in poetry, where desire is fully realized only because it is also recreated. They are fated to a recurrent and hopeless cycle of disappointments — "Leur femme les trompe, leur enfants les volent, leurs amis les raillent" — and can distinguish nothing "par haine de l'obscurité." They reject categorically the intimacy between contradictory values, the creative mixing and reversibility characteristic of the *pharmakon*. They are thus condemned to a life without distinction and a death without meaning:

> Le diamant de la création jette-t-il des feux
> obliques? Promptement un leurre pour le couvrir.
> Ils ne poussent dan leur four, ils n'introduisent dans
> la pâte lisse de leur pain qu'une pincée de désespoir
> fromental. Ils se sont établis et prospèrent dans le
> berceau d'une mer où l'on s'est rendu maître des
> glaciers. Tu es prévenu. (*NP* 17)

With only a "pinch" ("une pincée") of the wheat of despair, the bread they eat will never taste of joy, which is to say that, without the recognition that life unites without resolving different and contradictory values, they will only be blindly deceived by the barren neutrality of an experience without despair or hope, pain or delight, death or life. The poem warns the reader ("Tu es prévenu") against this folly, which, if it dreams of a mastery over life which is absolute, only leaves its practitioners the pathetic proprietors of their own frozen immobilized energy: "On s'est rendu maître des glaciers." They become what they behold, the fatally monotonous Apollonian stasis they have themselves produced, a redundant state of unchanging identity. They very element they have obsessively exiled, of difference and change, turns out to be the indispensable nourishment for want of which they are hopelessly famished. They have failed to consider the critical lesson of the poet's Friend in "Suzerain," who painfully teaches his pupil "combien la tentation se déprime chez qui s'établit," and that "Ce n'est pas le glacier qui nous importe." It is not the perpetuation of an Apollonian state that is important — "mais ce qui le fait possible indéfiniment, sa solitaire vraisemblance." What makes it possible is Dionysus, that dispersing force vital to an economy of energy whose primary motor is difference and change.

The foolish conduct depicted in "Le Mirage" is, in fact, a demonic parody of that creative but painful mode of existence advocated by the diabolic Friend and teacher in "Suzerain." It is curious, however, that if the former's conduct is such a parody, the mode affirmed by the figure of the serpent can be understood as a parody of a traditional ideology, whose views communicate in general the prudential and proprietary values condemned in "Le Mirage." The crucial difference is that the parody in "Suzerain" is not demonic but positive, or "infernal," like the radical reinterpretative reading of myth that we find in Blake's *Marriage of Heaven and Hell*.[23] It forces us to recognize that the true parody is the parodied: that is, the ideological deformations of reality by the work of repression. Parody penetrates these disguises and, by an equal counter-torsion, allows us to glimpse the real on the other side of ideology's distorting mirror. This process resembles Nietzsche's *Umwertung*, a revaluation that reverses the secure relationship between opposing values. So we find in Char's poem an image of the satanic, but revalued: the hated fiend and enemy is now the loyal adversary (as does Blake, Char recognizes that "Opposition is true friendship"),[24] the dangerous fugitive from moral justice and righteousness now a beneficial but irrationally persecuted force.

If in "Le Mirage," therefore, a certain "work ethic" is satirized in the proprietary obsessions of those attacked in the poem — owners, ultimately, not of tracts of land but of sterile fields of ice — opposed to this ethic is the provenance of the Friend in "Suzerain," who, we are told, comes from the "least obscure and laborious of suns" ("Du moins sombre, du moins ouvrier des soleils"). The exhausted and frozen energies of the proprietary are a demonic parody of the free and playful deployment of energy represented by the serpent. For if the sun is understood as the source of all energy, then the least obscure and laborious of suns provides the freest disposition of an energy not used up in work or rather, as we might suggest in the context, disposed of in a particular kind of work: the work of poetry and art, which realizes itself in the activity of play, the end and culmination of all work.

In a similar parodic reversal, we discover a radical reassessment of the values that a traditional ideology ascribes to the words and concepts of "temptation" and "church." The hard lesson of the Friend, which on the surface seems to be largely a show of destructive force ("Le coeur de mon Ami m'entrait dans le coeur comme un trident, coeur souverain égaillé dans des conquêtes bientôt réduites en cendres"), in the end shows the ephebe "how disheartened temptation can be for those who establish themselves, who surrender" ("combien la tentation se déprime chez qui s'établit, se rend").   Temptation and desire are positive things.   The Friend's Dionysian dispersing power realizes a positive temptation, measured against which the demonic temptation is in fact the dream of an acquisition possessed and secured against all loss ("Un butin s'amoncelait, dessinant le littoral cruel que j'aurais un jour à parcourir").   In spiritual terms, such acquisitiveness represents a radical failure and refusal to live in time; it reflects the hubristic desire for power over time and change.   This seems to be what is meant by the references to the establishment of a "church," when we are told that the secrets exchanged between the Friend and his disciple, "Nos confidences," "ne construiraient pas d'église."   On the contrary, the inheritor of all their powers is said to be silence ("le mutisme reconduisait tous nos pouvoirs").   This is because the serpent's power is such that it undercuts all proprietary mastery; it is a creative activity of which the decreative is an indispensable inaugural phase.   For in terms of creative energy, what is real is not the actual, not the properly established reality of things, but the potential of things to be precisely what they are not.   Creatively speaking, the real is, once again, the impossible.

> D'où venait cet Ami? Sans doute, du moins sombre, du moins ouvrier des soleils. Son énergie que je jugeais grande éclatait en fougères patientes, humidté pour mon espoir. Ce dernier, en vérité, n'était qu'une neige de l'existence, l'affinité du renouveau. Un butin s'amoncelait, dessinant le littoral cruel que j'aurais un jour à parcourir. Le coeur de mon Ami m'entrait dans le coeur comme un trident, coeur souverain égaillé dans des conquêtes bientôt réduites en cendres, pour marquer

> combien la tentation se déprime chez qui s'établit,
> se rend.   Nos confidences ne construiraient pas
> d'église; le mutisme reconduisait tous nos pouvoirs.
>
> (*FM* 193)

In a superficial reading of this passage, the serpent's wisdom, the stinging truth of what he imparts, may be too easily confused with the simply anarchic will to destroy whatever is order and established.   But this would be to resist the antidote he so subtly offers, as though it were a poison and nothing else, when in fact the two opposed effects, even in their opposition, are inseparable. In this ambivalence lies the very secret of creative energy.

What the Friend in "Suzerain" teaches is the necessity of destroying any resistance or obstacle to the free disposition of energy, not from a demonically wilful urge, but from a spontaneous creative impulse.   Analogous to Char's "satanic" wisdom is Blake's infernal perception of energy in *The Marriage of Heaven and Hell*: "Evil is the active springing from Energy. . . . Energy is the only life . . . Energy is Eternal delight."[25]   The serpent's energy is a manifold of diverse aspects: the patience of hope ("Son énergie que je jugais grande éclatait en fougères patientes, humidité pour mon espoir") which is the affinity for renewal ("l'affinité du renouveau") and wintering phase of desire ("une neige de l'existence"); the autumnal phase of despair corresponding to a dangerous ebbing in the cycle when the need for a disabusement of Apollonian illusion is at its most acute ("Un butin s'amoncelait, dessinant le littoral cruel que j'aurais un jour à parcourir"); and, in a dramatic conflict with the latter phase, the destructive stage of a Dionysian principle in which all conquests are immediately, in the very moment of their attainment, scattered and "bientôt réduites en cendres."

At this point in the poem the word "souverain" appears ("coeur souverain égaillé . . ."), which is a virtual synonym of the title "Suzerain."   It has become clear by now that these words designate a ruling or governing power which is at the furthest remove from anything like a proprietary mastery. Sovereignty is, on the contrary, the privilege of that being who, for one thing, can admit into a unity of creative activity the differing and contradictory phases of energy. On the one hand, the remarkable Dionysian propulsion of this energy seems to imply that our creative acts are to be always somehow cruelly deceived, because dispersed inevitably and disappointed. Yet this would be so only if intentions corresponded to what Derrida calls the "law of the house" or "law of the proper," which finds its extreme expression in the drive for appropriation. But a radically different "economy" is at play in the mode of existence affirmed by the figure of the serpent. According to its law even the work itself — the poem or poetic work — must be understood ultimately as a merely incidental and dispensable result, a product merely serving to punctuate, as one of its diverse phases, the continuum of creative energy.

Thus the apprenticing poet is taught by his Friend to "fly above the night of words, far from the stupefaction of ships at anchor" ("Il m'apprit à voler au-dessus de la nuit des mots, loin de l'hébetude des navires à l'ancre"). It is not the finished poem, understood as a final product with an established meaning, which is of ultimate significance. It is the active source of its production that is vital, and this source can be realized only as the renewal of a potential energy of meaning and therefore only at the cost of the actual. To say that "It is not the ice-field that matters to us but what makes it indefinitely possible, its solitary plausibility" is another way of saying that the poem is, to use again Char's metaphor of a successful marriage, "l'amour réalisé du désir demeuré désir" (*FM* 73). In the terms of a later poem, "Crible," the energy captured and preserved in the poem must be that of a continuingly active desire which "ne sème ni ne moissonne, ne succède qu'à lui et n'appartient qu'à lui. Il se désigne cependant comme le créancier absolu" (*NP* 85). It is desire that remains the poem's source and its successor, and thus can be said to be its "absolute creditor." The poem is the final product of a creative activity, but only as it contains within itself the principle of its own incompletion and of its continuing potential activity; it is both product and productive source. The pathetic proprietors of "Le Mirage des aiguilles" believe they have rendered themselves "maîtres des glaciers," masters of the frozen husk or shell left over after energy has been completely used up, proud owners of the detritus of entropy. But if a glacier is the end result of a dramatically ebbing energy, the incidental and frozen moment of energy's lowest phase, the poem must be the opposite of this: the preservation of a potential intensity, the realization of what in fact makes the poem possible in the first place, "ce qui le fait possible indéfiniment, sa solitaire vraisemblance." The poem expresses the energy that has gone into its making, and thus it must contain the possibility of its own decreation insofar as it is a product, a proper issue in a state of arrest, and as such lacks any further potential to be.

The act of decreation is represented in "Suzerain" as stemming ultimately from the command-like decision of an arbitrary will, one engaged in an elemental game of *fort-da*, that disappearing and reappearing act of the child described and analyzed by Freud in *Beyond the Pleasure Principle*. Near the end of the poem the poet tells us how the serpent's wisdom has been translated into his own experience: "Je nouai avec des haines enthousiastes qui j'aidai à vaincre puis quittai" — and then in the immediately following lines, couched in a seemingly innocuous parenthesis — "(Il suffit de fermer les yeux pour ne plus être reconnu)." It is this capacity of disappearance and reappearance, of binding alliance followed by disruptive separation, of identification followed by self-alienation, which characterizes what Char means by sovereignty. In one of the fragments of "Feuillets d'Hypnos" he writes: "Si l'homme parfois ne fermait pas *souverainement* les yeux, il finirait par ne plus voir ce qui vaut d'être regardé" (*FM* 101). The adverb "souverainement" means, among other things in the context, "arbitrarily," in the sense that any commanding act of the will must be arbitrary, the same being true of the creative will which, when it annihilates just as when it creates, must do so groundlessly, *ex nihilo*, or at least only on the ground of that which its own will brings into being. But this sovereign activity is two-fold and the goal of the vanishing act lies in the moment of recognition: "Je retirai aux choses l'illusion qu'elles produisent pour se préserver de nous et leur laissai la part qu'elle nous concèdent." To achieve its purpose, the poem must be capable of its own decreation, but only so as to continue to affirm that energy which remains vital and potential. Sovereignty consists in the capacity to hold together these contradictory and extreme expressions of the creative will: annihilation and affirmation, or, in Nietzsche's mythic terms, Dionysus and Apollo, and so to preserve in a single act of creation the tension that is born between them.

The closing theme of the poem concerns the fate of the serpent as the bestower of a creative energy opposed to any proper economy or "household law." Perhaps inevitably — these closing lines seem to suggest — we will find such a figure consigned to the margins of the social order. His kindred functionaries, the poet and the prophet, dwell voluntarily, as well as by force, on the margins to which they are expelled, like the "cursed share" in the political economy of which Georges Bataille speaks.[26] They inhabit the threshold of the house — that place of painful dif-ference described by Heidegger in "Language" —

or dwell outside the city gates, recognizing, in the words of the apprenticing poet in Char's poem, that "il n'y aurait jamais de femme pour moi dans MA ville." This is the lot of the prophet never heard in his own — his proper — country and therefore only properly heard in a place of exile. His *felix culpa* or "happy sin," spelling as it does the creative necessity of an alienation or estrangement of the proper, also turns out to be the burden of sin bestowed upon the ambivalent scapegoat, whose relentless persecution is the present state of freedom. MY city: there is no breathing space for the poet in the stricture that this emphatic personal pronoun expresses, implying in its possessiveness an entire network of propriety, property, and personal power. As Mary Ann Caws notes concerning the marginal being in Char, "the concept of marginality works in two senses: the word implies not only a situation on the edge of society, but a positive demand for a margin sufficient to assure his free path in a breathable space, suited to a being bare in his lack of heritage and heritors."[27] The poet seeks his gain in another economy, in a margin from which he profits and from which he prophesies, in that cursed and blessed share which, in its deficiency, exceeds the reappropriative reach of any proper social order. The extreme avatar of this poetic principle is the violent figure evoked in the closing stanza of "Le Mirage des aiguilles," who is radically contrasted with the wretched proprietors depicted in the first part of the poem: "Fidèle, méché, mais sans cesse vaguant, dérobant sa course par toute l'étendue montrée du feu, tenue du vent; l'étendue, trésor de boucher, sanglante à un croc" (*NP* 17). This figure's bloody violence is repeated in the fugitive serpent in "Suzerain," who in the eyes of society is a "wanted man." Through "the age of solitude" ("l'âge de la solitude"), the maturing poet of the poem climbs to his next dwelling place, in an ascent through deception and disillusionment much like that described in

"J'habite une douleur." The "tainted seat" that he now occupies is that of "L'HOMME VIOLET": the image of a violated humanity whose only recourse — like that of Char in his role as a leader in the guerilla actions of the maquis during the war — is an abrupt violence. For "violet" can also be read as *violé*, as well as, by the addition of a letter, violent.

But the significance of this "violet man" may be interpreted in another way. We may think of the poet's violence against the law of the proper, which must be violated to restore reality to its authentic, or "proper," image. This violation, potentially fatal, potentially restorative, and therefore fundamentally ambivalent, means again that we are within the mixed element of the *pharmakon*, an element suggested by the very colour violet — the colour of twilight veering between the calm of the day's blue and the violence of the sunset's purple, thus reflecting the state of being between two states, precariously and undecidably *between*. For those who would defend the "law and order" of the proper, the contradictory and undecidable nature of this violet, violating and violated, violent man makes him a notorious perpetrator of crimes against property and propriety, and like the figure of the serpent therefore justly persecuted as a "wanted man." The serpent's final epiphany in the poem, as we glimpse him for the last time slipping away and evading us, is in his double role as both an outlaw and a scapegoat, as both a violator of the proper and one violated by its law — a persecuted criminal. At the same time this figure is a sovereign, a suzerain. But like the god Theuth in Plato's *Phaedrus* he is not the king and father, but the prince and son, and like Theuth as well — or like his most dangerous invention, writing — he is the victim of a ritualistic expulsion. The serpent in Char's poem is the embodiment of that poisonous substance which must be expelled from the body proper. But at the same time he brings into play a *pharmakon,* concealing in his venom a potential remedy, a powerful medicinal and restorative influence, a viaticum of life-giving nourishment or provision, that very viaticum which fails to embellish the unwound serpents of those dealers in property in "Le Mirage des aiguilles." The serpent is the very figure, we might say, of writing — "Writing," as Derrida poses it in a "Plato's Pharmacy," "the outlaw, the lost son" (*D* 146) — of a writing which is perpetually exiled but which eternally returns as the indispensable, the *sine qua non,* the secret of good health.

> J'ai remonté ainsi l'âge de la solitude jusqu'à la demeure suivante de L'HOMME VIOLET. Mais il ne disposait là que du morose état civil de ses prisons, de son expérience muette de persécuté, et nous n'avions, nous, que son signalement d'évadé.
>
> (*FM* 193)

The Serpent's Health

A la santé du serpent

I

Je chante la chaleur à visage de nouveau-né, la chaleur désespérée.

II

Au tour du pain de rompre l'homme, d'être la beauté du point du jour.

III

Celui qui se fie au tournesol ne méditera pas dans la maison. Toutes les pensées de l'amour deviendront ses pensées.

IV

Dans la boucle de l'hirondelle un orage s'informe, un jardin se construit.

266

V

Il y aura toujours une goutte d'eau pour durer plus que la soleil sans que l'ascendant du soleil soit ébranlé.

VI

Produis ce que la connaissance veut garder secret, la connaissance aux cent passages.

VII

Ce qui vient au monde pour ne rien troubler ne mérite ni égards ni patience.

VIII

Combien durera ce manque de l'homme mourant au centre de la création parce que la création l'a congédié?

IX

Chaque maison était une saison. La ville ainsi se répétait. Tous les habitants ensemble ne connaissaient que l'hiver, malgré leur chair réchauffée, malgré le jour qui ne s'en allait pas.

X

Tu es dans ton essence constamment poète, constamment au zénith de ton amour, constamment avide de vérité et de justice. C'est sans doute un mal nécessaire que tu ne puisses l'être assidûment dans ta conscience.

XI

Tu feras de l'âme qui n'existe pas un homme meilleur qu'elle.

XII

Regarde l'image téméraire où se baigne ton pays, ce plaisir qui t'a longtemps fui.

XIII

Nombreux sont ceux qui attendent que l'écueil les soulève, que le but les franchisse, pour se définir.

XIV

Remercie celui qui ne prend pas souci de ton remords. Tu es son égal.

XV

Les larmes méprisent leur confident.

XVI

Il reste une profondeur mesurable là où le sable subjugue la destinée.

XVII

Mon amour, peu importe que je sois né: tu deviens visible à la place où je disparais.

XVIII

Pouvoir marcher, sans tromper l'oiseau,   du coeur de l'arbre à l'extase du fruit.

XIX

Ce qui t'accueille à travers le plaisir n'est que la gratitude mercenaire du souvenir.   La présence que tu as choisie ne délivre pas d'adieu.

XX

Ne te courbe que pour aimer.   Si tu meurs, tu aimes encore.

XXI

Les ténèbres que tu t'infuses sont régies par la luxure de ton ascendant solaire.

XXII

Néglige ceux aux yeux de qui l'homme passe pour n'être qu'une étape de la couleur sur le dos tourmenté de la terre.   Qu'ils dévident leur longue

remontrance.   L'encre du tisonnier et la rougeur du
nuage ne font qu'un.

XXIII

Il n'est pas digne du poète de mystifier
l'agneau, d'investir sa laine.

XXIV

Si nous habitons un éclair, il est le coeur de
l'éternel.

XXV

Yeux qui, croyant inventer le jour, avez éveillé
le vent, que puis-je pour vous? Je suis l'oubli.

XXVI

La poésie est de toutes les eaux claires celle
qui s'attarde le moins aux reflects de ses ponts.
Poésie, la vie future à l'intérieur de l'homme
requalifié.

XXVII

Une rose pour qu'il pleuve.   Au terme
d'innombrables années, c'est ton souhait.

(FM 194-99)

The poetic "work," for Char, is that activity whose required energy
expresses itself in the poem at the same time as an undwindling energy; it is the
translation of energy into a potential energy which is not used up.   In this lies
— to borrow an expression from Heidegger — "the workly character of the work
in the sense of the work of art," which differs from mere equipmentality in that
it does not waste away, dwindle, fall into disuse or turn into "mere stuff."[29]
Char formulates this preservative quality of poetry or art in his definition of the
poem as "l'amour réalisé du désir demeuré désir" (*FM* 73). This energy, which is
embodied in the serpent of "Suzerain," may be explored further in "A la santé
du serpent," where the conjunction in the poem's title of health and serpent
suggests the invocation of a *pharmakon*:   a potentially fatal poison which proves

to be, reversibly, a medicinal antidote. An aphorism from "Contre une maison séche" sums up this creative ambivalence: "Il en est qui laissent des poisons, d'autres des remèdes. Difficiles à déchiffrer. Il faut goûter. / Le oui, le non immédiats. C'est salubre en dépit des corrections qui vont suivre" (*NP* 121). The formulaic toast "à la santé" may remind us of the "health" that we find in the opening lines of another poem, "Joue et dors . . .": "Joue et dors, bonne soif, nos oppresseurs ici ne sont pas sévères" (*LM* 67). Play and sleep here act as a counter-poison or antidote, mysteriously easing and slackening a severe and possibly perilous oppression:

> Volontiers ils plaisantent ou nous tiennent le bras
> Pour traverser la périlleuse saison.
> Sans doute, le poison s'est-il assoupi en eux,
> Au point de desserrer leur barbare humeur.
>
> (*LM* 67)

Play and sleep are energy in the respective states of free deployment and dormancy, similar to the energy of the serpent in "Suzerain," who is said to come "du moins sombre et du moins ouvriers des soleils," that is, from a source of freely disposable, even idling energy which is used up not in work, but in play. The free use of energy functions, then, as a benign, medicinal action that combats a poisonous and possibly fatal constriction. The pharmaceutical effect of sleep, too, as working against a force of oppression is the idea behind the code name "Hypnos" of *Les Feuillets d'Hypnos*, which suggests a hypnotic or drug-induced sleep, an imitation of death or "playing dead" that is a strategy of survival and ultimately overcomes death and the powers dealing it, the mimetic image of the evil or poison being in the end the best remedy, the most effective *pharmakon*.

In "A la santé du serpent," as in "Suzerain," this health-giving force is symbolized by the serpent, a creature mythically known not only for its venom, but for its ambivalence and for the cure which contradictorily lies in its poison, a serpent without a sting being devoid of energy, a serpent without the power to wound being without the power to heal. In "Lettera Amorosa" Char addresses this enigma in raising the question: "Pourquoi le champ de la blessure est-il de tous le plus prospère?" (*LM* 95). The creative ambivalence of this prosperity stemming from the wound, of the vital benefit born from the potentially death-dealing blow, is what gives the series of diverse aphorisms in "A la santé" a concealed but compelling unity of intent. The "health" or toast of the poem's title is also the health afforded by the serpent, a wholeness realized only contradictorily and by a conversion of contraries, such as disease and health, poison and medicine, life and death. The initial aphorism, indeed, expresses a fundamental reversal: "Je chante la chaleur à visage de nouveau-né, la chaleur désespérée." A newborn warmth is a desperate warmth still cold; hope springs forth from the despair with which it mingles; heat comes forth from winter, in a crossing of contraries. This moment is that invisible turning point where opposites originally separate. Energy here does not take the form of a proper identity but is only known by its contradiction, its union of contraries. The reversal from despair to hope, winter to spring, cold to heat, is a manifestation of energy, of an energy in ascendance and which now awakens like a rising sun. If the serpent celebrated by Char in the title of the poem is symbolic of anything, it is, as it is described in Cirlot's *Dictionary of Symbols*, "symbolic of energy itself — of force pure and simple; hence its ambivalencies and multivalencies."[30]

The aphorism that immediately follows also expresses a reversal, but in addition is itself the reversal of the proverbial expression "rompre le pain": "Au tour du pain de rompre l'homme, d'être la beauté du point du jour." The proverbial breaking of bread by man becomes, in a turning of the tables, bread's breaking of man. This reversal corresponds as well to a new day born from night, to the turning-point of a recreated and ascending energy, which in this case announces a truly revolutionary situation, which would force humanity to redefine itself in a radical way. The reversal is also a verbal one. We find, for example, a similar effect in the final aphorism of the poem, XXVII, with its invocation "Une rose pour qu'il pleuve," although in this case the logic is causal not verbal, the normal order of causation ("Qu'il pleuve pour qu'il y ait une rose") being completely reversed. The form of aphorism II is especially significant, for it makes clear the proverbial nature of most of the formulations which make up the poem. Char's use of the proverb form is very reminiscent of Blake's use in *The Marriage of Heaven and Hell* where a counter or infernal wisdom is expressed as a parody of conventional proverbial wisdom; the same thing is to be found in Nietzsche's parody of proverbs and parables in *Zarathustra*. Another example is aphorism XXIII — "Il n'est pas digne du poète de mystifier l'agneau, d'investir sa laine" — which explicitly contradicts the innocence of the crucified Christ figured as the sacrificial lamb, the implication being that we are to understand such a spiritual "investment" as an ideological distortion and mystification of the authentic image of reality. In its place, Char asks for a revaluation along the lines of Nietzsche's *Umwertung* or of Blake's infernal interpretation of things. Blake, interestingly enough, shares a number of key terms with Char: contraries and contradictions, energy and desire.

The opening proverbs of Char's poem concern, then, a reversal announcing a reawakening creative energy which now begins to climb from the nadir of its ebb or decline. If the proverb and the wisdom it imparts are ideally directed towards the most successful employment of human energies, what Frye calls the "parody-proverb" aims at the destruction of a narrowly primitive concept of wisdom, one strictly oriented towards a careful sifting of past experience and tradition in view of a safe and prudent application in one's present life.[31]   This primitive wisdom is based on the conception of a limited proper economy of human energy, but it is only one of the forms of wisdom in the Bible.   In Frye's view the ultimate end of Biblical wisdom is a free disposition and deployment of our energies which would be creative in the fullest sense. This is certainly the point of the wisdom evoked by Char throughout his poetry and in particular in "A la santé."   But since we live in a world subjected to ideology (or to what Frye calls adjustment myth), the means of expressing that wisdom must often be indirect and parodic.[32]   In violent contradiction with that prudential and proprietary way of life satirized in "Suzerain" and "Le Mirage des aiguilles," creative energy is, by contrast, freed from any teleological stricture or law of the proper and is most reminiscent of the energy expressed in play, as opposed to work, or of that which we find in "the work-being of the work,"[33] to use Heidegger's words, in the sense of the work of art.   In a very suggestive discussion of the use of the proverb form in Ecclesiastes, Frye speaks of a wisdom and energy that are quite applicable to the intent of Char's poetry:

> Work, as we usually think of it, is energy expended for a further end in view; play is energy expended for its own sake, as with children's play, or as a manifestation of the end of goal of work, as in "playing" chess or the piano.   Play, in this sense, then is the fulfillment of work, the exhibition of what the work has been done for . . . . the point is even clearer in the Book of Proverbs, where Wisdom is personified as an attribute of God from the time of Creation, expressing in particular the exuberance of creation, the spilling over of the life and energy in nature that so deeply impresses the prophets and poets of the Bible.   The AV speaks of this wisdom as "rejoicing in the habitable part of the earth" (8:31), but this is feeble compared to the tremendous Vulgate phrase *ludens in orbe terrarum,*

playing over all the earth.   Here we finally see the
real form of wisdom in human life as the *philoso-
phia* or *love* of wisdom that is creative and not
simply erudite.   We see too how the primitive form
of wisdom, using past experience as a balancing
pole for walking the tightrope of life, finally grows,
through incessant discipline and practice, into the
final freedom of movement where, in Yeats's phrase,
we can no longer tell the dancer from the dance.[34]

As we have said, the first series of proverbs in "A la santé" concern
that moment of rebirth or recreation when an energy in decline is reversed
suddenly and begins to rise.   Aphorism III is another "parody-proverb," to use
Frye's term for Blake's proverbs in *The Marriage* which are "written from the
oracular or epiphanic point of view,"[35] this being an appropriate description of
Char's use of the form as well, since in his poetry the proverb also tends to
merge with the oracular.   The aphorism consists of the following cryptic
statement: "Celui qui se fie au tournesol ne méditera pas dans la maison.
Toutes les pensées de l'amour deviendront ses pensées."   He who trusts in the
sunflower is the poet who trusts in his creative energy, and thus relies on the
"tournesol" as that which turns towards the sun, the source of energy.   He will
not meditate in the house, because his thinking is naturally fugitive and evades
the law of the house or of the proper, escapes the stricture of the proprietary
and prudential.   "Epouse et n'épouse pas ta maison" (*FM* 95), Char writes in
"Feuillets d'Hypnos," a double imperative which perfectly expresses the contradictory balance the poet must learn as an inhabitant of the margins and guest
of the precarious threshold.   For poetry draws its strength from an economy of
energy which contradicts, and sometimes violently, the security and providence
of any proper order.   In the same "Feuillets," which is the notebook of Char's
violent experience as a resistance fighter during the war, we find the following
threatening caution addressed to the proprietary, who have sacrificed to the

interests of their own safety and property the truly "proper" concern of their "pays natal":

> AUX PRUDENTS: Il neige sur le maquis et c'est contre nous chasse perpétuelle. Vous dont la maison ne pleure pas, chez qui l'avarice écrase l'amour, dans la succession des journées chaudes, votre feu n'est qu'un garde-malade. Trop tard. Votre cancer a parlé. Le pays natal n'a plus de pouvoirs. (*FM* 92)

In this case, the proprietary has become an obsession and a disease, against which the only cure is an abrupt violence. In aphorism III of "A la santé," however, it is not a matter of violence against the conditions created by a sense of prudence and property that has grown too dangerous; what we discover is simply an avoidance and rejection of a narrowly primitive and provident wisdom. But if the poet is not provident, he may nevertheless prove providential, even in his apparent foolishness. This brings us to the second part of the saying: that "all love's thoughts will become his thoughts." Love is the nature, then, of the poet's meditation, which places his activity all the more in contradiction with the wisdom of prudence; to think only of love is condemnable as a dangerously foolish activity from the provident point of view. The idea that there is folly in thinking too much on love is, of course, itself quite proverbial, so that we can clearly see the parodic nature of Char's use of the proverb form as a counter-imitation or imitation-in-reverse of the traditional proverb.[36] What appears to be folly is actually a wisdom in the disguise of a parody of conventional wisdom.

The counter-wisdom espoused by Char prescribes a nonprudential but creative insecurity, where the state of good fortune is also one of risk and danger, where the opportunity for invention is also the chance of destruction. This fertile instability implies that for there to be a creative energy there must be the equal potential for contradiction and a meeting of contraries. This seems to be the point of aphorism IV: "Dans la boucle de l'hirondelle un orage s'informe, un jardin se construit." The "swallow's loop" points to the unity of a renewed energy; the swallow is the sign of springtime while the loop like the circle is the form of a unifying whole. Within this whole there is the potential contradiction of converging contraries: the building of a garden or inhabitable natural space is conjoined with the looming imminence of that force of destruction represented by the forming storm. The implication is that the circle of creative space must be a field of inherent instability and insecurity, and must include the possibility of violent contradiction, the very index of a freely disposable energy which in its ambivalence is able to go either way.

Aphorism V is another case of "parody-proverb," the wisdom it contains flying in the face of all prudent and provident concern: "Il y aura toujours une goutte d'eau pour durer plus que le soleil sans que l'ascendant du soleil soit ébranlé." Prescribed is almost a "lilies of the field" approach to the threat of an exhaustion of energy, in defiance of that primitive wisdom which anxiously voices the need for careful economical management. This is because an ever renewable source of ascending energy, "l'ascendant du soleil," is to be found in poetry, where desire remains, as it is put in "Crible," "le créancier absolu," the absolute creditor. By that very creative insecurity and instability which contradicts the proper, poetry paradoxically uses and keeps alive — uses without using up — an undwindling energy and desire, thus securing us against the possibility of the sun's ever being disturbed ("ébranlé"). The sun may be outlasted and overtaken by "a drop of water which will last longer than the sun," but the sun's ascent is not in peril; it will always be renewed, according to a general, unrestricted economy in which use and expenditure paradoxically leave the recreative potential of poetry undiminished.

Now follows a series of four aphorisms equally concerned with the reversal and freeing of creative energies, but this time from the perspective of a need actively to disrupt a dangerously constricted state of resistance and repression. Aphorism VI deals specifically with the necessity of contradicting the conventional idea of knowledge as an enlightenment governed by clarity and reason. Such an Apollonian conception is countered by an affirmation of secrecy and enigma, and of a knowledge actively produced — like poetry, made and created. Such knowledge must be contradictory, and presupposes a mixture of concealment and revelation, hiddenness and disclosure. Also, it is disruptive and runs up against the merely apparent reality of things, instigating disclosure by challenging and forcing open the disguises and deceiving appearances of the real. This disruption is suggested by the abrupt imperative of the prescription: "Produis ce que la connaissance veut garder secret, la connaissance aux cents passages." The image of this knowledge is the labyrinth or maze, which expresses the mixture and confusion of darkness and light, obscurity and revelation, multiplicity and unity. Opposed to this ambivalent element is the knowledge satirized in "Le Mirage des aiguilles," where the deluded take "pour de la clarté le rire jaune des ténèbres" and by the same token "n'en distinguent rien, par haine de l'obscurité. Le diamant de la création jette-t-il des feux obliques? Promptement un leurre pour le couvrir." But the very obliquity of knowledge, the indirection and obscurity contradicting the hubristic Apollonian desire for the full daylight of consciousness and clarity, form and definition, is vital in "A la santé." The key is the differential balance to be realized between concealment and disclosure, which the image of the labyrinth, with its hundred passageways, captures so well.   Authentic knowledge ultimately culminates in enigma, diverse forms of which pervade Char's poetry, from the emblematic riddle to the dark and prophetic oracle.   The success of the enigma depends on the tricky balance realized in the poem, since the failure to attain the proper balancing of forces destroys the creative economy of energy.   This failure is the subject of the poem "Pour renouer," whose title urges a retying of the enigmatic knot when the equilibrium has been treacherously tipped and the balance upset:

> Si ce que je te montre et ce que je te donne te
> semblent moindres que ce que je te cache, ma
> balance est pauvre, ma glane est sans vertu.
>
> Tu es reposoir d'obscurité sur ma face trop
> offerte, poème.   Ma splendeur et ma souffrance se
> sont glissés entre les deux.   (*LM* 134)

The need for a precarious stability "entre les deux," what Cirlot depicts as the "balanced duality" of the caduceus, comparable in its "precisely symmetrical and bilateral arrangement"[37] with the scales of Libra, suggests again the mixed element of the *pharmakon*.   In "Pour renouer" what is prescribed — since we are speaking of the "pharmaceutical," "prescriptions" are the order of the day — is the attainment of a measure, "une distance mystérieusement favorable et mesurée," a delicate differential balance between obscurity and disclosure.   If secrecy and concealment prevail for their own sake, or for the purpose of mystification, then the aim of the poem as "reposoir d'obscurité sur ma face trop offerte" becomes invalid.   Similarly, if the drive towards disclosure is too predominant ("Nous nous sommes soudain trop approchés de quelque chose dont on nous tenait à une distance . . ."), then the creative contradictory tension is destroyed and the energy of the poem dispersed.   In aphorism VI of "A la santé" the accent is placed on the disclosure, that force of revelation which combats the resisting concealment and hermetic mystery.   The crepuscular in this case, as in "Suzerain," is the twilight of daybreak and of the ascending solar energy celebrated in the opening aphorisms of the poem. In the later aphorism XX, the balance of successful enigmatic disclosure — with the emphasis again on the disclosure — is expressed as a solar ascendancy over darkness: "Les ténèbres que tu t'infuses sont régies par la luxure de ton ascendant solaire" (*FM* 198). If to release what knowledge wishes to mystify and keep secret, we must open up the concealed passageways of the labyrinth and throw light on the enigma, this does not mean the enigma is thereby destroyed. On the contrary, the disclosure merely restores the balance and untangles the creative knot, without untying it. The authentic enigma is always the furthest thing from an inhibiting, obscurantist obfuscation.

Aphorism VII provides us with yet another example of "parody-proverb": "Ce qui vient au monde pour ne rien troubler ne mérite ni égards ni patience." As in VI, this sentence affirms the need for a provocative disturbance of any order of things inhibiting creative activity. Poetry, for Char, is above all a "trouble-maker," because it brings difference and contradiction into the world of imposed order. In the words of one of the fragments from "Rougeur des matinaux":

> Nous sommes des passants *appliqués* à passer, donc à jeter le trouble, à infliger notre chaleur, à dire notre exubérance. Voilà pourquoi nous intervenons! Voilà pourquoi nous sommes intempestifs et insolites! Notre aigrette n'y est rien. Notre utilité est tournée contre l'employeur.
>
> (*LM* 80)

Poetry is not primarily an ordering, but a *dislocation* of any arrested and inhibiting order. "La réalité sans l'énergie disloquante de la poésie, qu'est-ce?" (*LM* 177) the poet asks in "Pour une Promethée saxifrage." According to a conventional wisdom, this sort of provocation or "trouble-making" is a proverbially foolish and destructive activity, and of course the serpent, as a diabolic agent *provocateur*, symbolizes such a disturbing force. Once again the image of the creative, for Char, is a parody and transvaluation of traditional understanding. Poetry does not bring harmony into the world, but relentlessly provokes contradiction.

Aphorism VIII urges human creativity by contesting the doctrinal perception of man's place in the universe as a creature removed from creation: "Combien durera ce manque de l'homme mourant au centre de la création parce que la création l'a congédié?" The primordial activity of human beings is *poieîn*, making and invention. In the terse terms of one of Blake's own proverbs from *The Marriage of Heaven and Hell*: "Where man is not nature is barren."[38] But human energies have turned from creation towards the exploitation of a submissive earth and dehumanized world. The remedy is that the human creature become a creator, as in "Suzerain" where the exile from a protected infantile sphere of innocence is also the possibility of an enhanced creative energy, capable of moulding the earth in a human image.

Aphorism XXII of the poem advises a similar change in human self-perception:

> Néglige ceux aux yeux de qui l'homme passe
> pour n'être qu'une étape de la couleur sur le dos
> tourmenté de la terre. Qu'ils dévident leur longue
> remontrance. L'encre du tissonier et la rougeur du
> nuage ne font qu'un.   (*FM* 198)

In this case, however, the accused is not a theologically inspired view of reality which tends to see the human creature indefinitely fallen out of creation, but rather an equally doctrinal scientific *episteme* which. if interpreted in a certain way, nihilistically conceives of humanity as nothing but the wretched product of a complex of impersonal and inhuman determining forces, such as History or

Evolution. In this regard, then, Char's humanism is highly romantic and quite close to Blake's in a number of respects.

Aphorism IX offers a parabolic image of the sterility that results when an Apollonian state of unchanging identity is sought at the exclusion of all creative energy:

> Chaque maison était une saison. La ville ainsi se répétait. Tous les habitants ensemble ne connaissaient que l'hiver, malgré leur chair réchauffée, malgré le jour qui ne s'en allait pas.
>
> (*FM* 195)

This ideal state of identity turns out to be a nightmare of hellish repetition, a gruesome parody of eternity. The need for contradiction and contraries becomes tragically clear. An unchanging reality is simply a world where energy has completely died, where unity has become uniformity and identity the monotony of the same. The oxymoronic "desperate warmth" of a reversible energy, celebrated as it begins its ascent in the opening aphorisms of the poem, is no longer possible when difference and contradiction have been fatally exiled. This refusal of contraries results in an unchanging winter where our desires, without the catalyst of difference, like left-overs served over and over again, are simply "warmed up" or "re-heated." "Without Contraries is no progression," Blake writes, which is a perfect way of explaining the death of energy depicted in IX. The only hope is that this state of monotonous identity be violently pulverized and shattered — "le poème pulvérisé" being at the same time the pulverizing poem — by the sheer impact of contradiction that the poet is capable of bringing into the world.

The need for contradiction and contraries is the subject of a number of the remaining "parody-proverbs" which make up the poem. Aphorism X, for instance, poses the contradictory relationship between essence and existence,

between an idealized higher reality and the opposing consciousness, or conscience, of the imperfect reality we inhabit:

> Tu es dans ton essence constamment poète,
> constamment au zenith de ton amour, constamment
> avide de vérité et de justice. C'est sans doute un
> mal nécessaire que tu ne puisses l'être assidument
> dans ta conscience.   (*FM* 196)

Char plays here on the fertile double meaning of the word *conscience* in French,
simultaneously consciousness and moral conscience. The contradictory nature of
reality is "un mal nécessaire," a sort of *felix culpa* or "happy fall," the necessary because ultimately creative evil of imperfection and alienation. Without
contraries is no progression, and therefore no energy, that energy which in
Blake's infernal view of things is "the only life." The poet seeks a balance
between the two poles of human existence, "La vitre-cloaque de Caliban" and
"les yeux tout-puissants et sensibles d'Ariel" (*FM* 65) as Char puts it in "Partage
formel." He seeks a point of gravity in a general instability, but he does not
try to overcome his insecurity by doing away with differences, but, as "l'homme
de la stabilité unilatérale" (*FM* 73) or as a "Magicien de l'insécurité" whose
satisfactions are only "adoptives" (*FM* 66), he looks for temporary — because
temporal — equilibriums among contradictory and contrary forces. The stability
gained by this "magician of insecurity" is "unilateral" precisely because the
poet's gravity is invented and not located outside himself. This "particularité,"
spoken of in "Rougeur des Matinaux," "parfois de nous balancer en marchant"
(*LM* 78) brings to mind Frye's words concerning a wisdom which "using past
experience as a balancing-pole for walking the tightrope of life, finally grows,
through incessant discipline and practice, into the final freedom of movement
where, in Yeats's phrase, we can no longer tell the dancer from the dance."[39]
The need for a self-created balance is a result of the poet's decision to dwell

between different worlds, in a threshold space and mixed element where the ground is fluid, mobile, and unsure. The poet, in fact, actively seeks out contradiction and contraries in order to measure himself and find his balance, which in the case of aphorism X is that point of suspension between the extreme poles of the ideal and the real.

Aphorism XIII puts the positive necessity of contradiction in negative terms: "Nombreux sont ceux qui attendent que l'écueil les soulève, que le but les franchisse, pour se définir." This is another way of saying, if we simply rephrase the aphorism: rare are those who seek their own contradiction and possible destruction; rare are those who look for adversity in order to define and create themselves. Rare and — according to a traditional wisdom — extremely imprudent and foolish. But rare in Char's peculiar view means both exceptional and privileged, and ultimately sovereign. If the prudent proverb runs to the effect that he who seeks adversity seeks his own destruction, the counter-wisdom of "A la santé" proclaims just the contrary, that — to borrow the words of Blake — "Opposition is true friendship." Aphorism XII, which immediately precedes this prescription of adversity, similarly affirms the image of a country of pleasure which it would be not only risky, but clearly foolhardy ever to try to realize: "Regarde l'image téméraire où se baigne ton pays, ce plaisir qui t'a longtemps fui." But the value that Char ascribes to such folly — as Blake writes, "If the fool would persist in his folly he would become wise"[40] — is again based on the potential creativity of contradiction. Sovereignty belongs to the self which is capable of balancing without dissolving the tension between different and opposing forces, which seeks its own contradiction, and even its own violent undoing. This capacity is what Nietzsche mean in *Zarathustra* by the need to will one's own downfall, *Untergang*, to will "zugrunde gehen."[41]

Char often speaks of another opposing self — adversary, contradictor, opponent — against which one pits oneself in the creative struggle for identity. It may be a man, a woman, even and perhaps most significantly: the poem itself. As he proclaims in "La Bibliothèque est en feu":

> Il n'y a que mon semblable, la compagne ou le compagnon, qui puisse m'éveiller de ma torpeur, déclencher la poésie, me lancer contre les limites du vieux désert afin que j'en triomphe.   Aucun autre. Ni cieux, ni terre privilégiée, ni choses dont on tressaille.   (*LM* 146)

The creative encounter for Char is a human encounter, not a sublime one, and is often depicted as an alliance or a marriage, which is at the same time a struggle of dominant wills where identity is born from contradiction and the matching and balancing of contrary forces.   There is little of the conciliatory in such a process.   Contradiction is not resolved or dissolved, but affirmed.   In the collision of the poet with his other self there is a transformation and — as an appropriate end of marriage — the birth of another being, in this case the poem, which represents a newly created identity and is the source of an intensified energy and increase of meaning.   In fact, far from resolved, contradiction in such a marriage has simply been *measured* and become ultimately an enigma, forming a knot which is a textual profundity, a depth of significance.   In the words of aphorism XVI: "Il reste une profondeur mesurable là où le sable subjugue la destinée."   This struggle with the sovereign opponent, who may also be the beloved, is also the contest of a labyrinth or maze, which one tries not to escape but to enter as a means of discovering — and not as a sign of having lost — the self.   In the closing apostrophe of "Le Mortel parténaire," the enigma of the poem is called a "dédale de l'extrême amour," a "labyrinth of extreme love," born from desire and energy, and epitomising what Char means by the poem as "l'amour réalisé du désir demeuré désir" and by desire as "le créancier absolu" (*NP* 85).

Several of the remaining "parody-proverbs" of "A la santé" focus on this difficult process of self-definition through adversity and contradiction. Aphorism XIV runs as follows: "Remercie celui qui ne prend pas souci de ton remords. Tu es son égal." An interaction ruled by narcissism and nostalgia, or by remorse and the desire for revenge, is only a failed encounter, treacherous in its self-deception and illusoriness. For its hidden motive is the revenge on time, the dream of recuperating a past identity, the refusal to admit the inevitable contradiction of one's identity in time, which is the reason for the Friend's correction of his disciple in "Suzerain": "*Ceci n'est plus*, avais-je coutume de dire. *Ceci n'est pas*, corrigait-il. *Pas* et *plus* étaient disjoints." To resist this disjunction is a reflex of the narcissistic desire for an eternalized identity, for an unchanging presence of self. Opposed to this yearning is the sovereign encounter of poetry which occupies a present without presence and affirms a presence without present. As stated in XIX: "Ce qui t'accueille à travers le plaisir n'est que la gratitude mercenaire du souvenir. La présence que tu as choisie ne délivre pas d'adieu." "Memory's mercenary gratitude" is another way of saying "nostalgia," an orientation towards the "no longer" of the past which is the ghostly continuity sought by a dangerously misled desire. The future orientation of desire, which is the direction of creative energy, is the essence of what is prescribed in XII where we are told to look at "l'image téméraire où se baigne ton pays, ce plaisir qui t'a longtemps fui," or in XI and XXVI:

XI

Tu feras de l'âme qui n'existe pas un homme meilleur qu'elle.

XXVI

La poésie est de toutes les eaux claires celle
qui s'attarde le moins aux reflets de ses ponts.
Poésie, la vie future à l'intérieur de l'homme
requalifié.   (*FM* 196, 199)

In nostalgia the self seeks its own eternalization and denies the contradiction of becoming in time, whereas the poet, in order to propel himself into the future of desire, must first of all be capable of self-forgetting ("Yeux qui, croyant inventer le jour, avez éveillé le vent, que puis-je pour vous? Je suis l'oubli," XXV), of choosing "a presence which delivers no goodbye." Thus, to return to XIV, thankfulness should not take the form of the "mercenary gratitude of memory" but of a gratefulness freely bestowed upon that being who, careless of one's remorse and nostalgia, comes forth as a "loyal adversary," as both a friend and an opponent, to contradict one. This capacity for contradiction, which means above all that one is capable of being contradicted, is what makes one sovereign. In the aphorism that immediately follows XIV, a similar point is made, in a form strongly reminiscent of Blake's infernal proverbs: "Les larmes méprisent leur confident" (XV). Again, this kernel of wisdom makes sense first of all as a parody of conventional wisdom, for it challenges the proverbial notion that friendship lies in sympathy of a confessional nature, and rejects it as a dangerous compromise. Through sympathy and confession one seeks not contradiction and adversity, but a confirmation of identity, which is the nostalgia for an unchanging self. "Tears scorn their confidant" precisely because, contrary to the gratefulness for contradiction prescribed in XV, they ask their confessor in an almost self-congratulatory way to be concerned with their remorse, with their nostalgia, with their revenge. They do not desire a sovereign equal in the other, a creative adversary, a definitive opponent and contrary, but an eternalized narcissistic image.

Aphorisms XVI and XVII, along with XX, directly concern the poem as the ultimate place of this extreme sovereign encounter between the self and the other:

XVI

Il reste une profondeur mesurable là où le sable subjugue la destinée.

XVII

Mon amour, peu importe que je sois né: tu deviens visible à la place où je disparais.

XX

Ne te courbe que pour aimer.   Si tu meurs, tu aimes encore.   (*FM* 198)

What such an encounter between self and adversary gives birth to is an extra dimension, the poem as an enigma, as a measured but insoluble contradiction which is an enduring future source of energy and desire.   Aphorism XVI calls this enigma "une profondeur mesurable," a measurable depth, the significance of which is the definitive result of a mortal and tragic encounter: that point at which "the sand subjugates destiny," that instance when time overcomes the human creator's will to self-creation.   We find in the later poem "Toute vie . . ." a similar representation of the enigma peculiar to the poetic work.   There we are told of a death and of a life born from that death, the work's life implying contradictorily the personal death of its creator.

Toute vie qui doit poindre
achève un blessé.
Voici l'arme,
rien,
Vous, moi, réversiblement
ce livre,
et l'énigme
qu'à votre tour vous deviendrez
dans le caprice amer des sables.
(*LM* 84)

The ultimate meaning behind the creation of the poetic work is tragic. Beyond the fact that in life we are all fools of fortune, in poetry this means primarily that the act of creation culminates in an ecstatic encounter with that most unavoidable of contradictions — one's death, the final expression of life in time. "Impose ta chance, serre ton bonheur et va vers ton risque" (*LM* 75), Char tells us in "Rougeur des Matinaux," which is the succinct wisdom of that sovereign being who has given himself over to a life ruled by fortune. The tragic *Amor Fati* of art demands in the end that one be capable of creating an identity, not simply in spite of that contradiction of contradictions which is death, but because of it, because of the creative opportunity it affords. Without death there is no enigma, and without enigma there can be no poem. For the poem, as is true of writing in general, is essentially testamentary, in and of itself.[42] Its very existence brings death into play: "Mon amour, tu deviens visible à la place où je disparais."

At the same time this encounter which gives violent birth to the poetic work is a nuptial moment, a union like marriage. It is an act of love, and implies death, as the act of creation implies ultimately the death of the creator. "Ne te courbe que pour aimer," as it is put in XX, "Si tu meurs, tu aimes encore." This aphorism resembles a saying from "Rougeur des Matinaux": "Enfin si tu te détruis, que ce soit avec des outils nuptiaux" (*LM* 81). The poem is an inviolable hymen, paradoxically born from a potentially fatal violence and violation, which also form a union, the marriage knot tied by the enigma of the poem. This nuptial and mortal encounter is the subject of "Le Mortel parténaire," where we read of a combat to the death which is also a scene of violent love-making, as well as a duel of riddling words. Poetry, for Char, shows itself to be both a martial and a marital art, not to mention a verbal one.

The confrontation in the poem takes place "On the white surface" of the page, which is also a bed sheet and the surface for a "boxing match." The opponents, or lovers, strike out at one another with blows; these blows are at the same time perplexing words, wounding to the point of death:

> A cet instant le premier dut à dessein prononcer à l'oreille du second des paroles si parfaitement offensantes, ou appropriées, ou énigmatiques, que de celui-ci fila, prompte, totale, précise, une foudre qui coucha net l'incompréhensible combattant.
>
> (*LM* 121-22)

The word which deals the death-blow in the poem to the "incomprehensible" — significantly not the uncomprehending — opponent gives birth to the poetic work as an ultimately unintelligible riddle. For these sovereign contestants owe their creative, and their destructive, power to the fact that they are enigmas, the riddling word of the one triumphing over the incomprehensibility of the other. In Char's poetry this violent moment is that critical point at which the wisdom governing life — since we have been concerned until now with a certain kind of wisdom — is overcome by life itself, and the proverb becomes the enigma, that is, a contradiction of the proverb, as life is the contradiction of all wisdom.

This is a moment similar to that in "The Second Dance Song" of Nietzsche's *Zarathustra* when the love of life and of life's folly becomes even stronger than the love of wisdom or philosophy. The passage in question also concerns the utterance of an incomprehensible word like the one spoken in "Le Mortel parténaire":

> "you think, O Zarathustra, I know it, you think of leaving me soon!"
> "Yes," I answered hesitatingly. "but you also know...." And I said something into her ear, in the midst of her tangled, yellow, foolish locks.
> "You *know* that, O Zarathustra? No one knows that."
> And we gazed at one another and looked out at the green meadow, over which the cool evening was

> spreading, and wept together. But then Life was
> dearer to me than all my Wisdom had ever been.[43]

The point at which life becomes dearer than all one's wisdom is of course the point of death, when the enigma of one's being, if one is a poet, becomes the enigma of the poetic work. The destruction of one's life, which nevertheless leaves the secret of that life inviolate and inviolable, coincides with the creation of the poem, that future source of energy and desire, that measurable, because inexhaustible, depth of meaning and significance.

> Certains êtres ont une signification qui nous
> manque. Qui sont-ils? Leur secret tient au plus
> profond du secret même de la vie. Ils s'en
> approchent. Elle les tue. Mais l'avenir crée. O
> dédale de l'extrême amour! (*LM* 122)

The Sovereign Text

Centon

> Vous recherchez mon point faible, ma faille?
> Sa découverte vous permettrait de m'avoir à merci?
> Mais, assaillant, ne voyez-vous pas que je suis un
> crible et que votre peu de cervelle sèche parmi mes
> rayons expirés?

> Je n'ai ni chaud ni froid: je gouverne.
> Cependant n'allongez pas trop la main vers le
> sceptre de mon pouvoir. Il glace, il brûle . . . Vous
> en éventeriez la sensation.

> J'aime, je capture et je rends à quelqu'un. Je
> suis dard et j'abreuve de lumière le prisonnier de la
> fleur. Tels sont mes contradictions, mes services.

> En ce temps, je souriais au monde et le monde
> me souriait. En ce temps qui ne fut jamais et que
> je lis dans la poussière.

> Ceux qui regardent souffrir le lion dans sa cage
> pourrissent dans la mémoire de lion.

> Un roi qu'un coureur de chimère rattrape, je lui
> souhaite d'en mourir. (*LM* 68)

The poetic text, for René Char, is an arena of creative, contradictory encounter between the self and the other. The text, in this sense, means above all a test: a sphere of sovereign con-test between the reader and the written. Throughout Char's poetry the proverb gives way to the enigma, the poem becoming that loyal adversary against which the reader is critically tested. The enigma is not, however, in some perverse obscurantist way, sought purely for its own sake, although this is the potential risk of all serious poetic writing. The enigma may seem to be an end in itself, but more importantly it must be a token of something that transcends it, the energy and desire that it preserves and is capable of bringing into play. As prescribed in XXI of "Rougeur des matinaux": "Imite le moins possible les hommes dans leur énigmatique maladie de faire des noeuds" (*LM* 79). But at the same time it is only through a riddling knot that the reader is tied to the text, enters into a contract of marriage with it ("Le poème est toujurs marié à quelqu'un," (*FM* 69), and what the poet has joined together let no idle and meddling reader tear asunder. This contract of marriage is equally a struggle between the reader and the text, like the struggle depicted in "Le Mortel parténaire." The Daedalian "labyrinth of extreme love" ("dédale de l'extrême amour") in that poem evokes the artifice of the mythic inventor, builder of the maze at whose centre awaits the enigmatic monster, the Minotaur, whose discovery and destruction are the task to be accomplished by the hero Theseus.

A single poem by Char seems to epitomize this enigmatic direction of his work, appropriately one of his most elusive and challenging poems for the reader, "Centon." On a first reading the poem clearly presents itself as a difficult riddle or enigma over which one must puzzle painfully in order to solve. The title provides at least a limited answer to the perplexity inasmuch as it suggests that what we may have in our hand is simply a piece of writing, of a very specific kind, a "cento," a patchwork text made up entirely of passages borrowed form other authors. The cento as a genre exemplifies the problem of writing as it is posed in Plato's *Phaedrus*, where Socrates uses the fable of Theuth as an authority in accusing any written text of inherent irresponsibility and potential danger. As Derrida points out in his analysis of this passage in "Plato's Pharmacy," Socrates condemns writing because unlike spoken discourse it cannot behave like someone present in person or attended by its originator, as a child might be accompanied by its father.[44] The cento, of course, is not only defined, as any piece of writing is, precisely by the absence of any such presence or assistance, but is furthermore, even for writing, an extreme case of alienated speech, since its every utterance is foreign to it, does not properly belong to it, but is a borrowing, a part of a series of sayings removed from their origin.

What is curious in *Phaedrus* is how Socrates uses the very fable of Theuth as an authority, in the same way — as he himself points out — that one might have recourse to the oracle. As with the oracle where the utterance seems compromised and made suspect by the absence of any presence or attendance, such a medium as this fantastic tale, which belongs to a tradition "that has come down from our forefathers" who "alone know the truth of it," would seem to invalidate whatever truth it is presumed to express. But in the case of the fable and oracle, the criteria of presence and origin are strangely waived or not seen to be pertinent in the same way. Indeed, Socrates accuses Phaedrus of unreasonably demanding from the oracle what he himself will later quite explicitly condemn writing for lacking, and chastises him to the effect that for him the truth should be enough in itself, whatever its origin, even from "trees or rocks":

"For you apparently it makes a difference who the speaker is, and what country he comes from; you don't merely ask whether what he says is true or false." With writing, however, it is not even important whether what it "says is true or false."[45] What is significant is the undecidability of its dangerous lack of presence and attendance, the uncertainty and unreliability posed by its inanimate nature and by the fact that it is divorced from its origin. Some of these features, of course, are equally characteristic of the fable, and presumably all of them of the oracle, and yet Socrates' criteria for the authority of their truth are somehow different. In an essay on Char's poem "La Bête de Lascaux," Blanchot comments on this link between writing and the oracle in *Phaedrus*:

> . . . la chose écrite apparaît essentiellement proche de la parole sacrée, dont elle semble porter dans l'oeuvre l'étrangeté, dont elle hérite la démesure, le risque, la force qui échappe à tout calcul et qui refuse toute garantie. Comme la parole sacrée, ce qui est écrit vient on ne sait d'où, c'est sans auteur, sans origine et, par là, renovie à quelque chose de plus originel. Derrière la parole de l'écrit, personne n'est présent, mais elle donne voix à l'absence, comme dans l'oracle où parle le divin, le dieu lui-même n'est jamais présent en sa parole, et c'est l'absence de dieu qui alors parle. Et l'oracle, pas plus que l'écriture, ne se justifie, ne s'explique, ne se défend: pas de dialogue avec l'écrit et pas de dialogue avec le dieu. Socrates reste étonné de ce silence qui parle. . . . Ce qui le frappe donc, ce qui lui paraît "terrible," c'est, dans l'écriture comme dans la peinture [Socrates speaks of painting as an analogy to writing, since paintings "stand before us as though they were alive, but if you question them, they maintain a most majestic silence"], le silence, silence majestueux . . . l'impossibilité de parler, de telle manière qu'ici le vrai n'a rien pour le soutenir, apparaît sans fondement, est le scandale de ce qui *semble* vrai, n'est qu'image et, par l'image et le semblant, attire la vérité dans la profondeur où il n'y a ni vérité, ni sens, ni même erreur . . .?[46]

Char's "Centon" is a perfect case of a writing that resembles the oracular inasmuch as what it expresses finally is a "majestic silence" and the "impossibility of speaking." But it is at the same time a writing that almost seems to compel us to question it closely; it presents itself as the riddling utterance of an enigmatic being who defies us to discover the secret of its proper name, who aggressively contests the possibility of our ever finding a solution to the puzzle it poses for us. It draws us into a questioning as we read, as though towards its centre, suggesting a contest of seemingly mythic proportions — the reader being a potential Theseus, the text Daedalus' maze, and the enigmatic creature seemingly speaking through the poem a sort of Minotaur. The oracular writing in "Centon" takes the form, then, of a ritualistic contest posed by the riddle of the text, oracles being of course notorious for speaking in riddles. As Frye writes in "Charms and Riddles":

> Those who consult oracles usually do so with a sense of uncritical awe, but oracles and oracular prophecies frequently turn on puns, ambiguous or double-faced statements, or sometimes, as in *Macbeth*, on quibbles that sound like feeble-minded jokes. There is a point at which emotional involvement may suddenly reverse itself and become intellectual detachment, the typical expression of which is laughter. . . . Similarly, the riddle is essentially a charm in reverse: it represents the revolt of the intelligence against the hypnotic power of commanding words. In the riddle a verbal trap is set, but if one can "guess," that is, point to an outside object to which the verbal construct can be related, the something outside destroys it as a charm, and we have sprung the trap without being caught in it.[47]

Char has a series of poems, "Quatre fascinants," which suggest precisely this tension between the charm and riddle. "Fascinant" of course means "charms," and these poems suggest that they are posing riddles that when solved will free the reader from their spell. The titles themselves seem to offer the solution, since they name the enigmatic creatures depicted in the sequence of emblem-like lyrics ("Le Taureau," "L'Alouette," "Le Serpent," "La Truite"), but this merely reflects the fact that the title is not the answer. "Le Taureau" and "L'Alouette" are, indeed, examples of what we might call meta-enigmas. They do not actually propose a solution to the riddles they present, but rather represent the creatures as beings whose very essence is enigma, whose secret name can be properly known only in its insolubility. The death of the bull in "Le Taureau" is the very image of a fatally wounding marriage knot: "Couple qui se poignarde unique parmi tous" (*LM* 106), while of the skylark in "L'Alouette" it is said, as might apply to one enigmatic being pitted against another in a contest, not so much of wills as of spells or charms: "Fascinante, on la tue en l'émerveillant" (*LM* 109).

For Char the solution of the enigma is not the point. What is of critical importance is its renewability, as in "Pour renouer," or as it is put in "Contre une maison séche": "Qui croit renouvelable l'énigme, la devient" (*NP* 124). Anyone who believes the enigma renewable becomes the enigma in the poetic work, the artifice of the poem where the heart of meaning is comprised perhaps only by "the answer which is not given." "Mais peut-être notre coeur n'est-il formé que de la réponse qui n'est point donnée?" (*LM* 119), Char writes in "Le Rempart des brindilles."

> Disparu, l'élégance de l'ombre lui succède. L'énigme a fini de rougir.
> *Nota.* — Cessons de miroiter. Toute la question sera, un moment, de savoir si la mort met bien le point final à tout. Mais peut-être notre coeur n'est-il formé que de la réponse qui n'est point donnée?
>
> Et la faculté de fine manoeuvre? Qui sera ton lecteur? Quelqu'un que ta spéculation arme mais que ta plume innocente. Cet oisif. sur ses coudes? Ce criminel encore sans objet? Prends garde, quand tu peux, aux mots que tu écris, malgré leur ferme distance. (*LM* 119)

The enigma of one's being, which in death "a fini de rougir," is conserved in the riddle of the poem. The purpose of the riddle is first of all defensive, apotropaic; it wards off what Nietzsche would call "die lesenden Müßiggänger," "the reading idler," whose intentions may be criminal.[48]   The poem should not be treated as a place of innocuous or frivolous verbiage, but as a place of dangerous contest where blood meets blood. For Char, as for Nietzsche, "Blut Geist ist."

The further intent of the riddle, linked to the protection of the poem's vital centre, is the preservation and renewability of significance, which seems to confirm Frye's observation in "Charms and Riddles" that "there seems to be some riddle behind all riddles which we have not yet guessed."[49]   The charm of certain riddles is that they fascinate us, like Char's "Quatres fascinants," without binding us compulsively or inescapably. Unable to solve them we return to them again and again, but with a careful detachment which allows us always to break the spell of our reading. Rather, they break their own spell by fascinating us only to frustrate consciously any attempt at a satisfying comprehension, as though they both promised and withheld a revelation that we hope to discover and yet also despair of ever discovering.

This is a perfect way to describe the experience of reading such a poem as "Centon." Like Socrates we are tempted to, we wish that we could, ask this riddling text to tell us more than we already know ("Written words . . . seem to talk to you as though they were intelligent, but if you ask them anything about what they say, from a desire to be instructed, they go on telling you just the same thing forever"),[50] to tell us more even than we seem to intuit without ever knowing. For like one of the remarkable creatures out of the Old English riddles to which Frye refers in his essay, this patchwork being of silent words act *as if* it were a speaking subject, throwing down the gauntlet of interpretation at the feet of the reader who, according to good etiquette, would like to know of course with whom he is in fact speaking: "And once a thing is put in writing, the composition, whatever it may be, drifts all over the place, getting into the hands not only of those who understand it, but equally of those who have no business with it; it doesn't know how to address the right people, and not address the wrong." The difference is quite clearly that unlike Socrates' vagrant writing, which is vulnerable and utterly defenceless ("And when it is ill-treated and unfairly abused it always needs its parent to come to its help, being unable to defend or help itself"), Char's "Centon," unattended as it is, is certainly able to fend for and to protect itself, perhaps even too able. We feel that if only this silent creature made up of nothing but a borrowed speech, made up of nothing but writing, were not so adept at the art of self-defence by which it wards off the meddling reader, then we could ask it the right question and if it could by the same token respond, we would have perhaps the clue or key, the flaw or breaking-point by which we could force and open up its defensive armature to our discovery. What we are after is in fact a proper name, we can almost feel it trippingly at the tip of the tongue, but it eludes us in a murmur, a mumbling just beyond the articulate and identifiable, as in the title of Char's poem "Marmonnement." This poem concerns precisely the tracking down of an unnamable creature: "Loup, je t'appelle, mais tu n'as pas de réalité nommable. De plus, tu es inintelligible. Non-comparant, compensateur que sais-je?" (*LM* 131). The secret name of this being is withheld perpetually and yet somehow endlessly promised to the poet in the relentless quest after "la double proie: toi invisible et moi vivace."

> Continue, va, nous durons ensemble; et en-
> semble, bien que séparés, nous bondissons par-

> dessus le frisson de la suprême déception pour
> briser la glace des eaux vives et se reconnaître là.
>
> (*LM* 131)

A "shiver of deception," we might suggest, is another word for the culminating point of any serious and critical act of reading. Deception is a necessary test of the self, an essential part of the contradictory exercise of one's creative sovereignty: one must be capable of being deceived, not just of deceiving. However we may respond, it is to this exercise that we are uneasily put by the creature addressing us in "Centon," whose undecidable nature makes us think of that figure Char salutes in the epigraph of "Rougeur des matinaux" as a being worthy of trust, but enigmatically only because of an uncanny power to delude and contradict: "Accolade à celui qui, émergeant de sa fatigue et de sa sueur, s'avancera et me dira: 'Je suis venu pour te tromper,'" (*LM* 73). Such a being is to be trusted unconditionally precisely because such contradiction is the mark of an authentic contestant ("Prenez garde: tous ne sont pas dignes de la confidence"), whose truth is personal ("La vérité est personelle"), and therefore an enigma ultimately inaccessible to another, and whose destiny which is married to or contracted with our own, like that of the poem to which the reader is freely but inextricably tied, is both tragic and momentarily illuminating: "O grande barre noire, en route vers ta mort, pourqoui serait-ce toujours à toi de montrer l'éclair?" (*LM* 73). The disclosure made possible by the poetic work arises from a union of struggling contestants, beings whose creative and destructive force derive from the enigmas that they in fact are, from the riddles they incarnate. As Frye points out: ". . . riddles often imply some kind of enmity-situation or contest, where you will lose a great deal, perhaps your life, if you don't know the answer."[51]

This kind of defiance on the part of the poet and of his poem, concerned with preserving the secret of a vital core of meaning from the reader, may leave one in a state of despondent irritation or of just plain frustration. It may on the other hand exhilarate and exalt one heroically in the contest and test of the text. The opening lines of "Centon" are addressed to a "Vous" which, although left indefinite, is unmistakably the reader who is formally accosted and challenged by the opponent text:

> Vous recherchez mon point faible, ma faille?
> Sa découverte vous permettrait de m'avoir à merci?
> Mais, assaillant, ne voyez-vous pas que je suis un
> crible et que votre peu de cervelle sèche parmi mes
> rayons expirés.   (*LM* 68)

The creature speaking here defies us to find our way past the shield of its enigmatic identity and to penetrate its aggressively defended centre. But it finally contests violently even the merest possiblity of such a success by the reader. The imagining of such a success is a dangerous deception which can end only in catastrophe — rather gruesomely, in an extreme dessication of the brain. The creature refers to itself as a "screen" or "sieve" ("un crible"), for which, interestingly enough — although the words are only homonymically related — another word in English is "riddle." This association of a screen and a written text is also suggested by Derrida in an essay entitled "Scribble (pouvoir/écrire)." The translator of the essay into English offers the following comments, which are pertinent to our present discussion:

> The title of the piece . . . requires some explana-
> tion. Derrida points out . . . that it refers back to
> the language of the original, "to scribble" meaning
> to write hurriedly for a living as well as to card
> wool (hence, to *separate* fibers: in French,
> *scriblage*), echoing also Joyce's "scribbledehobble."
> Pronounced Frenchly, the word yields *crible* —
> screen, sieve, and riddle (that is, both a grid, which
> organizes, and a device for sifting, winnowing,
> separating) — *scribe*, each functioning *critically*

(*krinein*) to select, to discern, to hierarchize. Superimposing one upon the other produces the stenographic nonce word *scrible*, which is intended to epitomize the system shadowed forth by such questions as "how to read?" and "how to write on writing?"[52]

Generally speaking, a screen or sieve suggests a process of differentiation, being an instrument that separates a given substance into more particular and discreet elements. It is a perfect metaphor for the operation involved in the solving of an enigma or riddle, since one necessarily proceeds by differentiation towards the guessing of the proper identity or name. But since the reader's "brain" is expressly threatened with destruction by this being's potentially fatal power of radiation, the further suggestion seems to be that the process of differentiation cannot end except by the disclosure of an identity which, if illuminating, must remain withheld and profoundly enigmatic. The reader is cautioned to keep a respectful — and vital — distance from the text's potent secret. The danger of unreservedly and idly penetrating an enigma is that it may rebound and redound catastrophically on the reader's head, which would be vaporized by the text's retaliatory force: "ne voyez-vous pas . . . que votre peu de cervelle sèche parmi mes rayons expirés." The fate of the unwary reader as warned in "Centon" is a disturbing one, and clearly reflects the seriousness with which Char regards the act of reading — all meddling readers beware, only the fully attentive need apply themselves here. The use of the word "cervelle" in this passage is significant, since it is the word for "brain" in French, which is opposed to *cerveau* when used to designate that part of the anatomy simply as matter, as in the brain of a slain animal which is to be eaten. But at the same time it can be used freely in a figurative sense to mean "reason, judgement, intelligence." Both meanings of the word coincide in Char's lines where the subject is a contest of wits which is at the same time potentially a physical struggle to the death. "Ecrasez-leur la tête avec un gourdin, Je veux dire un secret," Char declares in the title of one of his later poems (*NP* 135). Indeed, a large number of Char's poems might bear such a title: "Crush their heads with a club, I mean with a secret." The word "gourdin" sounds like a cognate of *gourde*, and even if it isn't it still suggests a similar emptiness at the core, implying that the "club" of the text, its defensive weapon, may somehow be nothing but its power to deceive, the nothingness of the secret it preserves from the reader. As Char poses it in "Toute vie . . .," recalling Mallarmé's words "Rien, cette écume, vierge vers"[53] which open "Salut": "Voici l'arme, / rien, / vous, moi, réversiblement / ce livre, / et l'énigme / qu'à votre tour vous deviendrez / dans le caprice amer des sables" (*LM* 84). To try simply to name the beast is perhaps, then, not the answer, but most of all because the intent and significance of the enigma lie not so much in the secret it conceals, but in the energy brought into play by the reader's effort to comprehend. This is in fact the significance noted by Frye in the Old English riddles where

> What one notices first of all in such poems is the tremendous energy of movement around the objects: the hard physical effort both in creating them and in using them is what is suggested. . . . Just as a picture may seem to us an arrest of energy, rhythm, and movement suddenly caught for a motionless instant, so these riddles show us a dissolving and reshaping movement that comes into a stationary focus as soon as we guess, that is, infer what the solid physical energy leads up to. The movement is towards identity rather than, as in Ovidian metamorphosis, away from it.[54]

In Char's poem, however, the enigma is preserved. The solution ultimately escapes us, which means that the energy is all the more intensely felt, since the tension is not released but recreated.

As Frye further observes in the same essay: "The object may be described by the poet, or the object may speak for itself and then challenge the

reader to guess its name."[55]   The latter is of course the case in "Centon,"
where the text addresses us as though it were a speaking subject, an animate
being endowed with the power of speech.   Derrida discusses this idea of the
logos as *zoôn*, as an organism or properly organized living creature, in his
analysis of Plato's *Phaedrus* in "Plato's Pharmacy":

> Logos, a living, animate creature, is thus also
> an organism that has been engendered. An *organism*:
> a differentiated body *proper*, with a center and
> extremities, joints, a head, and feet.   In order to
> be "proper," a written discourse *ought* to submit to
> the laws of life just as a living discourse does.
> Logographical   necessity   (*anangkè   logographikè*)
> ought to be analogous to biological, or rather
> zoological, necessity.   Otherwise, obviously, it would
> have neither head nor tail.   Both *structure* and
> *constitution* are in question in the risk run by *logos*
> of losing through writing both its tail and its head
> ... (*D* 79)

Derrida then cites the following passage from *Phaedrus*, which we will give in
English:

> Socrates: And to pass to other points doesn't his
> matter strike you as thrown out at haphazard?   Do
> you find any cogent reason for his next remark, or
> indeed any of his remarks, occupying the place it
> does?   I myself, in my ignorance, thought that the
> writer, with a fine abandon, put down just what
> came into his head.   Can you find any cogent
> principle of composition which he observed in
> setting down his observations in this particular
> order?
> Phaedrus: You flatter me in supposing that I am
> competent to see into his mind with all that
> accuracy.
> Socrates: Well, there is one point at least which I
> think you will admit, namely that any discourse
> ought to be constructed like a living creature, with
> its own body, as it were, it must not lack either
> head or feet; it must have a middle and extremities
> so composed as to suit each other and the whole
> work.[56]

The idea of the text as a *zoôn*, as having a living, engendered "proper
body," is linked naturally to its bearing a proper name.   But the title of Char's

"Centon" indicates a text which generically is in no way properly organized, but is a patchwork, a "quasimodo," whose matter is "thrown out at haphazard," without "any cogent principle of composition" to give it a "particular order." The cento is precisely a written discourse which runs counter to the imitation of a living speech, which contradicts the principle "that any discourse ought to be constructed like a living creature, with its own body, as it were," and lacking neither "head (n)or feet." The cento is made up entirely of elements from other texts, put together in apparently pêle-mêle fashion, so that to pursue the analogy we might think of it as a kind of monstrous being put together by a Dr. Frankenstein, and like Frankenstein's monster it can have no proper name — at the most the common name of "monster," designated only by the proper name of its inventor. We might apply indeed to such a text the exact words of Baudelaire in his dedication of *Petits Poèmes en prose* to Arsène Houssaye:

> Mon cher ami, je vous envoie un petit ouvrage dont on ne pourrait pas dire, sans injustice, qu'il n'a ni queue ni tête, puisque tout, au contraire, y est à la fois tête et queue, alternativement et réciproquement. Considérez, je vous prie, quelles admirables commodités cette combinaison nous offre à tous, à vous, à moi et au lecteur. Nous pouvons couper où nous voulons, moi ma rêverie, vous le manuscrit, le lecteur sa lecture; car je ne suspends pas la volonté rétive de celui-ci au fil interminable d'une intrigue superflue. Envoyez une vertèbre, et les deux morceaux de cette tortueuse fantaisie se rejoindront sans peine. Hachez-la en nombreux fragments, et vous verrez que chacun peut exister à part. Dans l'espérance que quelques-uns de ces tronçons seront assez vivants pour vous plaire et vous amuser, j'ose vous dédier le serpent tout entier.[57]

What Socrates understands purely in terms of a dangerous transgression of living speech which is for him the potential threat of all writing, Baudelaire praises in view of the "admirables commodités" allowing the reader the luxury and freedom of whatever organization seems fit. The reader is free to cut up and put together the text at will; the text will always relocate itself or not "sans peine," since it is in its very essence monstrously dislocated and improper. Its propriety is, in fact, its impropriety. In "Centon" as well the very commodity, the advantage of the text lies in its monstrosity, in the impossibility of ever discovering the secret of its organization or of assigning it a proper name. The poem's sovereignty stems indeed from its profound contradictoriness and ambivalences, from its essential undecidability.

> Je n'ai chaud ni froid: je gouverne. Cependant n'allongez pas trop la main vers la sceptre de mon pouvoir. Il glace, il brûle . . . Vous en éventeriez la sensation.
>
> J'aime, je capture et je rends à quelqu'un. Je suis dard et j'abreuve de lumière le prisonnier de la fleur. Tels sont mes contradictions, mes services.
>
> (*LM* 68)

Syntactically, the ambivalence of this textual creature is expressed disjunctively and paratactically: "neither hot nor cold" being a negative disjunction characteristic of what Blanchot calls the "neuter,"[58] and "It freezes, it burns" being of course a classical oxymoron. The disturbing undecidability of these attributes suggests not only the *pharmakos* but what Derrida refers to in "The Double Session" as the "hymen":

> What holds for "hymen" also holds, *mutatis mutandis*, for all other signs which, like *pharmakon*, *supplément*, *différance*, and others, have a double, contradictory, undecidable value that always derives from their syntax, whether the latter is in a sense "internal," articulating and combining under the same yoke, *hup'hen*, two incompatible meanings, or "external," dependent on the code in which the word is made to function. (*D* 221)

The undecidability of the hymen results from a marriage of incompatible meanings, a violent union of contradictory terms, which reflects as well the contract of the reader with the text, in what is both a marriage and a relentless contest.

Significantly, Char's use of oxymoron in this passage is of an almost Petrarchan turn, conforming with what may be rightly recognized as the courtly and chivalric element in his work. The idea of "loyal adversity," which is the very essence of the textual encounter in Char, bears comparison with courtly convention, and along with the omnipresent theme of the wound ("Pourquoi le champ de la blessure est-il de tous le plus prospère?" *LM* 95) suggests a fertile ground for conceits like the following one made by Shakespeare's Romeo: "I have been feasting with mine enemy, / Where on a sudden one hath wounded me / That's by me wounded" (II.ii.45-47).[59] It is precisely a wounding, an ultimately creative one, which is threatened by the repulsing sceptre and wielded sting ("Je suis dard") of the opponent or foe in "Centon." A wound, of course, demands a remedy, a *pharmakon*, which in Char as well as in *Romeo and Juliet* turns out to be the "physic" of a hymen or union — ultimately a tragic one in death — capable of joining incompatible extremes, a marriage of struggling contraries. In Char's poetry we never reach the point of resolving the meaning of the riddle. This is because the riddle is also the marriage knot the poet ties between the reader and his written text and like all good marriages, it is of little use if it does not last, whatever ruptures and separations may ensue. By virtue of this knot the poem is both a dangerous contest and a healing union. The healing power is a potential poison, just as the force of the marriage is a source of unremitting struggle. "J'aime, je capture et je rends à quelqu'un," the poem enigmatically proclaims, which is a suggestive way of affirming the hymen between the reader and the text, a test and contest as well as a loving encounter: a desiring, a seduction and a taking captive, and finally a yielding or submission. "Je suis dard et j'abreuve de lumière le prisonnier de la fleur," the creature continues in another riddling confession. The flower's prisoner is, to translate rather plainly, beauty's prisoner, the poem's captivated and captive reader, wounded by its sting and yet at the same time healed or mended by its disclosure, by the light with which the poem drenches the reader whose own sovereignty would be equal to the test. The contradictoriness of the text defines the nature of its precise service, the generosity of the disclosure that it makes possible being only a measure of the necessary concealment of the enigma. There would be no significance or surplus of meaning without a withholding of meaning, no identity that is not purely deceptive without an identity that is finally oppositional and ambivalent. In the poem's own words, "Tels sont mes contradictions, mes services."

The lines immediately following are precisely that: a contradiction, an inconsistent statement, a simultaneous affirmation and denial.

> En ce temps, je souriais au monde et le monde
> me souriait. En ce temps qui ne fut jamais et que
> je lis dans la poussière.   (*LM* 68)

The capacity to make such a statement and to dwell within the sphere of its consequences we have already met in the Friend of "Suzerain" who knows the need to live in the disjunction of the "*Pas* et *plus*," of that which isn't and that which is no longer. The opponent in "Centon" affirms the contradiction of one's identity which can only be lived in time. There is and is not an *illo tempore* ("En ce temps") of natural plentitude before the fall into history. There is in the idealization of one's imagination, but there is not in the adversity of reality where the capacity to live in the potentially creative contradiction of time is the supreme test of what Char calls sovereignty. The final two statements of the poem offer a threatening *caveat lector*. Those who believe they have mastered the enigma and that they command the contradictory nature of the sovereign being's identity will only become the victims of their own misprision and self-deception:

> Ceux qui regardent souffrir le lion dans sa cage
> pourrissent dans la mémoire du lion.

> Un roi qu'un coureur de chimère rattrape, je lui
> souhaite d'en mourir.   (*LM* 68)

"Mais tu as crevé les yeux du lion," the poet announces in "J'habite une douleur," "Tu crois voir passer la beauté au-dessus des lavandes noires . . ." (*FM* 178).   To put out the eyes of the lion or to watch this sovereign suffer in his cage is to imagine that one has destroyed the adversary or powerful con-tradictor which in Char's poetry is an analogy for the poetic text itself.   The belief in a command and mastery over the text is the most dangerous of deceptions — one only perishes in the lion's memory.   Such a project reflects the dream of a plenitude of meaning, of an identity that would also be a self-presence.   The believer in the text's full presence or meaning is said to be a "coureur de chimères," a "hunter of chimeras."   In this case the chimera could be understood to be "Centon," a deceptive monster of a text, like Baudelaire's collection of prose poems, "cette tortueuse fantaisie" of a scandalous serpentine organism.   To treat the enigma of the poem as though it were finally soluble, to act as though the trap set by the riddle of the sovereign being can be eluded and the being made captive at last, is to think that there is a truth that is not at the same time a contradiction, or a proper name that is not profoundly enigmatic.   Tellingly, both the chimera hunter and the being so vulnerable to such a capture may be confused easily by the syntax of the poem's final line. Although the reference in "Je lui souhaite d'en mourir" can supply grammatically only to "Un roi," there is the strong suggestion that it applies just as surely to "un coureur de chimères."   The implication is that both figures, the captured and the capturer, are cursed — it is a literal curse that closes the poem — but that they are cursed only by their own deception, which is to refuse the blessing of any text, that blessing being in fact a *blessure*, a wound. "I love him whose soul is deep even in its ability to be wounded, and whom even a little thing can destroy," Zarathustra proclaims in one of his anti-beatitudes.[60] For Char, the disclosure that the poem affords is at the same time dependent on the reader's potential for contradiction, that is, on the reader's capacity to be contradicted, to be wounded by the writing without whose wound one can never begin to read, nor ever hope to be cured.

Notes to Chapter 3

1. Friedrich Nietzsche, *Thus Spoke Zarathustra*, trans. R.J. Hollingdale (Harmondsworth: Penguin, 1969), p. 67.

2. See note 1 to Chapter 2.

3. For the connection between poetry and dwelling, see Martin Heidegger, "Building Dwelling Thinking" and ". . . Poetically Man Dwells . . . ," in *Poetry, Language, Thought*, pp. 143-61, 213-29.

4. Heidegger, "Building Dwelling Thinking," p. 161.

5. Plato, *Phaedrus*, trans. R. Hackforth, *The Collected Dialogues*, ed. Edith Hamilton and Huntington Cairns (Princeton: Princeton Univ. Press, 1961), p. 520.

6. I am following Derrida's reading of *Phaedrus* in "Plato's Pharmacy." As Derrida writes concerning Thamus's response to Theuth's gift of writing: ". . . without rejecting the homage, the god-king will depreciate it, pointing out not only its uselessness but its menace and its mischief. Another way of receiving the offering of writing. In so doing, god-the-king-that-speaks is acting like a father. The *pharmakon* is here presented to the father and is by him rejected, belittled, abandoned, disparaged. The father is always suspicious and watchful towards writing" (*D*, 76).

7. Blake, *The Marriage of Heaven and Hell*, p. 34.

8. Heidegger, *Poetry, Language, Thought*, p. 161.

9. Heidegger, *Poetry, Language, Thought*, p. 202ff.

10. Heidegger, *Poetry, Language, Thought*, p. 204.

11. Roger Laporte writes, as cited by Derrida: "You have, I suppose, dreamt of finding a single word for designating difference and articulation. I have perhaps located it by chance in Robert['s Dictionary] if I play on the word, or rather indicate its double meaning. This word is *brisure* [joint, break] ' — broken, cracked part. Cf. breach, crack, fracture, fault, split, fragment, [*brèche, casure, fracture, faille, fente, fragment.*] Hinged articulation of two parts of wood- or metal-work. The hinge, the *brisure* [folding-joint] of a shutter. Cf. joint" (*G* 65).

12. Mary Ann Caws, *The Presence of René Char* (Princeton: Princeton Univ. Press, 1976), p. 127.

13. I am using Caws's very apt translation of the line "Il n'y a pas de siège pur." Compare her analysis of "J'habite une douleur" in *The Presence of René Char*, pp. 126-29.

14. Serge Leclaire, *Démasquer le réel: Un essai sur l'objet en psychanalyse* (Paris: Éditions du Seuil, 1971), p. 7.

15. René Char, *Poems of René Char*, trans. Mary Ann Caws and Jonathan Griffin (Princeton: Princeton Univ. Press, 1976), p. 151.

16. Friedrich Nietzsche, *Ecce Homo*, trans. Walter Kaufmann (New York: Vintage, 1969), pp. 254, 290-91.

17. Nietzsche, *Ecce Homo*, pp. 326-27.

18. This is the version translated in *Poems of René Char*, pp. 150-51.

19. See Caws's analysis of the threshold, marginality, and marginal beings in *The Presence of René Char*, pp. 45n, 114-15, 165-68.

20. Northrop Frye, *Fearful Symmetry* (1947; rpt. Princeton: Princeton Univ. Press, 1969), pp. 233-36.

21. J. E. Cirlot discusses the caduceus in *A Dictionary of Symbols*, trans. Jack Sage (New York: Philosophical Library, 1962): ". . . the Mesopotamians considered the intertwining serpents as a symbol of the god who cures all illness, a meaning which passed into Greek culture and is still preserved in the emblems of our day" (35); "If all symbols are really functions and signs of things imbued with energy, then the serpent or snake is, by analogy, symbolic of energy itself — of force pure and simple; hence its ambivalence and multivalencies. . . . The symmetrical placing of two serpents, as in the caduceus of Mercury, is indicative of an equilibrium of forces, of the counterbalancing of the cowed serpent (or sublimated power) by the untamed serpent, so representing good balance by evil, health by sickness. As Jung has shrewdly observed, this much-used image is an adumbration of homeopathy — a cure effected by what caused the ailment. The serpent therefore becomes the source of the healing of the

wound caused by the serpent." (272, 276).

22. Friedrich Nietzsche, *Zarathustra*, p. 162.

23. See Northrop Frye's instructive reading of Blake's *The Marriage of Heaven and Hell* in *Fearful Symmetry*, pp. 198-201.

24. Blake, p. 41.

25. Blake, p. 34

26. Georges Bataille, *La Part maudite* (Paris: Les Editions de Minuit, 1967).

27. Mary Ann Caws, *The Presence of René Char*, p. 166.

29. Heidegger, *Poetry, Language, Thought*, p. 35.

30. Cirlot, p. 272.

31. Northrop Frye, *Anatomy of Criticism*, p. 298: "The proverb is a secular or purely human oracle: it usually has the same rhetorical features, alliteration, assonance, parallelism, that we find in the oracle, but it is addressed to the detached consciousness and the critical wit. Its authority comes from experience: for it, wisdom is the tried and tested way; only folly seeks what is new, and the essential virtues are prudence and moderation. The proverbs in Blake's *Marriage of Heaven and Hell* are parody-proverbs, written from the oracular or epiphanic point of view."

32. A similar overturning of the normally perceived relationship between wisdom and folly is at play throughout Nietzsche's *Zarathustra*. Zarathustra proclaims in his opening speech: " Behold! I am weary of my wisdom, like a bee that has gathered too much honey; I need hands outstretched to take it. / I should like to give it away and distribute it, until the wise among men have again become happy in their folly and the poor happy in their wealth" (39). This proclamation is itself a parody of the New Testament's presentation of its new message as a deceptively foolish "stumbling-block" for the understanding (1 Cor. 1.18 ff.), as a greater wisdom in the guise of folly.

33. Heidegger, *Poetry, Language, Thought*, p. 35.

34. Frye, *The Great Code*, p. 25

35. Frye, *Anatomy of Criticism*, p. 298.

36. Compare Nietzsche, *Zarathustra*: "*Love* is the danger for the most solitary man, love of any thing *if only it is alive*! Indeed. my foolishness and modesty in love is laughable" (175).

37. Cirlot, p. 36.

38. Blake, p. 37.

39. Frye, *The Great Code*, p. 125.

40. Blake, p. 36.

41. Nietzsche, *Zarathustra*, pp. 43-45.

42. Derrida, *Of Grammatology*, p. 69: "Spacing as writing is the becoming-absent and the becoming-unconscious of the subject. By the movement of its drift/derivation [*dérive*] the emancipation of the sign constitutes in return the desire of presence. That becoming — or that drift/derivation — does not befall the subject which would choose it or would passively let itself be drawn along by it. As the subject's relationship with its own death, this becoming is the constitution of subjectivity. On all levels of life's organization, that is to say, of *the economy of death*. All graphemes are of a testamentary essence. And the original absence of the subject of writing is also the absence of the thing or the referent."

43. Nietzsche, *Zarathustra*, p. 243.

44. Derrida, *Dissemination* p. 77: "*Logos* is a son, then, a son that would be destroyed in his very *presence* without the present *attendance* of his father. His father who answers. His father who speaks for him and answers for him. Without his father, he would be nothing but, in fact, writing. At least that is what is said by the one who says: it is the father's thesis. The specificity of writing would thus be intimately bound to the absence of the father."

45. Plato, *Collected Dialogues*, p. 520.

46. Maurice Blanchot, "La Bête de Lascaux," reprinted in *René Char* (Paris: L'Herne, 1971), p. 72.

47. Northrop Frye, "Charms and Riddles," reprinted in *Spiritus Mundi* (Bloomington: Indiana Univ. Press, 1976), p. 137.

48. Nietzsche, *Zarathustra*, p. 67.

49. Frye, "Charms," p. 141.

50. Plato, *Collected Dialogues*, p. 521.

51. Frye, "Charms," p. 138. Rimbaud's poetry frequently takes the form of a similar kind of contest by riddle. In "H" the poet closes the poem with the command "Trouvez Hortense," which is very reminiscent of the directions given at the end of the Old English riddles: "Untwist your mind and say what I mean" or "explain the riddle" or "If you can solve a riddle quickly / Say what this creature is called" or "Say who I am," etc. See *A Feast of Creatures: Anglo-Saxon Riddle Songs*, trans. Craig Williamson (Philadelphia: The Univ. of Pennsylvania Press, 1982), pp. 145, 119, 97, 141. In Rimbaud as in Char, any solution of the riddle, no matter how comprehensive, can only be partial and in need of indefinite supplementary readings. Rimbaud actually defies the reader in this regard. "J'ai seul la clef à cette parade sauvage," we are taunted in the closing line of "Parade," and in *Une saison en enfer* the poet abruptly declares

concerning his invention of a secret alphabet of colours: "Je réservais la traduction." See Rimbaud, pp. 162, 138, 120.

52. Cary Plotkin, translator's preface to Jacques Derrida, "Scribble (writing-power)," *Yale French Studies*, No. 58 (1979), p. 116.

53. Mallarmé, p. 27.

54. Frye, "Charms," pp. 139-40.

55. Frye, "Charms," p. 140.

56. Plato, *Collected Dialogues*, p. 510.

57. Charles Baudelaire, *Petits Poèmes en prose (Le Spleen de Paris)*, ed. Robert Kopp (Paris: Gallimard, 1973), p. 21.

58. See Maurice Blanchot, "René Char et la pensée du neutre," in *L'Entretien infini*, pp. 439-50.

59. William Shakespeare, *The Tragedy of Romeo and Juliet*, ed. Richard Hosley (1917; rpt. New Haven: Yale Univ. Press, 1954).

60. Nietzsche, *Zarathustra*, p. 45.

SELECTED BIBLIOGRAPHY

Ashbery, John. *Self-Portrait in a Convex Mirror.* Harmondsworth: Penguin Books, 1976.

Bataille, Georges. *L'Expérience intérieure.* Paris: Gallimard, 1954.

—————. *La Part maudite.* Paris: Les Editions de Minuit, 1967.

Baudelaire, Charles. *Petits Poèmes en prose.* (Le Spleen de Paris). Ed. Robert Kopp. Paris: Gallimard, 1973.

Bernu, Michèle, et al. *Séminaire César Vallejo.* Poitiers: Centre de Recherches Latino-Américaines, 1973.

Blake, William. *The Marriage of Heaven and Hell.* In *The Poetry and Prose of William Blake.* Ed David V. Erdman with commentary by Harold Bloom. Garden City, N.Y.: Doubleday & Company, 1965.

Blanchot, Maurice. "La Bête de Lascaux." In *René Char.* Paris: L'Herne, 1971, pp. 71-77.

—————. *L'Entretien infini.* Paris Gallimard, 1969.

—————. *Le Pas au-délà.* Paris: Gallimard, 1973

Bloom, Harold. *The Anxiety of Influence: A Theory of Poetry.* New York: Oxford Univ. Press, 1973.

—————. *Poetry and Repression: Revisionism from Blake to Stevens.* New Haven: Yale Univ. Press, 1976.

—————. *Wallace Stevens: The Poems of Our Climate.* Ithaca: Cornell Univ. Press, 1976.

Bové, Paul. *Destructive Poetics: Heidegger and Modern American Poetry.* New York: Columbia Univ. Press, 1980.

Burke, Kennth. *The Philosophy of Literary Form: Studies in Symbolic Action.* 3rd ed. Berkeley: Univ. of California Press, 1973.

Caws, Mary Ann. *The Presence of Ren Char.* Princeton: Princeton Univ. Press, 1976.

—————. and Jonathan Griffin, trans. *Poems of René Char.* Princeton: Princeton Univ. Press, 1976.

Char, René. *Fureur et mystère.* Paris: Gallimard, 1967.

—————. *Les Matinaux,* followed by *La Parole en archipel.* Paris: Gallimard 1962.

———. *Le Nu perdu et autres poèmes.* Paris: Gallimard, 1978.

Cirlot, J. E. *A Dictionary of Symbols.* Trans. Jack Sage. New York: Philosophical Library, 1962.

Cook, Eleanor. "Riddles, Charms, and Fictions in Wallace Stevens." In *Centre and Labyrinth: Essays in Honour of Northrop Frye.* Ed. Eleanor Cook et al. Toronto: Univ. of Toronto Press, 1983, pp. 227-44.

———. "Directions in Reading Wallace Stevens: Up, Down, Across." In *Lyric Poetry: Beyond New Criticism.* Ed. Chaviva Hosek and Patricia Parker. Ithaca: Cornell Univ. Press, 1985, pp. 298-309.

de Man, Paul. *Allegories of Reading: Figural Language in Rousseau, Nietzsche, Rilke, and Proust.* New Haven: Yale Univ. Press, 1979.

Deredita, John. "Vallejo Interpreted, Vallejo Traduced." *Diacritics,* 8 (Dec. 1978), 16-27.

Derrida, Jacques. *Dissemination.* Trans. Barbara Johnson. Chicago: The University of Chicago, 1981.

———. *Eperons: Les styles de Nietzsche.* Paris: Flammarion, 1978.

———. "LIVING ON: Border Lines." Trans. James Hulbert. In *Deconstruction and Criticism.* New York: The Seabury Press, 1979, pp. 75-176.

———. "La loi du genre" / "The Law of Genre." *Glyph 7.* Baltimore: The Johns Hopkins Univ. Press, 1980, pp. 176-232.

———. *Margins of Philosophy.* Trans. Alan Bass. Chicago: The Univ. of Chicago Press, 1982.

———. *Of Grammatology.* Trans. Gayatri Chakravorty Spivak. Baltimore: The Johns Hopkins Univ. Press, 1977.

———. *The Post Card: From Socrates to Freud and Beyond.* Trans. Alan Bass. Chicago: The Univ. of Chicago Press, 1987.

———. "The *Retrait* of Metaphor." *Enclitic,* 2, No. 2 (Fall 1978), pp. 4-33.

———. "Scribble (writing-power)." Trans. Cary Plotkin. *Yale French Studies,* No. 58 (1979), pp. 116-47.

———. *Speech and Phenomenon.* Trans. David B. Allison. Evanston: Northwestern Univ. Press, 1973.

———. *La vérité en peinture.* Paris: Flammarion, 1978.

———. *Writing and Difference.* Trans. Alan Bass. Chicago: The Univ. of Chicago Press, 1978.

Doggett, Frank, and Robert Buttel, eds. *Wallace Stevens: A Celebration.* Princeton: Princeton Univ. Press, 1980.

Eshleman, Clayton, trans. *Poemas humanos/Human Poems.* New York: Grove Press, 1969.

————, and José Rubia Barcia, trans. *César Vallejo: The Complete Posthumous Poetry.* Berkeley: Univ. of California Press, 1978.

Flores, Angel, ed. *Approximaciones a César Vallejo.* 2 vols. New York: L. A. Publishing Col., 1971.

Foucault, Michel. *Les Mots et les choses.* Paris: Gallimard, 1966.

Franco, Jean. *César Vallejo: The Dialectics of Poetry and Silence.* New York: Cambridge Univ. Press, 1976.

————. *Poetry and Silence: César Vallejo's Sermon upon Death.* The Seventeenth Annual Canning House Lecture, London, 1973.

Frye, Northrop. *Anatomy of Criticism: Four Essays.* 1957; rpt. Princeton: Princeton Univ. Press, 1973.

————. *Fables of Identity: Studies in Poetic Mythology.* New York: Harcourt, Brace & World, 1963.

————. *Fearful Symmetry.* 1947; rpt. Princeton: Princeton Univ. Press, 1969.

————. *The Great Code: The Bible and Literature.* Toronto: Academic Press, 1981.

————. *The Myth of Deliverance: Reflections on Shakespeare's Problem Comedies.* Toronto: Univ. of Toronto Press, 1983.

————. *A Natural Perspective: The Development of Shakespearian Comedy and Romance.* New York: Columbia Univ. Press, 1965.

————. *Spiritus Mundi: Essays on Literature, Myth, and Society.* Bloomington: Indiana Univ. Press, 1976.

Hartman, Geoffrey H. *Saving the Text: Literature/Derrida/Philosophy.* Baltimore: The Johns Hopkins Univ. Press, 1981.

————. *The Unmediated Vision: An Interpretation of Wordsworth, Hopkins, Rilke, and Valéry.* 1954; rpt. New York: Harcourt, Brace & World, 1966.

Hegel, Georg Wilhelm Friedrich. *Phenomenology of Spirit.* Trans. A.V. Miller. Oxford: Oxford Univ. Press, 1977.

315

Heidegger, Martin. "Heimkunft/An die Verwandten." In *Erläuterungen zu Hölderlins Dichtung*. Rpt. Frankfurt am Main: Vittorio Klostermann, 1981, pp. 9-31.

—————. *Nietzsche, Volume I: The Will to Power*. Trans. David Farrell Krell. New York: Harper & Row, 1979.

—————. *Poetry, Language, Thought*. Trans. Albert Hofstadter. New York: Harper & Row, 1975.

—————. *Sein und Zeit*. Rpt. Tübingen: Max Niemeyer, 1977.

—————. *What is Called Thinking*. Trans. J. Glenn Gray. New York: Harper & Row, 1968.

Kermode, Frank. *Wallace Stevens*. London: Oliver & Boyd, 1960.

Kierkegaard, Sören. *Either/Or*. Trans. David F. Swenson and Lillian Marvin Swenson. Garden City, N.Y.: Doubleday & Company, 1959. Vol. I

—————. *Repetition*. Trans. Walter Lowrie. New York: Harper & Row, 1964.

Krysinski, Wladmir. *Trois arts poétiques modernes: Francis Ponge, Wallace Stevens et Octavio Paz*. Actes du VIIe Congrès de l'Association international de littérature comparée. Budapest: Publishing House of the Hungarian Academy of Sciences, n.d.

Lacoue-Labarthe, Philippe. "Le détour (Nietzsche et la rhétorique)." *Poétique*, 5, 1971, 53-76.

Lanham, Richard. *The Motives of Eloquence*. New Haven: Yale Univ. Press, 1976.

Larrea, Juan. "Significado conjunto de la vida y de la orbra de César Vallejo." In *César Vallejo, poeta transcendental de Hispanoamerica: Su vida, su obra, su significada*. Actas del simposium celebrado por la Facultad de Filosofía y Humandiades de la Universidad Nacional de Córdoba. *Aula Vallejo*, No. 2, 3, 4 (1962), pp. 221-63.

—————. "Impropiedad del titulo 'Poemas humanos.'" In *Al amor de Vallejo*. 151-58.

Mallarmé, Stéphane. *Oeuvres complètes*. Ed. Henri Mondor and G. Jean-Aubry. Paris: Gallimard, 1945.

Miller, J. Hillis. "Stevens' Rock and Criticism as Cure." *Georgia Review*, 30 (1976), 5-31.

—————. "Impossible Metaphor: Stevens' 'The Red Fern' as Example." *Yale French Studies*, No. 69 (1985), pp. 150-62.

Nietzsche, Friedrich. *The Gay Science.* Trans. Walter Kaufmann. New York: Vintage, 1974.

————. *Nachgelassene Fragmente (Sommer 1872 bis Ende 1874).* Vol. IV of *Werke.* Ed. Giorgio Colli and Mazzino Montinari. Berlin: Walter de Gruytere, 1978.

————. *On the Genealogy of Morals* and *Ecce Homo.* Trans. Walter Kaufmann and R.J. Hollingdale. (New York: Vintage, 1969.

————. *Thus Spoke Zarathustra.* Trans. R.J. Hollingdale. (Harmondsworth: Penguin, 1969.

Parker, Patricia A. "Anagogic Metaphor: Breaking Down the Wall of Partition." In *Centre and Labyrinth.* Eds. Eleanor Cool et al. 38-58.

————. *Inescapable Romance: Studies in the Poetics of a Mode.* Princeton: Princton Univ. Press, 1979.

————. "The Metaphorical Plot." In *Metaphor: Problems and Perspectives.* Ed. Daid S. Miall. Sussex: the Harvester Press, 1982, pp. 133-57.

————. "The Motive for Metaphor: Stevens and Derrida." *The Wallace Stevens Journal,* 7 (1983), pp. 76-88.

Pascal, Blaise. *Pensées.* In *Oeuvres complètes.* Ed. Jacques Chevalier. Paris: Gallimard, 1954.

Plato. *Phaedrus.* Trans. R. Hackforth. *The Collected Dialogues.* Ed. Edith Hamilton and Hunington Cairns. Princeton: Princeton Univ. Press, 1961.

Riddel, Joseph. "Juda Becomes New Haven." *Diacritics,* 10 (June 1980), 29.

————. "The Climate of Our Poems." *The Wallace Stevens Journal,* 7 (1983), pp. 59-75.

Rimbaud, Arthur. *Poésies complètes.* 1929; rpt. Paris: Gallimard, 1963.

Shakespeare, William. *A Midsummer Night's Dream.* Ed. Willard Higley Durham. 1918; rpt. New Haven: Yale Univ. Press, 1957.

————. *The Tragedy of Hamlet Prince of Denmark.* Ed. Tucker Brooke and Jack Randall Crawford. 1917; rpt. New Haven: Yale Univ. Press, 1947.

————. *The Tragedy of Romeo and Juliet.* Ed. Richard Hosley. 1917; rpt. New Haven: Yale Univ. Press, 1954.

Shaviro, Steven. "'That Which is Always Beginning': Stevens' Poetry of Affirmation." *PMLA,* 100 (1985), pp. 220-31.

Stevens, Wallace. *The Collected Poems.* 1954; rpt. New York: Alfred A. Knopf, 1978.

—————. *The Necessary Angel: Essays on Reality and the Imagination.* New York: Random House, 1951.

—————. *Opus Posthumous.* Ed. Samuel French Morse. New York: Alfred A. Knopf, 1966.

Vallejo, César. *Poesía complete.* Ed. Jan Larrea. Spain: Barral Editores, 1978.

—————. *Contra el secreto profesional.* Lima: Mosca Azul Editores, 1973.

Vendler, Helen. *On Extended Wings: Wallace Stevens' Longer Poems.* Cambridge Mass.: Harvard Univ. Press, 1969.

Yeats, W. B. *Poems.* Ed. A. Norman Jeffares. London: Macmillan, 1966.